W9-BIR-234

The development of higher education

Titles in this series

IAU publications are obtainable from 6, rue Franklin, 75 Paris-16ᵉ.

teaching and learning

An introduction to new methods and resources in higher education

Norman MacKenzic, B.Sc. (Econ.),
Michael Eraut, B.A., Ph.D.,
and Hywel C. Jones, B.A.

Unesco
and the International Association of Universities

*First published in 1970 by the United Nations
Educational, Scientific and Cultural Organization,
Place de Fontenoy, 75 Paris-7ᵉ,
and the
International Association of Universities,
6, rue Franklin, 75 Paris-16ᵉ.*

2nd impression 1971

Printed by S.C. Maison d'Edition, Marcinelle - Belgique.

Preface

This inquiry into new methods and resources for teaching and learning in higher education has been carried out under the Joint Unesco-International Association of Universities Research Programme in Higher Education. The programme, which initiated a new form of co-operation between an inter-governmental organization and an international academic body, was brought into being at the end of 1959. Directed by a Joint Steering Committee, its purpose is to carry out under the auspices of the two organizations a series of detailed studies of important problems affecting the organization, operation and functions of institutions of higher education in the modern world.

The decision to embark on this particular study was taken by the Joint Steering Committee after a series of preliminary consultations and the work began with the convening of a small Meeting of Experts on Teaching and Learning Methods in University Institutions. This took place at Unesco House, Paris, from 23 to 27 September 1968 under the chairmanship of Professeur G. Mialaret, Directeur, Laboratoire de Psychopédagogie, Université de Caen, and with Mr. Norman MacKenzie, Director of the Centre for Educational Technology, University of Sussex, as Rapporteur. The other participants were: Professor S. B. Adaval, Head, Education Department, Allahabad University; Professeur D. Amor, Doyen, Faculté Polytechnique, Université Mohammed V, Rabat; Professor P. Bourdieu, Directeur (VI Section), École Pratique des Hautes Études, Paris; Professor R. Glaser, Director, Learning and Research Development Centre, University of Pittsburgh; Professor K. Härnqvist, Professor of Education, University of Göteborg; Professeur G. de Landsheere, Directeur du Laboratoire de Pédagogie expéri-mentale, Université de Liège; Dipl. Ing. H. D. Laubinger, Zentralarchiv für Hochschulbau, Stuttgart; Professor W. Meierhenry, Associate Dean of Education, University of Nebraska; Professor L. Nicolini Ghio, Director of Colegio Experimental Ruben Castro, Universidad Católica de Valparaiso; Professor Leone Smith Prock, Professor of Professional Foundations, Simon Fraser University, Burnaby; Professor A. M. Ross, Professor of Educational

Research, University of Lancaster; Professor B. Suchodolski, Director, Institute of Pedagogical Studies, University of Warsaw. The meeting reviewed the relevance of educational technology to teaching and learning methods in higher education and concluded that a new approach to the increasingly severe problems confronting the modern university was both possible and opportune. It identified a number of themes which appeared to demand further research and development. The Steering Committee is conscious of its indebtedness to the members of the meeting who, by examining the problems in an international setting and from their experience of a wide variety of educational situations, provided valuable background material for the present volume.

Instead of following the meeting of experts by the publication of a routine report the Steering Committee decided to invite the Rapporteur, Mr. MacKenzie, to use its findings as the starting point for a more intensive study. Work started in October 1968 and continued until the end of 1969 when the manuscript of the present volume was completed. Its authors are Mr. MacKenzie and his colleagues, Dr. Michael Eraut, Fellow of the Centre for Educational Technology and Mr. Hywel C. Jones, Research and Development Officer, University of Sussex, who were also present at the meeting. Since in the book they stress the importance of team-work in developing new methods and materials for teaching, they wish the book to be regarded as their joint work exemplifying this principle.

The Steering Committee is most grateful to the authors for deliberately seeking a fresh and constructive approach to teaching and learning in higher education and welcomes their concern for both the quantitative problems posed by expansion and the qualitative problems of increasing effectiveness. For expansion, if it is truly effective, leads to democratization, and improvement, if sufficiently profound, becomes regeneration; these are two great requirements of our time in education. Although the volume deals with many matters on the frontiers of educational research and development it is not addressed primarily to the specialist. By reviewing new potentialities for teaching and learning in the broad context of their complex and changing socio-political environment, and by examining the application of modern management concepts to higher education, the authors have indeed succeeded in producing a volume likely to be of interest and practical value to all who today participate in shaping the policy and directing the affairs of university institutions.

The Committee also expresses its gratitude to the University of Sussex for its readiness to allow the authors to undertake this task and joins with them in thanking the many individuals who supplied information and comments which contributed to the inquiry.

CONSTANTINE K. ZURAYK, RENÉ MAHEU,
President, IAU *Director-General, Unesco*
Co-Chairmen, Unesco-IAU Joint Steering Committee

Contents

Part one

Expansion and innovation

I. Introduction

The university began in a cloister, but it has become an arena; it started as a place where scholars could retreat from the world, but the urgent question for contemporary academics is the form and degree of their involvement in society. The world is entering the phase of mass higher education, which follows closely upon the emergence of mass elementary and mass secondary education. All three are expressions of the same phenomenon: a hunger for knowledge and skills so great that the appetite increases with eating. It is not simply that there are more people in the world; the revolution of rising expectations means that every year proportionately more of them want more education, and expect it to be provided.

In developed societies this process is already generating great political, social and economic pressures. As the wave of expansion moves through the school systems, it sweeps on inexorably into further and higher education. Developed societies, however, have at least had fifty years or more to establish their mass school systems, and they possess existing structures which can somehow expand to take the strain of increasing numbers. Developing societies are in a different situation; they cannot pass through the same process of evolution, and they are forced to face all aspects of educational expansion simultaneously. Their programmes must accommodate campaigns against illiteracy at the same time that they are seeking to provide primary, secondary, technical and higher education, and these programmes must all be attempted from a base of insufficient resources and experience.

We discuss what this means in terms of higher education in the next chapter, but we may briefly summarize it here. In the period 1930-34, it was estimated that in the thirty-nine countries then possessing some form of higher education, there was a total student enrolment of about 2.5 million [16].[1] By 1955-59, enrolments in these same countries totalled over

1. The figures in square brackets refer to the sources listed at the end of each chapter.

9 million, and Bowles has put the world enrolment in 1959 at 11.5 million [3]. Though no complete figures are available for the following decade—and errors of estimation mean that such totals are really orders of magnitude— all the evidence suggests that the world figure is now over 15 million and within the next few years it may well approach 20 million.

The expansion of higher education is no longer a matter merely of adding more students to a system that remains basically unchanged. That point was passed some time ago. In many countries, the growth of universities began to produce marked changes in kind as well as in scale sometime between 1950 and 1960, though these were at first seen as marginal reforms designed to assimilate larger numbers within the existing structure. During the decade which is just coming to its end, however, it became clear that the commitment to growth is inescapable and open-ended [11]. Though the waves of expansion will break irregularly over individual institutions, and even over university systems as a whole, they are waves borne on a rising tide which is steadily eroding the old fabric of higher education.

Whatever quantitative indicators are used, they underline the point. Whether one takes the growth in the number of institutions at the university and college level, the total of student enrolments, or expenditure on salaries, buildings and other facilities, the over-all pattern remains the same: the long-established structure of higher education is under unprecedented pressure to change, and to adapt itself to social demands. Older institutions which were once geared to the education of an élite must learn to admit and teach the masses; the precedents and experience that made them the carriers of past culture and values must be matched to an ability, and a willingness, to innovate; students who until recently were *in statu pupillari* must now be found a more nearly equal place in university government. New institutions have to cope with the problems of mass higher education at once; though they do not have to overcome the same difficulties of adaptation, they lack the experience and resources that older universities can draw upon. Everywhere change has begun to replace stability as a dominant characteristic of the modern university.

Change does not necessarily imply improvement; the change may be for better or worse. But the scale on which change is occurring is shown by the number of times the word 'new' is easily coupled with the word 'university' as compared, say, with only fifteen years ago. There are new universities, new types of university, and universities in new countries that had none previously. There are new sources for the student population and new problems of scale in student numbers, new academic disciplines and new courses, and new kinds of learning facilities for libraries, laboratories, class-rooms and other buildings; there are new kinds of students, new sources of finance, new management techniques, new relations with government, or the school systems, or with industry or the public at large. And, the special concern of this book, there are new media for educational communication, new ideas of learning and new methods of teaching.

All these new developments show the relationship between society and the universities has been altering in recent years. The concept of the State as patron to a community of scholars dies hard, because it has many attractive features; but in that simple form it cannot survive in the modern world. As universities increasingly become large-scale public enterprises, so they become less isolated (and less protected) from their social environment. Even the most autonomous institution today is subject to forms of indirect and direct control which link it to the processes of change which affect society as a whole—changes in values and attitudes, in social structure, in economic resources and technology. The radical reform of the university system in France is only one dramatic exemplification of a trend which can be seen throughout the world: traditional structures are unable to contain the pressures which are being generated.

It is the structures which are under most immediate pressure, and are being changed first, because questions of scale can be dealt with more easily than questions of quality—and much of the change in quality is slow, subtle or unrecognized. It is relatively easier to create new forms of university government and administration, to recruit different types of student population, and even to forge complex new links between universities and the societies they serve, than it is to modify the academic concepts and practices which have been central to the classical idea of a university. Many virtues reside in that classical idea, not least the values of independence, academic integrity and the disinterested pursuit of knowledge. But it offers strong in-built resistances to innovation, especially in the sphere of teaching and learning, and especially to any shift from élite to mass higher education. For increasing numbers seem to threaten the quality of university education; they provoke the fear that 'more means worse' and induce anxieties about falling academic standards.

Change is creating many contradictions of this kind within higher education —between old forms and new content. It is not merely universities that are having to adapt under pressure, without clear guide-lines of theory and experience, and in a relatively short space of time; similar strains are being felt by all types of post-secondary education, as the demand for vocational, technical and professional training increases. As a result, there is a growing realization that our concern should be with the whole spectrum of further and higher education, and with the interrelationship of the different institutions which are ranged along it, rather than with treating each type as a law unto itself. In the next decade, one of the most important questions for governmental agencies is how to plan for an increasingly integrated post-secondary sector, and to apply new procedures and methods systematically to all its component parts. The Organization for Economic Co-operation and Development (OECD) has already taken note of the need to do this, and in a number of countries the education ministries have begun to appreciate that the pressures of mass higher education may well impose radically new patterns of organization, not least the elimination of many of the traditional distinctions between universities and other types of institutions.

This change has already been reflected in the character of student agitation, which is displaying remarkably similar patterns throughout the world. The wide range of issues on which student discontent has focused shows in how many places the pressures are breaking through: it has erupted in institutions as different as Haile Selassie I in Addis Ababa, the London School of Economics, the University of Tokyo and the University of California at Berkeley: it seizes on issues as diverse as the Viet-Nam war, fees, examinations, cafeterias, racial policy and teaching methods [14]. But in all places, and in all cases, it arises basically from the same source—the impact of quite new social and economic circumstances upon the traditional system of higher education. In all cases, moreover, such agitation (or merely the fear of it) is serving as the immediate point of this reaction, giving the most powerful impetus to self-appraisal and reform that the university world has ever experienced. No discussion of the future of higher education can now take place without the participants referring to the context of student pressure. (It is sometimes difficult to get them to refer to anything else, whatever the topic that is nominally being debated!) How, it is asked, can there be a rational consideration of such matters as the planning and administration of universities, or problems of the curriculum, teaching methods or research policy, when students are on strike, occupying the premises, or demanding radical changes in the values and goals of their institutions and in the ways they set about achieving them?

It is a fair question in present circumstances, when many universities and colleges are genuinely concerned about their prospects of survival as institutions in which new knowledge is seriously pursued and existing knowledge is conscientiously transmitted. Yet it is equally fair to ask for a sense of proportion. Despite the publicity they have received, the most extreme forms of unrest have so far afflicted only a minority of institutions, and involved only a tiny percentage of the millions of students enrolled in higher education throughout the world. The interests of the majority of institutions and of their students have to be borne in mind; and it may be that by critically examining their own structures and activities, universities and colleges will find that the most constructive means of facing what is loosely called 'the student problem' will also prove to be relevant to the other problems to which it is related. To say that one cannot discuss vital policy issues because no one knows whether one's university will be open next week or next year, or because one does not know what changes student pressure will have brought about, is a counsel of despair. It can lead only to a loss of nerve and growing indecision at a time when strong nerves and decisive leadership are qualities that academic faculty and administrators need above all.

The problems of change in universities need to be seen and tackled as a whole, rather than as a bundle of separate difficulties that can be dealt with by a process of piecemeal reform. In this book, we are primarily concerned with the ways in which new methods of teaching and learning are relevant both to the quantitative problems posed by expansion and to the qualitative problems of more effective teaching and learning. But teaching and learning are central functions of any university or college, and they cannot be meaningfully discussed in isolation from other aspects of higher education. Student unrest, for instance, has shown how they can be disrupted or, in some cases, reformed by changes that are not directly related to the instructional process. The same can be said of financial considerations. The manner in which a university conducts its teaching may be determined as much by the money it is given to provide staff, buildings and other facilities as by any pedagogic principle. It will also be affected by such matters as admissions policy, which controls the numbers and academic level of the student population; by the balance between academic faculty and professional administrators in decision-making; and by the relative importance of research activity in the institution.

What has been true in the past applies with even greater force to the future. Innovations in teaching and learning methods cannot be considered on their intrinsic merits alone: they will inevitably be judged at least as much by their extrinsic implications as by their possible contribution to more effective learning [10, 12]. At this early stage, indeed, there is bound to be a bias towards innovations that promise relief from logistic pressures. More students have to be admitted every year, and anything which seems likely to help in assimilating and teaching them will be welcomed, above all by academic administrators and government departments. It is much more simple to decide whether an innovation makes an impact on the number of students that can be taught, for instance, than to estimate what it will do to make their learning more effective. The installation of a closed-circuit television system, to take a case in point, may enable an institution to make better use of class-room space and faculty time, and both these factors can be measured and costed: it is another matter to judge how it alters, and whether it aids teaching and learning, or what effects it has on faculty behaviour or student morale [6]. Some innovations, moreover, are designed to modernize the curriculum, and improve the ways in which it is taught, yet they will do little to cope with larger numbers or nothing to reduce unit costs: because they may need smaller classes or more expensive preparation of materials, they may actually add to the cost of teaching. They are not likely to be favoured unless the evidence to support them is more obviously conclusive than is usually the case with educational innovations.

It is scarcely surprising that, even in institutions that are seeking to introduce new methods of teaching, two parties have often emerged—those for whom innovation is basically a means of offering the old teaching programme to more people, and those for whom it is a way of bringing the curriculum and the teaching-learning process itself more into line with modern conditions. Each of these two parties has different objectives, and consequently adopts different strategies. One of the major difficulties that has to be faced in introducing new methods is that the more conservative group has the weight of precedent, the leverage of power, and the pressures of logistics and finance on its side [5].

There is, of course, a major difficulty about almost all educational innovations: they are seldom clear-cut operations whose character can be precisely defined, neatly distinguished from other variables in the system, and evaluated without uncertainty. The nature of the educational process is different from other enterprises, and it does not lend itself to decisive or unquestioned breakthroughs of the kind that one may experience in medicine, for instance, by the discovery of new drugs or surgical techniques, or that laboratory experiments can produce in the natural sciences. Educational change involves concepts, attitudes and behaviour; it is intellectual, social and interactive in character [9]. And it is much less easy to deal with changes of this order than with those that involve the manipulation of things rather than people [1]. For this reason, the first responses to the demand for modernization in higher education are likely to be practical rather than intellectual: it is always possible to admit more students, or construct more buildings. Growth at the margins of the existing structure is the easiest short-run answer, and it leaves the central assumption about the teaching-learning process largely unchallenged. This is bound to happen in the early stages of change, when the pressures creating it are largely external and the initiative for change within the structure is much weaker. In any case changes of quality are slow and long-term in nature and cannot be secured by immediate reforms however radical [2].

Indeed, but for the pressures that expansion is generating, it is unlikely that any great interest would be shown in new ideas about teaching, or that improvement of the learning process would be given very high priority in the allocation of resources. It is noteworthy that the cycle of curriculum reform and interest in new teaching methods has moved up through the educational systems of the world almost in phase with the wave of expansion. A serious concern with new curriculum and with teaching procedures appeared in universities as large-scale expansion started. Hitherto, universities had given little thought to the way teaching is carried on or to ways of measuring its effectiveness. It has required the duress of growth to make them do so: and if, by some miracle, that source of pressure were removed, it is probable that the majority would rapidly and with relief regress to the old mean. In themselves, few of the arguments for innovation would convince. New equipment may be developed, new techniques demonstrated, new concepts proposed: yet they would be wholly disregarded—or else consigned to an audio-visual ghetto or the purdah of departments of education—were it not for a growing recognition that they may be relevant to the problems created by the need to cope with the rising tide of numbers, to the demands

of students for more relevant and imaginative teaching, and to the requirements of more effective learning.

There are, of course, other important reasons for the fact that teaching
methods have so far been the last, rather than the first resort of the innovator.
Some are academic or professional; some are psychological; some are simply
due to ignorance or suspicion of alternative ways of teaching at the university
level. But all of them have contributed to an astonishing neglect by universities of the actual processes whereby their faculty teaches and their students
learn. We return to this neglect later, in Chapter III, but we note here that
institutions of higher education have hitherto invested miniscule proportions
of their annual budgets, and comparably small amounts of time and effort,
on studying either the theory or practice of their own operations. Scientists
familiar with research and development programmes, or with the significance
of operational research, may show very little awareness that such procedures
may be directly relevant to their own academic environment. Happily, a
slowly awakening interest in higher education research is one of the by-
products of the present crisis, but the very poverty of the research to date is
an indication of how much has hitherto been taken for granted. Even where
universities have shown some concern with teaching and learning problems,
this has usually arisen from psychologists in departments of education who
have concerned themselves with school teaching and childhood learning. It
is true that a good deal has been written in broad terms about university
education, but much of this is not research at all, but a reaffirmation of
intuitive beliefs and subjective experience. At best, the literature is descriptive,
quantitative, and prone to rely on untestable philosophical or moral
assumptions; and, at its worst, like so many debates on academic committees,
it is anecdotal, full of special pleading and lacking in any real analytic rigour.
Many aims of university education are either implicit, or else are expressed
in general terms—such as 'encouraging students to think for themselves'. Such
general aims reflect an attitude or state of mind on the part of academics
rather than offer an operational description of the curriculum.

The result is that relatively little is known about the current state of
teaching in higher education—of the extent to which, for instance, various
techniques are employed, or the combinations of them to which students are
exposed—and even less is known about their effectiveness in terms of student
learning. Very few studies exist, even on an institutional basis, let alone
nationally, and cross-national summaries or comparisons are simply not
available. This may matter a little less than appears at first sight, since the
repertoire of techniques is basically similar in most universities and colleges
the world over: lectures, seminars, tutorials, work in laboratories and
libraries, essay writing and other conventional teaching methods are found
everywhere. The differences between universities affect the 'mix' of these, the
size of classes, the number of contact hours between teachers and taught, and
the standard of the teaching they offer. But even before we ask the basic

17

question (which is how the effectiveness of such teaching is measured, and with what conclusions) we can see the difficulty of generalizing about teaching methods when particular information about them is lacking.

This raises one of the serious problems about this present study. It is hard to make useful comments about new teaching methods when there is such a dearth of relevant data on the old [7]. On what basis can one be compared to the other? How can we judge the effectiveness of innovations when we must plainly confess that we are unsure how to assess the effectiveness of what we are doing already; when, for instance, the normal criterion of achievement is a grading or examination system that is geared to the conventional methods? What if it turns out—as some research suggests —that the need to 'pass' in the required fashion may have more influence on what a student learns and the way he learns it than does the formal pattern of teaching? What of suggestions that the socio-economic status of students may be more decisive than any other variable in determining the subjects they study and their level of achievement in them? What evidence is there that effective learning depends upon a high level of contact between faculty and students? How valid is the widely held belief that there is a significant and positive link between teaching and research? We know of no study which satisfactorily demonstrates that link, yet the belief that it exists is continually used as an argument that undergraduate colleges without a graduate division offer inferior academic opportunities. It is also this special link that is usually cited as the reason for exempting university faculty from the need to receive any professional training as teachers, such as teachers of school children are given.

Such questions highlight our ignorance. They also, curiously, provide one of the more subtle lines of defence for preserving the present teaching pattern. If it cannot be proved that current methods of teaching are good, by the same token it cannot proved that they are bad—and meanwhile, it is argued, the existing system continues to turn out millions of graduates who manage to become reasonably successful doctors, scientists, teachers, administrators and the like. Teaching, it is said, is an art acquired by experience, and something essential is lost to the craft when efforts are made to support it through scientific analysis and techniques. Disregarding the complacency implied by this view, leaving on one side the element of self-fulfilling prophecy which is built into most teaching-examination systems, and even ignoring the more radical argument that much student learning occurs informally and independently (almost in spite of rather than because of the formal instruction) we must reply that this defensive line of argument misses the point. It is not necessary to insist that present teaching methods are bad, or that the wealth of past experience should be arbitrarily discarded. We simply have to ask whether there is any possibility of improvement, and how we should go about devising techniques for measuring the learning that occurs with both old and new methods—and thus be able to use our experience constructively.

Yet the world community of higher education has grown and diversified so much since the end of the Second World War that it is hazardous to make general statements that go much beyond numerical summations. Even quantitative data are collected and presented in so many different ways that one has little confidence that comparisons show more than orders of magnitude; and once one goes on to questions about the character and consequences of higher education, to the analysis of aims, to descriptions of operating procedures, summaries of resources or accounts of research projects in education the task becomes so difficult that it is not surprising that it is seldom attempted. We could well ask some further questions. What, for instance, are the significant differences between higher education systems (such as those of the U.S.S.R., Sweden and Italy) where there is a considerable amount of central planning and control, those (such as the United States and the Federal Republic of Germany) where there is much decentralization and even autonomy for individual institutions, and those (such as the United Kingdom and several Commonwealth countries) which have institutional autonomy within an increasingly planned over-all system? [4, 15, 18]. To what extent should a university be regarded as a moral enterprise, responsible for transmitting certain social values to the emerging professional cadre, as a training establishment for specialists, and as a centre of scholarship and research? [8]. What responsibility should a university assume for the retraining of teachers and other professional groups, for part-time and continuing education, for finding new ways of educating the socially deprived, minority groups, the physically handicapped and other elements in the population whose access to higher education has been restricted by élitist concepts?

If there are so many obstacles to an analysis of this kind, one may well ask how there can be a transfer of experience occurring between one country and another. Yet, if we are discussing innovation, we must either conclude that new methods are idiosyncratic and thus incapable of transfer, or seek for some way of describing them which, with all the necessary qualifications, permits them to be tried out and adopted in a suitable form by any institution. Clearly, we have to attempt the latter, and this—as well as the space limitation which imposes constraints on the case description of any given innovation—has unavoidably led us to present much of our material in the form of general statements. There are great drawbacks in such an approach, not least that it may give the impression that the whole process of innovation is more straightforward than is actually the case; an impression which has its dangers for developing countries which understandably want quick answers to their very great problems, for it may make them prey to high-pressure salesmanship, raise premature expectations, and lead to disappointment. What we have endeavoured to do is to offer an introduction to new methods, not a definitive description of what they are or of the immense variety of ways in which they can be implemented according to the structure, problems and resources of any and every institution.

19

As authors, we have drawn upon our own experience in different aspects of the development of a new British university; on our visits to many institutions of higher education in Europe, the United States, Canada and elsewhere, and on our participation in a number of conferences on educational technology and university management, at which we have been able to discuss teaching problems with colleagues from more than thirty countries. We have also undertaken an extensive review of the relevant literature, and addressed a postal inquiry to more than 500 universities, college and research centres throughout the world. Though their replies have provided valuable background information, and in Chapter V we quote a range of examples from them, they also show that, outside North America, innovation in teaching and learning methods has been tentative, small in scale and weak in theory.

For this reason, we have based our account substantially upon American work in this field—though no cultural, political or value judgement is thereby implied. We have done so in full awareness of all the differences that exist between the American situation and that prevailing in other countries, because the new methods of teaching and the new concepts of the learning process which we shall be discussing have been developed further and with more diversity in the United States than elsewhere [13]. The scale of that development and its diversity is demonstrated by any indicator one selects, whether it is expenditure on new equipment, the number of institutions attempting to innovate, and the totals of professional and academic staff involved in innovation, the level of research into teaching and learning and, not least, the volume of available literature [19]. This last point is of great importance. Outside the United States the literature is fragmentary, and often difficult to obtain, whereas the American literature is comprehensive, covers in depth almost all the issues we wish to discuss in this book, and can be secured with relative ease.[1] It is unlikely that anyone anywhere can do serious work on the development of teaching and learning methods who has not at least some acquaintance with the extensive American literature in this field.

It is worth adding a further note on this matter. Why should this be the case? The answer to this question is relevant to the general problem of introducing new methods. The United States has gone a long way down the road towards mass education at all levels; its educational system is also extraordinarily diverse, mixing public and private systems and offering examples of almost all known educational theories and practice. The United States system, moreover, is coping with educational problems that range

1. We wish to make one bibliographic comment. We have tried to keep references to the minimum: with such a wide range of subject-matter it has been necessary to be highly selective, and in choosing references we have opted for those that seem to us most helpful, recent and relatively accessible. We have marked a limited number of books with an asterisk: these we consider to be particularly valuable as general or background sources for those unfamiliar with the literature. All references are listed in alphabetical order at the end of the appropriate chapter.

from the illiteracy of poverty-stricken children in rural areas and urban ghettos to the provision of the most advanced research programmes. It therefore produces many models for study and, somewhat surprisingly, models that are of potential value to developing countries. It does so, moreover, in a society with an advanced technological base, especially in electronics and communications, where there is a large publishing industry concerned with the educational market, and where very large public and private funds have lately been available to promote and support innovation. It is also a society in which the cultural climate is favourable to innovation, and where the experience of the economy encourages efforts to shift the emphasis of any occupation from a labour-intensive to a capital-intensive base. All these and other factors have been conducive to experimentation in educational method. We are not arguing that all the consequences have been positive, or that waste, frustration and failure have not occurred. But even negative results have value, in indicating approaches that are best avoided, while positive achievements provide a fund of experience which can be drawn on by those who have come later to the field of innovation. Whether we are discussing the quantitative pressures for change, or the need to secure qualitative improvements in the learning process, we can usually find appropriate analogues in their experience which will enable us to see our own problems and possibilities in a new light—and that, after all, is the way most effective changes begin.

Our task has therefore been to indicate ways in which institutions of higher education, afflicted by all the stresses of transition, can begin to reconsider their methods of teaching and learning, not to offer neat or immediate remedies. For though potential remedies exist, none has been tried long enough, on a large enough scale, or evaluated with sufficient rigour to justify any sweeping claim that one method or another is necessarily more effective, cheaper, more convenient or even academically desirable. The situation is so complex, and the potential remedies are at such an early stage of development that caution is required as well as optimism. The best that can be done, in terms of our brief, is to set problems of teaching and learning within the wider context of the changing university, to indicate the nature of the emerging repertoire of resources which bear on the extension and improvement of the learning process, to comment on the conceptual changes that are occurring, and to note some of their implications for the organization and management of learning resources.

REFERENCES

1. BARNETT, H. G. *Innovation: the basis of cultural change.* New York, McGraw-Hill, 1953.
2. BENNIS, W. G.; BENNE, K. D.; CHIN, R. *The planning of change.* New York, Holt, Rinehart & Winston, 1961.

3. Bowles, Frank. *Access to higher education.* Vol. I. Paris, Unesco-IAU, 1963.
4. Council of Europe. *Réforme et développement de l'enseignement supérieur en Europe.* Strasbourg, 1967.
5. Dietrich, John; Johnson, Craig F. A catalytic agent for innovation in higher education, *Educational record (Washington),* vol. 48, 1967 p. 206.
6. Evans, Richard; Leppman, K. *Resistance to innovation in higher education.* San Francisco, Jossey-Bass, 1967.
7. * Gage, N. L. (ed.). *Handbook of research on teaching.* Chicago, Rand McNally, 1963.
8. International Association of Universities. *The expansion of higher education.* Paris, 1960.
9. Katz, E.; Levin, M. L.; Hamilton, H. Tradition of research on the diffusion of innovation, *American sociological review* (Washington), vol. 28, 1963.
10. Miles, Matthew B. *Innovation in education.* New York, Teachers College, Columbia University, 1964.
11. Niblett, W. R. (ed.). *Higher education : demand and response.* London, Tavistock, 1969.
12. Rogers, Everett. *Diffusion of innovations.* New York, Free Press of Glencoe, 1962.
13. * Saettler, Paul. *History of instructional technology.* New York, McGraw-Hill, 1968.
14. Smith, G. Kerry (ed.). *Stress and campus response.* San Francisco, Jossey-Bass, 1968.
15. Unesco. *The development of higher education in Africa.* Paris, 1963.
16. ——. *World survey of education.* Vol. IV. Paris, 1966.
17. ——. *Access to higher education in Europe.* Paris, 1968.
18. Wardenburg, J. J. *Les universités dans le monde arabe actuel.* Paris, Mouton, 1966.
19. * Weisgerber, Robert A. (ed.). *Instructional process and media innovation.* Chicago, Rand McNally, 1968.

II. The age of expansion

The shortage of information about the structure, procedures and activities of universities reflects the privileged position they have so long enjoyed as relatively autonomous institutions. They have been permitted to govern themselves, establish their own admission policies, devise their own syllabuses, set their own examination standards and decide their own research priorities. Even in higher education systems with considerable central control, they have in practice had much independence in academic matters; in decentralized systems they have been more a law unto themselves, especially where they possess control over their own budgets. As a result, they have not in the past produced the flow of statistical and other data which is available in most countries for the lower levels of education and makes it possible to describe and analyse them in a systematic manner. Neither individual universities nor national systems of higher education normally have had access to the kind of information which is required for serious sociological or operational research. It is true to say that the sociology of higher education is still in its infancy.

This fact has recently been underlined by a number of attempts to discover how particular universities operate, and how sufficient data can be secured to make meaningful comparisons between them. One such project is now being currently undertaken by the International Institue for Educational Planning in Paris, entitled 'Planning the Development of Universities', which is endeavouring to collect information about planning mechanisms and adaptive techniques [6]. Another has been an OECD project on the growth of higher education, and a number of planning authorities (such as the State boards of higher education in the United States) have begun to tackle this task [11, 12]. They are all encountering considerable difficulties, both methodological and practical, in this work, not least because many universities and colleges themselves lack the statistical information required [4].

In an age of expansion, such ignorance has become a serious constraint, not merely on the investigator but also on the effective management of individual institutions. For it inhibits planned development, and in particular prevents the rational allocation of resources to priority objectives. In the first stage of expansion, it led to an underestimation of the capacity for growth as recently as 1960: many institutions were simply unaware of their potential for expansion and some were reluctant to upset their established way of life by attempting it. (The debate in the United Kingdom at the time of the Robbins Report clearly demonstrated this view). When, however, it proved possible to enlarge existing universities and establish new ones on a hitherto unprecedented scale, this success led to a reversal of attitude. It seemed likely that future expansion might continue along much the same lines, and that universities, colleges and higher education systems could thus look forward to a decade after 1970 in which the pattern of expansion laid down between 1955 and 1970 would continue to serve [13]. There are already signs that this may not be the case; that, just as many institutions previously doubted their ability to grow rapidly, they may now be under-estimating the hidden momentum of further growth—and therefore failing to make adequate preparation for it. It would be risky to assume that the problems of the next decade can be tackled effectively by the emergency measures that were used in the first phase of expansion. Some different solutions may be necessary [8].

They should, perhaps, be warned by the fact that almost every planning forecast of expansion of demand has proved in a few years to be short of the mark—even when such forecasts have been based more on the estimated capacity of the system to absorb students than on the demand for places that is likely to arise. They should be warned, too, by evidence that resources to meet expansion may not be available on the same scale as in the last ten years. The demand from ministries of finance and of education (as well as from the public) is that universities should accept more students but, at the same time, reduce the unit cost of educating them; there is also a clear tendency to cut back on library, research and peripheral facilities that have hitherto been rather generously provided. There is the growing difficulty of recruiting sufficient teaching staff of high ability, certainly on a world scale. Though higher education seeks to absorb a significant proportion of its graduates into teaching and research, it is meeting stiffer competition in the labour market from industry, government, communications and leisure indus-tries as well as from other sectors of education that are also being forced to expand.

Studies of the supply of teachers for higher education have been few in number and have not been particularly rigorous in their quantitative estimates or adequately analytical in terms of the subject-disposition, the quality of training and levels of professional competence, or the relationship between the supply and standards of university teachers in relation to comparable sectors of the manpower market. Though such questions are integrally linked to any realistic discussion of the need for and the character of new methods of teaching and learning, it is not possible in most countries to move far beyond informed guesswork in this respect; research has neither produced suitable data nor guide-lines for applying it to the prospects of changes in teaching and learning methods. This is only one more of the urgent research tasks that a systematic approach to this problem demands [5].

It is hard to quantify matters of this kind when there is insufficient reliable data, and when individual institutions know they must grow but find it difficult to work out the specific implications for themselves of an over-all expansion. Yet the evidence, mainly on the growth of student numbers, slowly accumulates; either expansion must be cut back, or systems of higher education must change their character and their methods of work to accommodate a faster rate of growth than in the past. The study by Frank Bowles, for instance, has shown the scale on which expansion is occurring in South-East Asia [1]; comparable developments are occurring in China, the U.S.S.R. and Latin America. More recently, a study by OECD has brought out some new and important aspects of expansion in its twenty member countries which probably has more general implications [10]. This inquiry, which covered all students in higher education in the 20-24 age-group, is based upon the decade 1955/65, and thus underestimates the recent position. In these countries, in 1955, there were 3.9 million students in universities and 0.7 million in non-university institutions of higher education, such as teacher-training and technical colleges of various kinds. By 1965, these totals had risen to 7.9 million and 1.8 million respectively.

It is interesting to note that, in a group of countries with such different cultural backgrounds, higher education systems and available resources, the accelerating upswing of expansion seems to be running on very much the same time-table, and that it is not greatly affected by these differences. OECD remarks that the growth rate has been remarkably homogeneous:'. . . it seems that no country can reasonably claim that the increase in its university enrolments during the last ten or fifteen, years was "out of proportion" compared to any other country.'

Certain other conclusions follow from the OECD analysis. It has sometimes been assumed that economic forces (the availability of resources for higher education, on the one hand and, on the other hand, the requirements of the economy for skilled specialists) might account for some part of the recent expansion. This does not appear to be the case, at least in the sense of direct and short-term effects. It has also been assumed that countries with a very high *per capita* income (gross GNP *per capita*) could afford the fastest growth. While this obviously applies to Sweden and Canada, very rapid expansion has also occurred in countries at a relatively low level of economic development, such as Greece and Turkey. It must equally be observed that some developed countries (such as the United Kingdom and Switzerland) and some fairly poor countries (Spain and Ireland) have lower growth rates. No obvious correlation therefore exists between *per capita* income and expansion rate. Nor is there any immediate connexion between enrolment patterns and the degree of central control over the university system. High rates are certainly found in the centralized systems of France and Sweden, but they are also evident in the relatively autonomous universities of Canada and Yugoslavia.

OECD found it impossible to establish some other correlations that had been expected on *a priori* grounds. Although a relatively faster rate of expansion might have been expected in countries where there is open access to higher education (and this holds for Canada, France and Austria), Norway has had a high growth rate despite selective entry, and some 'open' systems (e.g., Italy and Switzerland) have had comparatively slow rates of growth. Over the decade under examination, moreover, some countries have experienced changes in growth rates without any changes in their admission methods. Of equal relevance to the theme of this book is the finding that there appears to be no significant correlation between high growth rates and either the degree of student unrest or the scale on which radical innovations have been introduced. Though the OECD study suggests that an innovative propensity may be produced by previous, existing or anticipated increases in numbers—and this hypothesis underlies our own approach in this book—it is clear that there are other as yet unexamined variables which lead to student unrest, or innovation, or both.

It has also been found that the relative rate of expansion over the decade is broadly similar for university and non-university-type institutions of higher education: in both types, moreover, the proportion of female students is rising—a fact of considerable social significance and growing relevance to decisions about logistics, curriculum, teaching methods and the career patterns of students. This trend, too, seems to be accelerating. In 1950, women accounted for 20 per cent of the student population in only seven OECD countries, whereas by 1965 some seventeen countries were past this point.

The regularities that emerge from this data are all the more interesting when one realizes that they apply with such uniformity in countries such as the United States, where over 30 per cent of the age group at least begins some form of higher education, and Turkey and Portugal, where the comparable percentage is still just under 5 per cent. Although the OECD study does not reach a definitive conclusion about the reasons for these regularities, it does cast doubt on the demographic explanation commonly advanced to explain the expansion of higher education (the 'population bulge') and suggests that the really important factor is the development and structure of the secondary school systems: '. . . the size of the graduating class (from the secondary schools) appears to be the most immediate cause of the changing growth rates of higher education enrolments (in fact, of new entrants). . . In most OECD countries the secondary school system represents the real selection mechanism for higher education admission.'

It is necessary to be cautious in extending these conclusions to the different circumstances of African, Asian and Latin American universities, partly because studies comparable to those just made by OECD are not available, and partly because the circumstances vary greatly in these regions. Higher education in most of Africa, for example, is still at an early stage of development, and it is emerging in the context of still undeveloped primary and secondary schools. The period after 1980 is likely to be the critical one in Africa. In Asia, however, the situation varies between the quantitatively well-developed system of higher education in Japan, to the nascent higher education systems of South-East Asia where, of the 86 institutions in 7 countries reviewed by Howard Hayden, only 7 had existed prior to 1945 [3]. The Latin American situation is different again. There are many old-established universities, and a number of new ones, some of which have very large student populations, which have the greatest difficulty in changing their traditional structure and have serious deficiencies in an administrative sense and also in providing adequate staffs of full-time teachers. It is possible that, of all the continents, Latin America is the one in which the universities will find it hardest (for cultural and political as well as organizational reasons) to cope with large-scale expansion.

Despite the diversity between these major regions, however, despite the differences between countries and institutions within them and despite the shortage of staff, money, facilities and, at this stage, sufficient suitably prepared candidates for admission in certain places, it is clear that in the next decade the level of enrolments will continue to rise rapidly. The demand side for higher education is growing, and it will go on growing, and neither government policy nor shortage of resources is likely to do more than contain the relative rates of growth. This, of course, is the value of the OECD study: it suggests that the growth rate can only be marginally affected and over short periods of time by factors which have hitherto been thought to control it—the demand for trained personnel in the labour market, for instance, or attempts to restrict entry to numbers which the universities feel are manageable. It may be possible to switch the flow of aspirants between one type of institution and another—from universities, for instance, to colleges of technology or polytechnics—but the demand for growth in the higher education systems as a whole is unlikely to be greatly affected by such measures. For growth, it seems, is the product of a change further back in the system: once the decision to create mass secondary education has been implemented, the only real question is how long it will take for the higher education system to respond to the pressure this eventually generates. This is the source of the 'hidden momentum'.

If the OECD reasoning is correct, the rate of expansion over the next decade may well make the development of the last ten years seem like a period of steady and relatively restrained growth. Even if expansion continues at the average rate of the quinquennium 1960/65, broadly speaking this would mean for the OECD countries an approximate doubling of numbers (an annual rate of 6 to 8 per cent cumulative). But it is probable that the rate is already accelerating. If developed countries are actually beginning to follow the United States down the path of mass higher education, then it may be more realistic to expect that, by 1980, some of them may have the same proportion of the age group in higher education as is now the case in the United States. The educational, financial and social implications of that are enormous.

Attempts will undoubtedly be made to hold down numbers, on academic grounds, for reasons of cost, and because it will be said that the labour market cannot absorb such a large supply of graduates and other trained personnel. (Some developing countries at the present time have an excess of graduates over suitable employment prospects: this both raises political problems and indicates a serious mis-match between the output of higher education—not least in the subjects studied by undergraduates—and the manpower needs of the society.) Even so, all the foreseeable constraints are likely to do no more than act as drag-lines on a process which is already launched. And though various constraints may do something to slow down the rate at which new applicants from the schools present themselves for admission, they will probably be offset by other demands that will be made upon the higher education system (for example, from persons already qualified and employed, who need retraining and specialist courses). Teachers are an obvious case in point, but the evidence suggests that many other professional groups will be in need of post-experience courses in the years ahead. It is significant that already, in Sweden, the number of enrolled students in vacation periods exceeds that of the term-time enrolment, and many of these are adults receiving retraining. The extension of education through the life-span will not only demand that universities provide more part-time and short courses: it is likely over a period of time to have a considerable impact on their curricula, staffing, teaching methods and to change their relationship with other educational institutions.

The absolute growth in student numbers, however, is only part of the problem. The OECD study has already shown that the rate of growth in some poorer and less developed countries is running at much the same pace as in developed countries: if the hypothesis that expansion is a product of mass secondary education is correct, then it is likely that as secondary provision improves in developing countries the flow of qualified applicants towards higher education will increase proportionately faster. That is to say, the time-scale over which expansion will occur will be condensed—and the expectation, so common only a decade ago, that the evolution of higher education in developing societies will repeat the evolutionary cycle followed by European universities, will prove to be false.

This raises very serious questions indeed, for higher education systems in developing countries labour under a number of disadvantages. They have no backlog of experience on which to draw, no substantial capital investment in libraries, laboratories or even teaching space which can be worked more intensively, few or no research staff, and their teaching must often be done either by expatriate or newly trained impatriate faculty. Even where governments are prepared to spend money on a reasonably generous scale, there are some things that simply cannot be bought or, at least, bought quickly. There is, for instance, a lack of what may be called general cultural facilities: the wealth of sources outside formal full-time education (such as museums, galleries, libraries, radio and television services, bookshops, theatres and cinemas) available to students in developed countries for informal learning. And there is a similar lack of other institutions which can make a contribution to higher education, such as hospitals, industrial establishments and research centres, all of which supply background support, physical facilities and even teaching staff to institutions of higher education in developed societies. In such circumstances, expansion necessarily takes place on a much weaker base, and it cannot be assumed that the teaching pattern which serves the needs of a sophisticated university system is necessarily the best for higher education where needs are great and resources inevitably slender. That is why dealing in gross numbers alone disguises the nature of the problem. There is a world of difference between adding 1,500 students to an established British university with an enrolment of 10,000 and adding 1,500 to the University of East Africa.

Comparable factors affect the composition of the new student populations that are emerging. Teaching cannot be discussed as if it were some kind of abstract function which can be performed without reference to the student body to whom it is addressed. That fact is so obvious that it is embarrassing to state it, but much of the literature on teaching methods ignores it—the reason being that, until fairly recently, there was an implicit assumption (transferred from Europe to many new colleges in Africa and South-East Asia) that all university degrees were more or less equal and that all student bodies were more or less equal too. This never was true, even as between one British university and another, and even as between different departments within the same university. While it was a polite and convenient fiction, it helped to inhibit serious work on student learning problems which derive from social, intellectual and personal differences. In this respect the OECD study draws attention to some obvious changes in the gross composition of the student population in member countries. There is the steady rise in the number of women entering higher education; there is a slower rate of increase in the proportion of children from working-class families, though this may pick up speed as more children of skilled and unskilled workers go trough to complete secondary education. There is certainly, with expansion, a much larger proportion of students who are the first in their family ever to receive higher education—a phenomenon in quantitative terms most marked in the United States and the U.S.S.R., and this has some obvious implications both in terms of learning habits and the expectation students have about their academic and subsequent careers.

Unless such factors are taken into account (and this requires detailed analysis at all levels, from the national system to the characteristics of students in a particular class or course), it will be difficult to design the most appropriate forms of the teaching-learning process and to apply them to the specific situation in any institution. For current research not only suggests that differences in socio-economic background may produce greater variations in learning than do differences in the methods or conditions of instruction; it also indicates that more progress towards effective learning may be made by concentrating attention on the needs and activities of the learner than by approaching the problem from the standpoint of the teacher. Though this research originates in European and North American contexts, and much more work needs to be done urgently along these lines in developing countries, it is more than a reasonable hypothesis that this principle will apply in these countries—more than reasonable because the diversity of students entering a nascent system may be more significant and troublesome than the diversity of those admitted to a mature one, not least because the opportunities for informal learning outside the organized pattern of instruction are so much greater in developed countries.

At the same time that numbers are rising, an equally important and even more rapid process of expansion is going on—one that also bears directly on the content and methods of higher education. This is the 'knowledge explosion', the fact that the amount of human knowledge is increasing exponentially [7]. As a consequence, to put the matter baldly, the ability to memorize is becoming less and less relevant, for knowledge is both too extensive in any field and too liable to obsolescence, especially in sciences, technology, medicine, and some social sciences. The ability to find one's way to a specific item of information, to retrieve it in usable form, and apply it to the solution of a problem, however, is becoming commensurately more important. Such a shift of emphasis will inevitably transform both what is taught and the way it is taught, and the way we assess student skills and behaviour: the only question is how long it will take to make such an adjustment. We may, indeed, already be approaching the point where it is more relevant to ask how a university organizes knowledge (into what disciplines and cross-disciplines), how it classifies it, what facilities it offers for storing and retrieving it, what training in information processing it gives to its staff and students, and what opportunities it offers to apply information to the solution of problems, than to ask simply how it teaches. We may also expect, it may be added parenthetically, that new methods—including automation—will develop more rapidly in this sphere than in that of conventional teaching.

This expansion of knowledge is certainly as powerful an impetus to innovation as the expansion of numbers, and its scale has been graphically expressed in many ways. It has been said that half of all the research and development work undertaken since the dawn of civilization has been completed in the last decade; that 70 per cent of all the scientists who have ever lived are now alive; that the accumulation of scientific data doubles every eight years; and that as far back as 1960, research generated 60 million pages of reports each year, published in 55,000 journals in sixty languages. It is not possible to quantify such statements with any great accuracy, but such illustrations indicate the orders of magnitude involved. It may be that higher education is in even greater danger of being swamped by information than by students! [2]

The growth and diversification of knowledge is also expressed in curricular terms—in the changing content of the courses that students are expected to follow. As the store of knowledge expands and alters, the curriculum must be adapted and new 'maps of learning' must be drawn. The fact that many of the growing points of knowledge in recent years are found at the intersection of traditional disciplines is one of the factors promoting interdisciplinary inquiry; at the same time the need to reflect these new intellectual relationships in the course structure is expressed in a movement towards interdisciplinary teaching. But this it not all: apart from these academic motives for creating a new curriculum pattern, one must note the impact of student demands for 'relevance' in their courses, which is as much part of the dynamics of higher education today as such external pressures as the skilled manpower needs of a society and its changing employment patterns. Many difficulties ensue from such attempts to reform the curriculum—some intellectual, some organizational, some that are a question of teaching methods and resources, and some that raise basic problems of course design and evaluation. Not the least of the dangers is the possibility that the search for novelty and relevance may lead to vague courses with undefined boundaries which prove to be almost unteachable or unlearnable and, possibly, of a low academic standard. Quite different organizing concepts and operating skills may be required for both faculty and students by the curricular pattern that is emerging [9].

As a practical matter, it is necessary for an institution to deal with a whole series of problems about acquiring, classifying, storing and communicating knowledge as they arise; the expansion and the diversification of the curriculum as well as changing social requirements demand flexibility in this respect. But all the developments now occurring in higher education underline the need to extend our concern with knowledge-getting and knowledge-using beyond the limited framework of conventional methods of teaching and learning. The most important conceptual change, perhaps, is to view the provision of information within a university or a college as whole; that is, as part of a single system in which the library, the computer and media facilities (as well as increasing provision for self-instructional procedures) are seen as related components in an over-all learning environment, and components, moreover, which may play just as active a role in the learning process as formal teaching.

From the standpoint of the learner, what matters most is not the formal instruction he is given but the kind of learning resources to which he has access, and also the range of competencies he acquires which will enable him to make good use of these resources to achieve his aims. That is why, for example, no planning for the future is realistic that does not set new goals for and enlarge the sphere of activity of the university library, not least because the library is the immediate point of impact for the knowledge explosion, just as the class-room, the lecture-theatre and the laboratory are for the expansion of student numbers.

As all these pressures upon the university increase, they produce symptoms of stress. The initial response of many institutions has been to look for means of accepting larger numbers while alleviating the symptoms of the strain they create: this situation is like that of a man suffering from bronchitis who insists that he is capable of smoking another twenty cigarettes a day if only the doctor will give him medicine to stop his coughing. But the time has come when palliatives are proving inadequate, and more radical remedies are required. We can already observe this change occurring in a number of aspects of university organization and activity.

In the first place it affects the way in which universities are financed. From the national point of view, in any country, the prospects of continuing expansion are alarming: whether the gross rising costs are considered as a proportion of the national income, of government expenditure as a whole, or of the total educational budget. In the United Kingdom, for instance, the share of all three categories devoted to post-secondary education has been rising relatively faster in recent years than almost any other form of public spending. Projected into the next decade, it becomes clear that in a number of countries there will be political as well as economic resistance to a continuing rise of the same magnitude. Experience over the last decade in all countries, moreover, indicates that there is a tendency for unit costs to rise as well—although future expansion may only be manageable if there is a relative reduction in the cost for each student place so that 'productivity' in a general sense is increased. Such considerations are now forcing governments, and also individual universities, to take a fresh look at the way in which funds are allocated, in which they are controlled and in which better 'value for money' can be achieved. It is the growing awareness of this fact that is beginning to force a change in the relationship of central university authorities and specific institutions, and also in the methods of budgetary control within universities.

Cost factors bear on the wider question of resources. In the past, when many older universities possessed a reasonable amount of spare capacity (such as under-utilized lecture-theatres, libraries and laboratories, partly owing to the practice of closing for a quarter of the year during vacations), strict resource control might well have created more bureaucratic problems than it solved. An institution could use that spare capacity, which included relatively light teaching loads, as a means of ensuring some flexibility, and it also served as a reserve which could be used to permit marginal and *ad hoc* changes such as fluctuation in the distribution of students between courses or even in total numbers from year to year. But things have become tighter in the last few years and this is no longer the situation. If the pressure of numbers is to be relieved, the use of resources must be optimized. Building and other plant must be used as efficiently as possible; support facilities, such as staff, equipment, library and laboratory provision, must be brought into balance; and the teaching programme of the academic faculty must be adjusted to get the best possible returns from the large sums of money spent on salaries. This cannot be done when decisions in all these respects are taken as issues arise, and often without much cross-reference between them, or a review of their total implications. It is quite common to find decisions taken about building programmes on the basis of capital budgets, without regard to staffing, let alone academic criteria; and these may even be taken by different government agencies, quite apart from arbitrary administrative divisions in a university table of organization. Institutions of higher education are beginning to find that they have to undertake systematic resource planning, involving all their component divisions, and they are also discovering that this needs new models, new techniques and new management structures.

We have already referred to the curriculum pattern. But the pressures now exerted on universities and colleges are imposing changes in the course pattern for resource reasons as well. When the admission rate rises, there may be a need for a different type of introductory course; and experiments are now going on with changes in the duration and intensity of courses, in the mixture of formal and informal instruction, and in the time and place at which learning activities are conducted. Many American institutions, for example, are finding that opportunities for independent study, such as access to self-instructional laboratories for science and for languages, need to be open for many hours in the day on the same basis as libraries. At the same time, experiments are being made in several countries in the use of broadcasting, correspondence and other media for forms of higher and continuing education, thus permitting students to study at home, or in their places of employment, or in other situations outside the formal class-room system.

It is in this context that one must consider the teaching and learning process. Because it is the central purpose of any educational institution and at the same time most sensitive and difficult to change, it has taken longer for the pressures of expansion to affect it—or even to create a situation in which the need to reconsider conventional methods is becoming widely accepted. Yet it is increasingly apparent that the methods that have done duty for so long are not necessarily suitable for an age of mass higher education (not least because of their cost), and even if the cost factor can somehow be managed, there are other grounds on which the present methods are open to criticism and reform. It can be argued, indeed, that even where pressure of numbers is not a matter of prime importance, it is desirable to consider the new concepts and techniques that are becoming available, because they hold out some hope that learning can be more effective as well as more extensive and, after all, more effective learning may in the long run be one way to achieve economies, because it means that resources are better used, that students may learn more or learn more quickly.

In the following chapter, therefore, we consider how universities approach the most vital of all their functions: that is, the way in which they teach and their students learn.

REFERENCES

1. BOWLES, Frank. *Access to higher education.* Vol. I. Paris, Unesco-IAU, 1963.
2. DE SOLLA PRICE, Derek J. *Little science, big science.* New York, Columbia University Press, 1963.
3. HAYDEN, Howard. *Higher education and development in South-East Asia.* Paris, Unesco-IAU, 1967.
4. HENDERSON, A. D. State planning and co-ordination of public and private higher education, *Educational record* (Washington), vol. 47, 1966.
5. INTERNATIONAL ASSOCIATION OF UNIVERSITIES. *The staffing of higher education.* Paris, 1960.
6. UNESCO/INTERNATIONAL INSTITUTE FOR EDUCATIONAL PLANNING. *Planning the development of universities.* Paris. (In press.)
7. MACHLUP, F. *The production and distribution of knowledge in the United States.* Princeton, Princeton University Press, 1962.
8. MAYHEW, Lewis B. (ed.). *Higher education in the revolutionary decade.* Berkeley, McCutcheon, 1968.
9. MEIERHENRY, W. C. The relationship of media and the curriculum. In: R. A. Weisgerber (ed.), *Instructional process and media innovation.* Chicago, Rand McNally, 1968.
10. ORGANIZATION FOR ECONOMIC CO-OPERATION AND DEVELOPMENT. *The development of higher education.* Paris. (In press.)
11. PALTRIDGE, J. G. *California's Coordinating Council for Higher Education: A study of organizational growth and change.* Berkeley, Centre for Research and Development in Higher Education, 1966.
12. ——. *Conflict and coordination in higher education: the Wisconsin experience.* Berkeley, Centre for Research and Development in Higher Education, 1968.
13. WILSON, Logan (ed.). *Emerging patterns in American higher education.* Washington, D. C., American Council on Education, 1965.

III. A crisis in teaching ?

Teaching in a modern university is a highly complex business, very different from the classical conception expressed in the phrase which describes 'Mark Hopkins at one end of a bench and the student at the other'. Though that tutorial relationship remains the ideal, both as a value and a practice, it is far from the reality for the majority of students in higher education throughout the world. They are instructed through lectures, seminars, and laboratory demonstrations, through practical work, field-trips, projects and case-studies; they read books, journals and other printed materials, watch films, slides, and television programmes; they use sound recordings, and operate many pieces of equipment. The variety of learning situations to which they are exposed, as these instructional resources are combined in different ways (too often, in an arbitrary and haphazard manner), is so great as to defy simple classification or summary. Both the methods employed and the quality of the teaching they provide differ from one course to another, from one institution to another, and from one national system to another. The complexity of the teaching pattern is such that even within one university it can only be reported in general terms, and even then most reports still tend to be descriptive rather than analytical. Only a tiny minority of institutions have ever attempted to review their methods of teaching course by course or subject by subject, to consider the resource implications of various 'mixes', or to relate systematically the objectives, teaching methods and evaluation techniques of any course [1]. In the absence of such studies, even generalizations are little more than summaries of random impressions.

Yet, despite the lack of comparative data on teaching methods (and on the ways in which the effectiveness of teaching is assessed) there is a widespread and growing impression that they are less than adequate to meet the needs of universities today—an impression expressed by many as 'a crisis in teaching'. What do people mean when they say this ? They certainly do not mean any sudden discovery that the long-accepted methods by which instruction in higher education proceeds are hopelessly and inevitably ineffective: that would fly in the face of the evidence that universities and colleges obviously do manage to educate large numbers of students to acceptable levels of knowledge and reasonable standards of professional competence. But there is a sense of dissatisfaction which stems from several sources. There are the common complaints (reported from many countries) by students: objections to poor teaching, routine, boring, ill-prepared and ill-delivered lectures, to the impersonality of large classes and the lack or real contact between faculty and students. There are also criticisms about outmoded or irrelevant elements in the curriculum, about the emphasis placed upon formal instruction and traditional examination procedures, about the failure to pay sufficient attention to the ways in which students learn and to new techniques for assessing their performance, and about the stress laid on teaching as opposed to learning [12]. There is, on the part of faculty, a feeling that the standards of academic work cannot be maintained if additional numbers are continually absorbed into the system, and if faculty are forced to give up creative research in order to spend more hours on assembly-line teaching—especially if this has a 'training' or 'vocational' rather than an academic emphasis. There is also a belief in at least some countries that the pressure of expansion has led to the recruitment of teaching staff of inferior academic qualifications and experience. Finally, it is argued that the concepts and methods of university teaching have not advanced in line with contemporary knowledge of human learning and behaviour—in short, that education has failed to keep pace with developments that have been transforming other sectors of society.

The criticisms are well known, even if they have not been quantified: some of them, indeed, have been well known for years: one is tempted to paraphrase Mark Twain's comment that everyone talks about the British climate but no one does anything about it. The difficulty is partly that it has been hard to see what can be done to make significant improvements, especially when attitudes and habits are ingrained in the whole structure of higher education, and partly that universities have lacked appropriate means for carrying out changes even when the need for them is apparent. Though marginal adjustments are being made all the time, the essential features of the system persist unaltered.

This point comes out clearly when the faculty of any institution begins to consider its teaching problems. The usual point of departure is to consider what can be done to improve the existing pattern, rather than to ask whether the pattern itself requires reform. Indeed, the temptation is to modify the content of the curriculum rather than the methods whereby it is taught, that is, to transmit new knowledge through old channels. Even when this temptation is resisted and the methods themselves are examined, attention is often focused on means of improving existing methods, especially performance skills, rather than on possible changes in method or on more fundamental questions about the teacher's role in the learning process [1].

That is why a common and understandable line of criticism has been to complain that university faculty are poorly prepared for their professional task as teachers. The argument has been well put by Paul Klapper [20]: 'The large classes, the inexperienced teachers, the long teaching day, the heavy teaching assignments—these are not the primary causes of ineffective teaching in our colleges and universities today: rather, they are the secondary causes which have intensified it. The fact remains that our teachers in institutions of post-high-school levels have not been prepared to teach. We have persisted in the assumption that good teachers are born, hence cannot be made, and, further, that anyone who really knows can teach because the converse—he who does not know cannot teach—is true. . . Aimlessness is the most important single cause of ineffectiveness in teaching and of frustration of educational effort. Again and again one looks for evidence of purpose in classroom, lecture hall and laboratory.'

There is a great deal to Klapper's criticism: it is so patently applicable to many teachers in higher education, not just in the American institutions of which he was writing but elsewhere in the world. While some university systems are beginning to pay more attention to the pre-service and in-service training of university faculty, and to deciding what competencies they require (for instance, in the U.S.S.R., some European countries, in Australia, and in a number of United States universities) such programmes are usually on a small scale, normally directed at entrants to the profession, and are considered more as pilot projects than as established procedures. A case in point comes from Sweden, where the Office of the Chancellor of Swedish Universities has appointed a special Committee for University Training Methods (UPU), whose purpose is to investigate the methods of university instruction and examination. This is an interesting example of a co-ordinated national effort in this field; UPU is sponsoring research and development work in language laboratories, programmed instruction, counselling in study techniques, methodology of goal analysis and evaluation, the conditions of student study, the reorganization of budget techniques, and the training of university teachers by special courses. In this last respect, UPU has participated in a Nordic expert committee in university training methods appointed by the Nordic Cultural Commission. UPU has also prepared a compendium on university training methods for use in courses for university teachers. Attention should also be paid to the special faculty training institutes in new methods which have been organized as summer courses at a number of centres in the United States, with the support of funds from the Federal Government, and to the rather sudden burst of interest in faculty training lately shown by such bodies as the National Union of Students, the Association of University Teachers, the Committee of Vice-Chancellors and a number of individual institutions in the United Kingdom.

37

Hitherto, however, it is fair to say that the academic profession as a whole, indeed, has always regarded professional training as something more suitable for school-teachers than for scholars, and there has been resistance—even overt hostility—to changes that attempted to meet Klapper's point. The outcry in the United Kingdom, for instance, against the proposal in early 1969 to link academic salaries to teaching performance, was predictable (and, in the crude form it was put forward, understandable). Only five years previously the Hale Committee, investigating teaching methods in British universities, had reported that [13]: '... we are clear that any proposal to make a full-time course of training lasting for, say, a year a necessary qualification for a university appointment would receive no support at all. Any arrangements which were obligatory ... might act as a serious deterrent to the recruitment by universities of men and women whose primary interest was in scholarship and research.'

The objections then offered to systematic training were too much even for the Hale Committee, though it generally took a rather complacent view of the situation, and published a report which was more a quantitative review of university teaching than one which took into account the research literature and the current controversies about teaching and learning. It therefore added somewhat dolefully: 'On the other hand, the present arrangements, if such they can be called, seem to be more haphazard than is desirable, and result in much university teaching being less effective than it should be.'

The English are known to have a talent for meiosis. It would have been nearer the mark to say that much teaching in higher education seems to be poor, and that in so far as any means of assessing it are viable, too much of it seems to be ineffective, especially when one considers the resources of skilled manpower that it absorbs. While we lack touchstones which would enable us to put the matter more precisely, or to make acceptable comparisons, simple heuristic procedures reveal too many faults for comfort. Any serious study of class-room practice by university and college teachers would probably reveal a shocking 'failure-rate' in terms of teaching competencies [25]. We are not arguing that academic faculty should be judged solely in terms of class-room competence: there are too many instances where personality and academic distinction seem to ensure that students are well motivated and taught by scholars who, in a formal sense are 'bad' teachers. But there is enough evidence to support Klapper's argument that even a limited investment in training university teachers might pay reasonable short-term dividends in improved performance—that, if necessary, the conventional methods, could be made to work better than they do [24].

As matters stand, the whole pattern of recruitment of academic staff is an extraordinarily chancy business: its peculiar features are highlighted by the fact that this is a profession which puts a premium on high standards, on precision in scholarship and research, and on complex procedures for admitting and examining students, yet adopts the most unsystematic criteria for recruiting newcomers to its ranks [18]. It is generally assumed that outstanding academic performance, as an undergraduate, coupled with a period of supervised research, is necessarily correlated with the skills—or even the personality factors—required of a teacher. The result is the recruitment of faculty who are somehow expected to acquire by experience a wide range of competenties, to become teachers, researchers, administrators and student advisers by turns, and between times to write books, serve on public committees, and act as consultants to government and industry. The remarkable feature of this system, in Dr. Johnson's phrase about the preaching woman, is not that it is done well but that it is done at all.

We are not immediately concerned with ways in which all the various competencies required can be developed or, at least, a better division of labour between them can be secured. The present need is to explore more closely the factors that inhibit even an elementary attempt to improve teaching, for these factors will certainly operate even more stringently against attempts to make more radical changes [3]. The first of these is the fact that there is no agreement as to what is meant by 'good' teaching. The phrase may mean that a teacher is popular, that he seems to interest and motivate his students, that they get better examination results, that their subsequent professional careers are more successful, that more of them take up academic careers themselves—or all these things. But even in the most general and subjective sense, few 'good teachers' at the university level have ever had professional training, despite the fact that even a naturally good teacher can improve his performance if he is helped to acquire some formal pedagogic skills. Under present circumstances, if a member of a university faculty teaches well it is usually because he was fortunate enough to be well taught himself (one of the most important sources of teaching behaviour is the model older teachers provide for young ones, since imitation is not only a form of flattery but also of learning), or because he prizes his role as a teacher and takes personal pains to do it well [29]. Even the best of such teachers, however, will probably be unable to offer a coherent theory of teaching or learning; at best they can rationalize good habits that seem to work, while at worst the university teacher rationalizes bad habits with a rag-bag of prejudices and false inferences. They cannot even be said to proceed by trial and error: each trial is simply a random shot unless the error is noted and corrected. 'He who aims at a target all day must sometimes hit it,' said Cicero, and the same applies to a teacher. But how much sooner and more frequently will he hit it if he adjusts his aim as he proceeds, so that each new effort lies closer to the centre of the target.

The second of the inhibitory factors was well summarized by the Hale Committee in terms which apply far beyond the British academic context to which they referred [13]: '. . . . there are certainly factors in university life which are unfavourable to the study of teaching methods. A person who adopts the career of university teacher does not do so in most cases because his main object is to teach. A more usual motive is to pursue research in a subject which had engaged his attention as a student, *teaching being regarded as a duty incidental to a life of scholarship*. And, whatever the motive which first led him to adopt an academic career, he soon realizes that it is on his achievement as a scholar rather than as a teacher that his advancement in his profession will depend . . . there is certainly little to tempt anyone to give a study of teaching methods time which both inclination and self-interest would lead him to devote to his own subject.' [*Italics added.*] The point can be underlined by contrasting the frequency with which university faculty speak positively of 'research opportunities' but negatively of 'teaching loads'.

In such circumstances the suggestion that anything significant might be done to study and actually to alter teaching methods can seem something of a threat. Quite apart from the criticism that is implicit in any proposal for 'training', such an idea strikes directly at the rationalizations with which a college or university teacher supports his professional role. As long as he is able to believe that innovations in teaching methods are unlikely, unworkable, too expensive, ineffective or otherwise undesirable, he need not make any effort to find out whether these propositions are true, and he is relieved of any need to experiment or to modify his own attitudes and behaviour. For too long, too much of the academic profession has clung to the conviction that little can be done to improve teaching and learning—a conviction that is easily elided into the complacent assumption that present methods are not too bad, or into the pessimistic conclusion that all attempts to change the situation are foredoomed to failure.

This state of mind has deeper springs than the priority given to research over teaching, with its associated but untested beliefs that good teaching is vitally dependent upon successful research, and that promotion should be determined on the principle of 'publish or perish'. It reflects a further inhibition on change, which relates to ideas which are philosophical or moral in nature. Many institutions of higher education throughout the world, outside the European and American contexts from which they emerged, have uncritically inherited the assumptions on which university education was first established. One of these is that the pursuit of knowledge is the primary objective, and that its communication is a secondary function that may be little more than a by-product. It follows that the pattern of teaching corresponds to the pattern in which knowledge has traditionally been organized into specific disciplines. Another is that 'education' is superior to 'training', the latter term often being employed in a somewhat derogatory sense. There are many philosophical origins for this individualist view, from Rousseau to Froebel and Dewey, and these affect all levels of education from the infant school to the graduate seminar. But they all amount to much the same thing: the concept of 'respect for the developing person', which underlies much of university precept and practice.

There is no reason at all to reject that concept: as part of a system of values for a university, it embodies the best traditions of humanism. But every society has its accepted value system which it promotes through a process of socialization and attitude-formation which begins in infancy and extends through life. The real issue, in any educational context, is how those values are translated into a curriculum and then transmitted to the learner [10]. Once that question is faced, the inadequacy of the 'personal development' philosophy as a theoretical base for instructional procedures becomes increasingly apparent: there is a gap which is hard to bridge between the philosophical aims and what actually happens, and there is no obvious way in which one can be translated into the other. The philosophy, that is to say, has attitudinal but not operational significance. It does not provide any means of setting academic priorities, of providing any criteria whereby success or failure can be evaluated, of deciding what is effective learning, or of developing strategies for teaching.

Consider, for example, how the idea that exposure to what is 'good' is linked to the concept of 'maturation'—the belief that the variety of experiences that a student is offered contribute over time to his development as an individual who is capable of organizing knowledge and applying it to the infinite range of situations he will encounter in life. There is nothing wrong with such a concept in a general sense; indeed, unless we assume that some such process is occurring in students, much of the learning that actually happens is inexplicable. The trouble is that we too often draw the wrong conclusion from this observation: that it is the time-factor, rather than the nature of the experiences, that is critical. Time may well be relevant to personal development, yet it is much less obviously relevant to training in skills and techniques; the experience of medical and science departments in universities, as well as of training programmes for industry and the armed services, suggests that in some circumstances intensive learning experiences are just as effective. Yet most of any education system remains time-bound, largely for administrative reasons, but also because the length of time allocated to a learning task is governed by hidden assumptions about the learning process, assumptions which may not be as well-founded as they superficially appear. We talk about class-periods, the school day, the academic year. We describe courses of study in terms of their duration—the one-term course, the three-year degree—and we set assignments, like examinations, by the hours. Yet the mere passage of time is not necessarily significant, or well correlated to academic achievement, for learning is not time-bound in the same way for each student, although the 'lock-step' method of teaching has to assume that it is, and is directed at a notional 'average student'. Students actually learn at different paces, through different learning styles, and from different types of stimulus. At its best, of course, the 'exposure-maturation' system endeavours to recognize this fact; it may even work reasonably well in a university which can afford favourable staff-student ratios and a flexible tutorial mode of teaching, such as that for which Oxford and Cambridge have been particularly noted. But it does not work so well in most institutions of higher education, which have unavoidably to cope with large numbers of students and work them through a highly formalized syllabus and mass examinations—a situation in which most universities find themselves in an age of mass higher education.

It is also doubtful whether the 'exposure-maturation' approach has ever been so relevant to scientific education and a whole range of professional courses as to the humanities. J. B. Conant has noted the difference between what he calls the 'theoretical-deductive' approach of the humanities, where the validity of actions is derived from theories, and the 'empirical-inductive' methods of science and medicine, where results are measured against hypotheses. For this reason, it is often much easier for a scientist or a medical professor to grasp the nettle of effective learning than it is, say, for a historian or a teacher of literature. It is noteworthy, indeed, that most progress towards new teaching methods in recent years has been made in scientific, technological and medical faculties, where their effectiveness can be most visibly demonstrated.

What now seems clearly to be needed is some means of giving the student the skills and the opportunity to develop his learning capacity, to participate more in the learning process, and to judge his performance by criteria other than the ability to regurgitate information in a written examination [27]. It is therefore necessary to ask why education in general and universities in particular should have been so little influenced by developments in the behavioural sciences, let alone by research on learning [21, 23]. One has only to compare how little has been done to study and improve ways in which we teach and learn (though education is now a major industry) with the investment that has been made to improve the effectiveness of advertising. This is not to say that education should adopt the techniques of persuasion which are used to sell soap, but one of the most striking contrasts in modern society is the difference between the effort that is put into changing the way people behave as consumers (or voters) and that which is devoted to new ways of influencing them as learners. Part of the answer, perhaps, is that we cannot easily measure whether people learn, whereas commercial operations —which anyway attract more money—can be subjected to the test of the market-place. Yet there is more to it than that.

For one thing, teachers tend to pick up only those elements of the behavioural sciences which can be fitted into their original philosophic assumptions. One notes, for instance, the persisting influence of *gestalt* psychology on education, though this happens to be the psychology which has least to say in operational terms about the way in which learning conditions can be manipulated to best effect. Another explanation lies in the fact that, lacking professional training programmes and other regular means of acquiring information about advances in the behavioural sciences (or, indeed, about new ideas and their applications), the majority of teachers in higher education are simply unaware that there is anything useful to be gained in this respect [5]. Even when they are aware of new developments, moreover, their interest is often restricted by a suspicion that the behavioural sciences have a formal and even a mechanistic bias, which conflicts with the professional ethic that teaching is fundamentally an art which requires flexible interpersonal relationships. This state of mind is enhanced by the apparent association of new pedagogic concepts based upon the behavioural sciences with the trend towards automatization and standardization which is assumed to be implied by the use of teaching machines and other devices based upon the new technology of communications. There is even a further fear: the argument against innovations sometimes rests on an anxiety that they will render a teacher's professional skills obsolete and even create technological unemployment. It is noteworthy that Sidney L. Pressey, the founder of the movement towards self-instruction through teaching-machines, came to the conclusion late in his career that 'the educational world is not yet ready for any such innovation', and that 'the major part of this work was done in the Great Depression; then, there were no funds for innovation . . . and, with thousands of teachers unemployed, any possibility of creating technological unemployment was to be avoided'. Under present pressures, when teachers are in short supply, the anxiety is not usually expressed in that form, but many individual teachers apparently do fear all that is embodied in the cant phrase that 'the machines are taking over' [28].

It would be valuable to have a careful study of teacher attitudes and rationalizations towards innovation in teaching methods, for the literature as a whole contains very few case-studies, and a beginning has scarcely been made at the level of higher education. There are clearly strong elements of resistance, some of which have quite legitimate conceptual and practical backing, not least the desire for clear and convincing demonstrations that new methods actually work and can be translated from the level of experiment to general practice.

There is also a recurring demand for a comprehensive theoretical framework to justify the introduction of new methods (a demand which reflects the enduring influence of the 'theoretical-deductive' approach especially upon those concerned with the theory and practice of education). This demand is much harder to answer than a request for empirical evidence that innovations actually work. For the reasons we have given earlier, it is virtually impossible to develop general theories of teaching which can satisfy the assumptions of the traditional educational philosophy. It is more than sixty years since Edward L. Thorndike, whose work provides an early antecedent for much of the progress made in the last decade, remarked that [31]: '. . . there is no chance for a simple general theory. . . . The true general theory must be the helpless one that there can be no general theory, or that it must be made up of such extremely vague conclusions as the features common to all human natures and the changes everywhere desirable allow. Such conclusions are

43

on a level for helpfulness and illumination with the inane tautologies of hygiene books: "Good air, nutritious foods and proper exercise are bound to assist health".'

Much the same point has been made more recently by Hatch and Bennet, who write [14]: If the research reported . . . is representative of our present state of knowledge we should abandon hope . . . that a miracle can be worked by discovering and employing some one "general method" of instruction. . . The consensus of studies made since 1920 is that no one mechanical teaching device, in and of itself, is better than another. Teaching by the lecture, recitation, discussion, tutorial, reading-study, reading-quiz, correspondence, or several different laboratory teaching methods (the regular, the drawing or the physiological type), has not been demonstrated to be intrinsically better than some other technique. The effect of research on the effectiveness of teaching should be shifted from the "tactics" of teaching to the "logistics" of learning to methods which in contradistinction to the pedagogical, may be described as the methods of scholarship, of inquiry, of problem-solving or of critical thinking.' The conclusion was reinforced only two years ago, by Dr. Ruth Beard, editing a British symposium on research into teaching methods in higher education, who argued [2]: ' . . . not only is there no theory of teaching to turn to when problems arise, but theories of learning are too numerous and too little concerned with human learning to provide a framework for action. Teachers cannot design courses taking into account the numerous variables in learning and personal interactions, but must introduce innovations largely on the basis of induction from their observations.'

The attraction of a general theory, of course, is obvious. It is often said that education needs a science of man, and seeks it in psychology; because it is also a moral enterprise, it equally needs a philosophy. The search for a general theory, therefore, has been an attempt to combine these two goals, to find a theory which has a scientific base and a social character. But, as we have indicated above, the situation in this respect has not greatly changed since Thorndike's day; and if innovations aimed at the improvement of learning are to come in the foreseeable future they clearly cannot wait until the development of a comprehensive theory of learning. Some other, less ambitious and less extensive theory is required—a theory, above all, which permits us to formulate testable hypotheses about learning activities and enables us to make some form of empirical evaluation of them [9].

Where, then, should we look for the help we need? It is possible that we have so far been formulating the problem in a misleading manner, and have therefore been looking in the wrong direction [32]. The discussion of teaching and learning has largely focused in the past on two aspects of the question—at the lowest level, on methods of teaching, and at the highest level of abstraction, on theories of learning. It has, furthermore, sought to judge teaching methods against the touchstone of values, and to apply to learning theories the test of practical validity. It is scarcely surprising that muddle ensues. More progress might have been made if the order had been reversed, if the emphasis had been placed on theories of teaching and methods of learning. But even such an arbitrary reversal is unsatisfactory: it still assumes a dichotomy between teaching and learning—and it is this dichotomy which creates the unbridgeable gap, that leads us to say that we can do nothing about one until we know more about the other [8].

Fortunately, it is conceivable that the assumption is fallacious; otherwise we should really be unable to hope for much progress. The dichotomy disappears when we speak of a teaching-learning process which occurs in a teaching-learning system. For we can then begin to study systematically the nature of the system, what actually happens in that process, and consider what occurs when we manipulate different variables that affect it. We do not have to concern ourselves immediately with why anything happens, because it is not necessary to explain the results that are observed in order to make practical use of them. This concept is surprisingly simple, but it underlies almost all the important innovatory work done in recent years; and it permits us to move towards a systematic (even, in some respects, a scientific) base for the teaching-learning process without having to wait upon a theory that interprets all the phenomena involved.

This is the main reason why we now speak of a developing technology of education, for a technology means simply the application of systematic procedures that have objective purposes and lead to demonstrable results— unlike a science, which goes on to interpret these results. The history of human knowledge is full of examples of such procedures, which produce observable (and even regular) results though the links between cause and effect remain unknown. The treatment of diabetes is a notable instance; another is the emergence of a viable technology of metals some two millenia before there was any science of metallurgy; and there are many other examples to be found in both science and medicine.

Education may well be passing through much the same sort of evolution; it may be possible to develop a viable technology even in the absence of scientific explanation. After all, the educational system as we know it is only about a century old. As an instrument for instructing the mass of the population to higher levels of knowledge and skill it is a modern phenomenon. We are only just beginning to realize that it is a system which is actually amenable to types of research and development procedures which have already proved their worth in other fields of human endeavour. Education passed, first, from a mystery to an art; and it is now passing from an art to a technology. There is much yet to be done before we begin to speak of it as a science.

It is for this reason that we must take very seriously the insistence of those who urge that we should now focus our attention upon the facts of the instructional process rather than on interpreting them. The point has been powerfully made by Ernest R. Hilgard, among others [16]. Once we do this, as he points out, it is possible to make headway even when learning theorists are in disagreement or when there is not an appropriate theory for the set of facts under review. If, to take a simple example, there is agreement that rewarding sucessful performance strengthens the possibility that the next attempt at a task will be successful, it does not greatly matter at the first stage whether the explanation offered is contiguity, reinforcement or communication theory. For the fact that rewards produce better results can be established empirically, and it can then be used heuristically to tackle a further problem.

It is this line of argument that has led Hilgard to reject the belief that a sophisticated and accepted learning theory is a pre-condition of any systematic principle of instruction. It was not necessary for the Wright Brothers to possess an advanced theory of aerodynamics before their plane first flew at Kitty Hawk, and several generations of aircraft were off the ground before some of the basic concepts involved were identified and understood. Hilgard equally objects to the related proposition that teaching is an art in which more is somehow learned from 'good class-room experience' than by systematic study. This, he observes, is like returning to pre-scientific medicine in the belief that, since the cause of cancer is unknown, the best recourse is to cultivate a good bedside manner. It has also been remarked that the present relationship of learning theory to education is more like that of physiology to medicine than that of medicine to the patient.

What we are discussing here, in fact, is one aspect of the shift that is clearly occurring from a concern with teaching to a concern with learning, from what is presented to what is received [17]. Lawrence M. Stolurow has criticized what he calls the 'communication-learning fallacy', which assumes that 'information transmitted to the student is always learned' [30]. Though, in a crude form, this is clearly fallacious, and known to be so, the essential assumption still underlies many discussions of teaching methods—and has even been carried over into the earlier stages of research into new methods, especially, as we show below, into research on the use of media as teaching aids. By concentrating on the problems of improving the presentation of stimulus materials, and working with some of the cruder concepts of communications theory, much of this research concerned itself in a lop-sided fashion with ways in which information was transmitted to the student without exploring too closely what was learned, and by whom, and at what speed, for what purpose. Understandably, this led to a passive attitude towards student response: the student was seen in a dependent situation, relying upon information directed at him, whether through the agency of media, or through the more traditional forms of the lecture and the textbook.

Learning, however, is a dynamic and interactive process, in which the role and experience of the student are vital components, in which he should contribute as well as receive, in which his perception of what is happening is quite as important as the perception of his teachers, and in which his assessment of its value may be more relevant than that of his examiners [26]. Good conventional teaching, of course, has always sought to take account of the learner, but its structure and methods have greatly inhibited it. The inflexible style imposed by large numbers, by the needs of time-tables and the availability of teaching space, by the conventional practices whereby courses are designed, and by teaching based upon the format of an accepted academic discipline, has meant that the 'teaching' emphasis has remained paramount. Once we accept that learning rather than teaching is the point of departure, we have to ask some different and searching questions. We can accept the approach made by Professor Jerome S. Bruner [7], and consider what experiences will motivate the student, and enable him to learn, what ways knowledge can be best structured for a given learner or group of learners, what sequences and modes will present the material most effectively, what should be the nature and pacing of rewards or penalties, and how we can gradually move a student from a reliance on extrinsic rewards to those which are intrinsic.

It is at once apparent that such an approach leads away from straightforward problems of teaching and learning to much wider issues: it forces one to ask what the student is expected to learn, as well as how it can best be learned. Thus both the implicit and explicit goals of the curriculum are then called into account. Though Professor Bruner retains the phrases 'theory of instruction' to describe this process, his work has itself been a major contribution to this change of emphasis, and he has summed it up in this way [6]: 'Finally, a theory of instruction seeks to take account of the fact that a curriculum reflects not only the nature of knowledge itself, but also the nature of the knower and the knowledge-getting process. It is the enterprise *par excellence* where the line between subject-matter and method grows necessarily indistinct. A body of knowledge, enshrined in a university faculty and embodied in a series of authoritative volumes, is the *result* of much prior intellectual activity. To instruct someone in these disciplines is not a matter of getting him to commit results to mind. Rather, it is to teach him to participate in the process that makes possible the establishment of knowledge. We teach a subject not to produce little living libraries on the subject, rather, to get a student to think mathematically for himself, to consider matters as a historian does, to embody the process of knowledge-getting. Knowing is a process, not a product.'

If the revision and renewal of the curriculum is seen as an integral part of the teaching-learning process, a change must also occur in the roles and interrelationships of teachers, students and others who are involved in it [27]: the system becomes much more complex than the conventional linear model, and it demands much more from those who have to design, manage and operate it. To put it epigrammatically, the teacher becomes a learner himself, and the learner undertakes some part of the teaching role [22]. This happens because the teacher learns more about teaching, and the learner begins to assume a greater responsibility for his own progress. Moreover, the roles of other participants change, and new roles have to be created [4]. Some of the new methods now being tried for instance, not only require that librarians move out of their traditional sphere into a more dynamic type of activity: they also need the services of professional staff, artists, photographers and technicians, and the co-operation of educational technologists and psychologists [15, 23, 34]. In fact, the ecology of a teaching institution changes once its primary function is redefined in terms of learning [19].

What we have endeavoured to do so far is to sketch the main features of the movement away from a discussion of teaching methods within a conventional framework towards a consideration of a learner-based system [11]. This movement is necessary, because the older methods are proving inadequate, and possible, because new means of making learning effective are becoming available [21]. But before we proceed to examine these new procedures in greater detail, it is desirable to look more closely at the repertoire of resources which are now on offer for this purpose. We need to do so, first, because much of the literature on innovation deals with what are loosely called 'new media', and it is desirable to consider what these are and what is involved in using them. And, secondly, it is logically appropriate to move through a sequence which begins with pressures and problems, through an analysis of the resources which can be applied to them, to a study of the procedures whereby they can be most effectively applied.

REFERENCES

1. AXELROD, Joseph. *Model building for undergraduate colleges: A theoretical framework for studying and reforming the curricular-instruction subsystem in American colleges.* Washington, D.C., U.S. Dept. of Health, Education and Welfare, 1969.

2. * BEARD, Ruth M. (ed.). *Research into teaching methods in higher education.* London, Society for Research into Higher Education, 1968.

3. —— (ed.). *Innovation and experiment in university teaching methods.* London, Society for Research into Higher Education, 1968.

4. BRIGGS, Leslie J. The teacher and programmed instruction: roles and role potentials. In: F. G. Knirk and J. W. Childs (eds.), *Instructional technology.* New York, Holt, Rinehart & Winston, 1968.

5. BROWN, James; THORNTON, James W. Jr. *College teaching.* New York, McGraw-Hill, 1963.

6. BRUNER, Jerome S. Some theorems on instruction, illustrated with references to mathematics. In: R. Hilgard (ed.), *Theories of learning and instruction.* Chicago, University of Chicago Press, 1964.

7. * ——. *The process of education.* Cambridge, Mass., Harvard University Press, 1960.

8. DUBIN, Robert; TAVEGGIA, Thomas C. *The teaching-learning paradox: A comparative analysis of college teaching methods.* Center for the Advanced

Study of Educational Administration, University of Oregon, 1968.

9. GAGE, N. L.; UNRUH, W. R. Theoretical formulations for research on teaching. *Review of educational research*, vol. 37, June 1967.

10. * GAGNÉ, R. M. *The conditions of learning.* New York, Holt, Rinehart & Winston, 1965.

11. GLASER, Robert. Psychology and instructional technology. In: R. Glaser (ed.), *Training research and education.* New York, Wiley, 1965.

12. ——. Ten untenable assumptions of college instruction. *Educational record*, (Washington, D.C.), vol. 49, 1968.

13. HALE, Sir Edward (chairman). *University teaching methods.* London, HMSO, 1964. (Committee Report.)

14. HATCH, Winslow; BENNET, Ann. *Effectiveness in teaching.* Washington, D.C., U.S. Government Printing Office, 1960. (New Dimensions in Higher Education No. 2.)

15. HEINICH, Robert. The teacher in an instructional system. In: F. G. Knirk and J. W. Childs (eds.), *Instructional technology.* New York, Holt, Rinehart & Winston, 1968.

16. HILGARD, Ernest R. A perspective on the relationship between learning theory and educational practice. In: E. R. Hilgard (ed.), *Theories of learning and instruction.* Chicago, University of Chicago Press, 1964.

17. * —— (ed.). *Theories of learning and instruction. Sixty-third yearbook of the National Society for the Study of Education.* Chicago, University of Chicago Press, 1964.

18. INTERNATIONAL ASSOCIATION OF UNIVERSITY PROFESSORS AND LECTURERS. *The recruitment and training of university teachers.* Ghent, 1967.

19. JANOWITZ, Morris; STREET, David. The social organisation of education. In: P. H. Rossi and B. J. Biddle (eds.), *The new media and education: their impact on society.* Chicago, Aldine, 1966.

20. KLAPPER, Paul. The professional preparation of the college teacher. *Journal of general education* (University Park, Pennsylvania), vol. 3, 1959.

21. LUMSDAINE, A. A. Educational technology, programmed learning and instructional science. In: E. R. Hilgard (ed.), *Theories of learning and instruction.* Chicago, University of Chicago Press, 1964.

22. MAYHEW, Louis B. *Innovation in collegiate instruction: strategies for change.* Atlanta, Southern Regional Education Board, 1967.

23. MCKEACHIE, Wilbert J. Research in teaching: the gap between theory and practice. In: C. B. Lee (ed.), *Improving college teaching.* Washington, D.C., American Council on Education, 1966.

24. * ——. Teaching at college level. In: N. L. Gage (ed.), *Handbook of research in teaching.* Chicago, Rand McNally, 1963.

25. ——. *Teaching tips: a guidebook for the beginning college teacher.* Ann Arbor, Mich., Wahr, 1960.

26. PERLBERG, Arye; O'BRYANT, David C. *The use of videotape recording and microteaching techniques to improve instruction on the higher education level.* Urbana, Ill., University of Illinois, 1968.

27. * POSTLETHWAIT, S. N.; NOVAK, J. D.; MURRAY, H. *An integrated experience approach to learning.* Minneapolis, Burgess, 1964.

28. PRESSEY, Sidney L. Auto-instruction: perspectives, problems, potentials. In:

E. R. Hilgard (ed.), *Theories of learning and instruction*. Chicago, University of Chicago Press, 1964.

29. PULLIAS, Earl V. Factors influencing excellence in college and university teaching. *Educational record* (Washington, D.C.), vol. 44, 1963.

30. STOLUROW, Lawrence M. Programmed instruction and teaching machines. In: P. H. Rossi and B. J. Biddle (eds.), *The new media and education: their impact on society*. Chicago, Aldine, 1966.

31. THORNDIKE, Edward L. *Educational psychology*. New York, Lemcke and Buechner, 1903.

32. WOODRING, Paul. Reform movements from the point of view of psychological theory. In: E. R. Hilgard (ed.), *Theories of learning and instruction*. Chicago, University of Chicago Press, 1964.

33. New teaching strategies, I. *Audiovisual instruction* (Washington, D.C.), October 1968.

34. New teaching strategies, II. *Audiovisual instruction* (Washington, D.C.), November 1968.

Part two

The impact of new media

IV. New resources for learning

It is a reflection on the rate of innovation in education that the phrase 'new resources for learning' is normally considered to include resources such as film (first used regularly in education in about 1910) and slides (first used in education in about 1890) [45]. Nevertheless it is true that for most college and university teachers the use of any resource other than chalk, talk and book is regarded as something special if not as a novelty. The purpose of this chapter is not to suggest which resources should be used but merely to outline which resources can be used. Our reason for including it at this stage is to ensure that our subsequent discussions on resource selection are based on the total repertoire of potentially available resources; and to eliminate some of the common misapprehensions about the nature, use and abuse of 'new' learning resources. Wherever possible we give references to fuller accounts of the applications and potential of each kind of resource. By this means we can avoid superfluous description for those who are already familiar with the resource repertoire without ignoring the needs of those who are seeking further information.

There is no obviously convenient or generally accepted system for classifying learning resources, so we shall use one which is based primarily upon information sources. Our first three sections will be on television, the language laboratory and other audio-visual resources. We include teaching machines in a section on feedback devices and reprographic equipment in a section on accessing devices. These are followed by a section on new resources for the 1970s, which describes some of the new equipment now being developed and its possible implications for higher education, and a section on the computer as a learning resource. Programmed learning is left to the final section because all the previous sections are potentially relevant to it. Programmes are different in kind from the other resources described in this chapter in that they are neither hardware nor confined to one particular medium. Indeed, most of the resources listed are capable of being incorporated into a programme, since we define programming as a process for developing resources which is independent of the medium of communication.

TELEVISION

The glamour of television as an entertainment medium has at least brought it to everybody's notice, and it has probably received more attention in education during the last decade than any of the other new media. Its potential for education lies in three main directions: (a) it can show things that would otherwise be difficult to see because they are of an inconvenient size, too far away or too complex; (b) it can transcend the limits of space and time either by open-broadcast, closed-circuit or recorded transmission; (c) it can be used for evaluation of performance; for instance, an athlete, an actor or a teacher can be recorded as he performs and his performance can then be viewed in a replay by himself and others. More detailed discussions of these applications and of the technical problems involved can be found in the appropriate books and journals [5, 7, 14, 15, 32, 33, 48, 61].

But few of these discussions give much account of the cheap portable video-tape recorders (VTRs) which have recently come on the market. A simple camera, recorder and receiver can now be purchased for about $ 1,500 and operated off a battery power supply by virtually anyone. These camera-recorder chains are well suited to the evaluation of performance and can also be used for demonstration or for recording if quality is not critical and the intended audience is small (thirty or less). We believe that cheap VTRs will find increasing use, that their price will fall and that their pattern of use will soon resemble that of the ordinary sound tape recorder. Indeed it may eventually become more popular.

In marked contrast to this cheap equipment is a closed-circuit television installation, complete with studio and distribution system. These installations cost much more (up to $ 300,000 for a large system) and while small systems (about $ 10,000) can be found at the departmental level in American, European and some other institutions, they will more usually be set up at the institutional level. They are a commitment which should never be undertaken lightly or hastily because their costs are nearly always greater than has been originally foreseen. It is easy to underestimate the need for professional and technical staff, for graphic and photographic support, for studio space and for expensive distribution networks; especially when a high rate of work is necessary in order to secure economies of scale. Of course, a beginning can be made with new equipment and techniques without a commitment to such long-term and large-scale implications—and a beginning is usually made in this fashion. If innovators had to wait until their institutions were ready to commit big sums of money, it would be hard to make any start at all. But it is essential to note that many media projects have been started without adequate consideration of what may eventually be involved.

LANGUAGE LABORATORIES [3, 4, 13, 24]

Discussion of the use of language laboratories is inevitably coloured by the fact that the laboratory is a fixed installation. This poses practical problems, but they ought not, in the first instance, to obscure the basic principles involved. What is normally termed a 'language laboratory' might best be regarded initially as a series of facilities lending themselves to use in certain circumstances for the fulfilment of limited tasks. It is usually (though not inevitably) true that for reasons of convenience these facilities are housed in one place, as opposed to being portable or mobile, and this introduces factors not directly related to the degree of efficiency of the 'laboratory' to fulfil the tasks allotted to it. The financial implications of housing the facilities in a fixed spot are considerable and must not be ignored once a decision has been made on pedagogical grounds concerning the need for, and the availability of, the facilities.

It is therefore logical to proceed from an analysis of the language-teaching problems to a consideration of the number, type and arrangement of the facilities required to deal with them. But the facilities are only means of exploiting material, and it is frequently the need for adequate supplies of specialist materials that is overlooked and underbudgeted when language laboratories are discussed. Unless such materials are accessible, or provision is made for their manufacture and multiplication (i.e. that the requisite facilities are available), even the provision of a laboratory will be of very limited use.

A second premature conclusion sometimes imposed by the fixed nature of a conventional laboratory, and the cost involved in installation, is an exaggerated estimate of the use and function of the laboratory in an over-all teaching programme. Over-use and inappropriate use lead inevitably to discouragement and disillusion, and this is an all-too-familiar pattern. At its crudest, the laboratory is appropriate in the teaching of a certain amount of certain registers of language to certain people for certain purposes in certain circumstances; unless all these conditions are fulfilled, there will be a decrease in efficiency and consequent psychological reaction.

A laboratory—whether fixed or otherwise—must be fed and serviced. Its consumption of raw tapes, spools, boxes, labels, etc., will vary according to use, but will always be considerable (perhaps an annual outlay of about one-fifth of the original cost). The maintenance of the complicated electronic components is a highly skilled job, requiring an appropriately skilled staff. Certain less-skilled servicing tasks are also essential to smooth running. And finally the problem of random access to materials must be solved by a carefully defined and administered system of classification, storage and retrieval, requiring certain library skills. All these must be costed in advance, before decisions about installations are taken.

The language laboratory has proved its worth within the parameters indicated above. But it is not a panacea for the production of instant linguists, it will not replace the teacher; essentially it provides certain quantities, types and combinations of facilities for learning.

OTHER AUDIO-VISUAL RESOURCES

Further information about other audio-visual resources can be obtained from general audio-visual references [1, 5, 7, 16, 20, 46]. For the sake of completeness the common types of resources are listed in Table 1.

Many institutions have established central agencies to provide audio-visual services and the advantages of centralization include economies of scale and the ability to attract professional staff of the appropriate quality. While we do not dispute that some audio-visual services can be best provided by a central agency, we feel that it is important to note certain disadvantages which can only be overcome by careful planning. The professionals who run

TABLE 1

Presentation equipment	Materials	Production equipment
Sound		
Record players	Records	
Tape recorders	Tapes	Tape recorders
Radio		
Still pictures		
Slide projectors	Slides	Cameras
Filmstrip projectors	Filmstrips	Photographic equipment
Overhead projectors	Transparencies	Graphic equipment
Epidiascopes	Photographs	Heat copiers, etc.
Micro-projectors	Wall charts	
Still pictures with sound		
Record/Filmstrip systems		
Slide/Tape systems		
Motion pictures with or without sound		
Loop projectors		
(8 mm and super 8 mm)	Film loops	Cine-cameras
Cine-projectors	Silent film	
(8 mm and 16 mm)	Sound film	

such agencies are bound to measure their success by the total value of their equipment and by the extent to which their facilities are used. Indeed it is difficult to imagine how other success criteria could replace those of size of budget and intensive use without altering the whole administrative structure of the institution. But valuable assets and high turnover do not necessarily imply profit: there is no obvious relationship between the quantity of audio-visual materials produced and improvements in the quality of learning. It is the planned use of audio-visual resources which is most likely to improve quality, and most of the planning and preparation time will have to come from the faculty concerned rather than the audio-visual specialists. But how does one reconcile the provision of a service to all who demand it (and most central agencies go out canvassing rather than just sit and wait) with the observation that the use of audio-visual resources without adequate faculty planning usually increases the cost of teaching without increasing its effectiveness? We return to this question again in Chapters XIII and XIV.

Another important development is the increasing emphasis on the use of audio-visual resources for independent study. This has led to the concept of the learning resource centre [5, 6, 7, 8, 12]. While in our view this should be a natural extension of the library—or at least closely associated with it—it has often developed quite independently. Usually a learning resource centre has learning booths (or 'carrels') in which individual students can use slides, filmstrips, film loops, tape recorders and books. The more ambitious examples even include viewing facilities for television. They must seem forbiddingly expensive to visitors from developing countries, yet much can be achieved at a relatively cheap level. Very similar learning situations can be set up with cheap battery-operated slide viewers and small battery tape recorders. And it would not surprise us if someone was to demonstrate that a proper exploitation of this cheap portable equipment gave better value for money in developed countries as well.

FEEDBACK DEVICES

The purpose of feedback devices is to supply knowledge of results when a student or a group of students are questioned on what they have learned. When the question is also presented by the device it is called a 'teaching machine'; but when the question is posed by a teacher it is usually referred to as a 'feedback class-room'. The feedback class-room gives knowledge of results to the teacher as well as to each of his students.

Teaching machines are normally divided into three categories, adjunctive, linear and branching [19, 45, 49, 50]. The adjunctive machines developed by Pressey and his co-workers provide knowledge of results to students answering multiple-choice test questions. Methods of giving feedback include lighting a bulb, allowing a punch in the correct answer space to penetrate more clearly, and having chemically treated paper change colour. The term adjunctive is used because these machines are adjuncts to the main teaching-learning process. They only contain tests and they are used to test and revise material which the student has already encountered elsewhere. Linear and branching machines present original material as well as questions and answers and can therefore assume total responsibility for teaching a topic. The linear machine presents questions step by step in a predetermined sequence, gets the student to answer each question in turn and gives him immediate knowledge of results. The branching machine allows the student alternative routes through the material and uses his mistakes to determine his route, but it can only accept multiple-choice button-pressing responses. None of these machines has so' far been shown to have any learning advantages in higher education over programmed texts; and they impose considerable restrictions on the person writing the material. Many of the other resources discussed in this chapter can, however, be used as teaching machines with considerable advantage. The slide projector and the tape recorder are both useful for presenting material in media other than print, and the computer has all the flexibility which the traditional teaching machines lack. We shall return to this in the final section when we discuss programmed learning.

The feedback class-room is essentially an electronic response system, which permits a teacher to pose questions to a class in which each student is equipped with a press-button device which registers on a scoreboard visible to the teacher [25]. In its simplest form the student switch registers 'Yes' or 'No' and an appropriate light showing the student's response appears on the teacher's indicator. More elaborate versions permit a choice of up to five possible answers, indicate to the student by a green or red bulb whether his response is correct, and then tabulate the individual and group scores, both for individual answers and series of them. In its most sophisticated shape, such a device punches a paper tape which can then be run through data processing equipment to give print-outs and analyses of student response.

Some of the same purposes, however, may be achieved much more cheaply by using pairs of cardboard discs. One disc is divided into five sectors, marked A, B, C, D and E on one side and coloured on the other side; then a second disc of the same size with one sector cut out is pinned to it centrally. If each student is given a pair of discs be can use it to answer a multiple-choice question by putting his chosen sector at the top where the second disc has been cut out. When he holds the discs up his teacher will only see the colour appropriate to his choice, e.g. blue, because the other colours will be masked by the rest of the cut-out disc. This enables the teacher to judge the approximate distribution of his students' answers by rapidly assessing the colour distribution held up before him. A multi-coloured cube can be used in a similar manner [52]. More accurate measurement and recording of student answers is given by the more sophisticated 'feedback class-room' but it is questionable whether this greater accuracy is significant in view of the extreme variability of the teaching performance.

ACCESSING DEVICES

At the moment most accessing devices can be divided into two categories: reprographic devices, which enable the student to take away copies of a resource and which require the physical presence of an original [23, 53]; and dial-access devices, which enable the learner to examine a data bank located at some distance but do not give copies to take away. A third type of device, which permits the examination of a distant data bank as well as enabling the student to take away copies of the information he requires is likely to emerge in the not-too-distant future.

The impact of reprographic devices on education is already considerable. The paperback revolution has become institutionalized [26] and now we are in the midst of a photocopying revolution. There are copyright problems involved in this [2, 11, 57], but we are here concerned with the technique. The price still needs to come down if photocopying is to become economic for general teaching purposes but many of its advantages are already becoming apparent. It is possible for students to work at home with copies of articles or chapters instead of having to buy or borrow whole books and the pressure on library resources can be thereby diminished. It is possible for all the students attending a discussion to have read the same short background paper beforehand; and it is possible to copy a student's paper and circulate it for discussion. All these advantages offer an escape from the use of a single textbook or a few scholarly works as the main sources of information.

The earliest form of dial-access device is the telephone, though it is still rarely used in education. It is particularly useful in remote teaching situations and access to a tutor by telephone can be a valuable supplement to a correspondence course. With suitable amplification a telephone can also be used by a class to question an expert at some distant location. This is particularly valuable when the group has already read an article or listened to a recording made by the expert or one of his colleagues. A sophisticated addition to this 'tele-lecture' or 'tele-discussion' is the 'electro-writer' system, often referred to as 'blackboard-by-wire'. This system makes it possible for a person to write with a stylus on the surface of the electronic equipment, for the image to be transmitted over telephone lines and for his message to be projected on to a screen at the receiving end. Both written materials and simple diagrams can be transmitted as they are produced [1, 7].

So far we have discussed the use of the telephone for obtaining access to a distant person. It can also be used for access to stored information in a Dial Access Information Retrieval System (DAIRS) [7, 42, 59, 60]. The simplest version of such a system allows a student to dial for a sound tape or a record instead of having to fetch it and play it back on his own machine. This is particularly valuable when the student can listen in his home as well as in the library/resource centre; and it tends to be used for listening to lectures or for language study. Its main disadvantage is that the student has little control over pacing, stopping or starting: he cannot choose to listen to excerpts as he can when operating his own machine. For this reason it is best to view the simple DAIRS as reducing the demand for student-operated equipment rather than replacing it. A video-channel can be obtained either by adding decentralized ancillary equipment which the student operates himself or by expanding the distribution system to carry visual information in addition to audio-information. Some of the more expensive systems now in use allow the student to dial a television programme or a film, though the store of visual information to which he has access is very limited in size. As with sound-only systems, he cannot easily browse or select excerpts from a particular programme.

NEW RESOURCES FOR THE 1970s

Until now cost and complexity have limited the development of visual recordings. Even the cheapest VTRs are still too expensive for one to consider installing them in learning carrels for regular student use and their picture quality is too low for many purposes. Movie projectors are not quite as expensive but films are costly and it is very difficult to select excerpts from them. But the need for a motion-picture equivalent of the long-playing gramophone record or audio-tape recorder is likely to be at least partially met during the next decade by the emergence of a new class of machines, a class which may be broadly described as teleplayers or devices for retrieval television.

The first of these to be announced, in 1968, was the Electronic Video Recording (EVR) player [58]. This device, developed in the laboratories of the Columbia Broadcasting System in the United States, stores pre-recorded programme material on a narrow film contained in a sealed cartridge about the size of an audio-tape reel. Each cartridge contains up to thirty minutes of material on each of two tracks, or, in the version still under development, thirty minutes of colour programme, using the second track in this case for the colour coding. The film cartridges are printed from a master tape, prepared in an electron-beam recorder, which will accept television film originals.

The quality of picture and sound is high—superior to that obtained from broadcast television on most video-tape recorders—and the projected cost of a one-hour cartridge and of the player are both well below current prices for either video-tape or video-tape recorders on which to play it. The manufacturers claim that quite small production runs of cartridges—between 100 and 200—are economically usable and practicable, and of course all cartridges are compatible with all players.

The three virtues claimed for EVR are (a) that it permits relatively cheap central production of materials for presentation through television; (b) that it permits audio-visual materials to be presented whenever a normal television set is available and that this can be done without some of the difficulties, such as blackout, that are involved in film presentation; and (c) that the 'stop-frame' capacity of EVR has great potential for education. The last of these three claims is particularly significant. While a single frame can be held on modern video-tape recorders, and on some film projectors, there is usually a loss of quality and it is extremely difficult to find a particular frame (individual picture). The EVR player, however, presents a still picture of good quality, and has an attachment that permits the user to advance or retard the film frame by frame. It can therefore be used for presenting one or more single frames (such as a filmstrip) mixed with motion picture and sound. This means that it begins to approach the desirable model of a single, relatively simple, all-purpose audio-visual device. Looking further ahead, it is possible to foresee what has been called 'reference EVR': the development of a search or retrieval system which would enable the user to locate any one of the 180,000 frames which make up the EVR film cartridge. Once this occurs, large numbers of maps, diagrams and photographs could be held in compact form, and made accessible to teachers and students. All necessary illustrations for an anatomy course, for example, might be contained in a single cartridge, and comparable advantages for such information storage capacity can easily be projected for other academic disciplines.

The EVR player and cartridges are still under development, and the first models are expected to be available towards the end of 1970. But other manufacturers are working on competitive devices. In the middle of 1969 the RCA Corporation in the United States demonstrated a prototype of a device called Selectavision, similar to EVR in that it uses pre-recorded material, but using a different film base and employing laser techniques for reading out the recorded signal; it was stated that Selectavision, promised for the market within two years, would have colour capacity from the outset [17]. Reports are circulating in trade circles that other types of teleplayers are under development in the United States, the United Kingdom, the Federal Republic of Germany, the Netherlands and Japan.

In the long run, manufacturers entering this field must be expecting to sell their players and recordings for domestic use as a means of entertainment, as well as enrichment and self-instruction. That, after all, is where the mass market lies. But it is significant that all of them view education as a potential market. The immediate use of such devices in higher education is likely to be limited, partly because the market for pre-recorded teaching or learning materials is likely to be relatively small, though teleplayers might become convenient alternatives to the use of 16 mm film. Yet where a larger audience exists—say, for Open University or similar programmes, or for series with a wider appeal, like introductory-level courses in science or mathematics—the ability to replay at will could be very attractive. Within ten years it seems certain that devices of this kind will have found a useful and expanding role.

THE COMPUTER AS A LEARNING RESOURCE

It is certain that the use of computers in higher education will extend most rapidly and extensively in dealing with problems that are common to education, science, business and public administration; that is, for high-speed computation and data processing [10, 18, 43]. Already the use of the computer in higher education for the purposes of administration and research is becoming a major item in a university budget and before long it may be the single most costly item next to faculty salaries. But the proposition that a computer could also become a potent new vehicle for teaching and learning is more recent, though it is being taken up with considerable enthusiasm [9, 22, 31, 50, 59]. Serious research programmes are now under way, not only in the United States, but also in Belgium, Canada, France, Japan, the Netherlands and the U.S.S.R., some sponsored by commercial enterprises producing computer and associated software, some underwritten by State agencies. Many research studies, conference reports and other materials are already available on this theme [36, 37, 38, 39, 55, 56].

The potential applications of the computer to teaching and learning are of two main types: those which are essentially similar to existing applications of computers and which are only delayed by problems of cost; and those which are dependent for their realization on the development of new techniques. Naturally the latter are more contentious but they are not necessarily more important. One application that is only delayed by cost is that of providing computational and data-processing facilities for students. The widespread provision of these facilities could have a marked effect on the curricula of higher education. It would allow a much greater use of problems involving computation, since the student would still be able to concentrate on the main principles without being unduly distracted by routine computational demands; and it would encourage successive approximation approaches to optimal solutions. Related to this is the use of computers for simulations, as for example when data relating to a model environment and the way it reacts to certain changes is stored in a computer and a student or a group of students explores the environment by making decisions and assessing their consequences [44, 51].

Computer-assisted learning (CAL), in which the computer is used as a highly sophisticated teaching machine which can replace and sometimes surpass many but not all of the functions of a human tutor, is the natural focus for the 'educational futurists'. But its long-run potential tends to blind people to its short-run uncertainty. Even though pilot schemes of this kind are already in operation and some American institutions are using them to present parts of regular courses, there is little evidence that any of the present uses are either very economic or very effective [7, 28]. Nor do they even begin to use the full potential of the computer. There is no way to by-pass the problem of our ignorance about how people learn and this limits the way we can programme the computer. The use of computers in the tutorial mode will undoubtedly accelerate research into the learning process but it can never replace it. Within five or ten years there may well be a place for CAL in many courses in higher education though only for relatively short sections of those courses. There are signs that these limitations are now being increasingly recognized and most publications in the last year have been much more realistic about the likely rate of development of CAL [38, 41]. We believe that curriculum changes in higher education will be at least as important as new programming techniques in determining the rate of adoption of CAL. The further the curriculum moves from its present preoccupation with the transmission of content, the more difficult it will become to use CAL. The same trend may, however, lead to a rapid increase in the use of the computer by students for computation, data processing and simulation.

The use of the computer for the management of learning represents an intermediate stage between its use for computation and data processing and its use in CAL. Computer-managed learning (CML) derives originally from the use of computers for the analysis of test and examination data. Automatic marking does not necessarily require computer capacity but computers can provide a rapid and much more detailed analysis of a student's achievement and abilities, and they can keep an up-to-date record file of each student's progress, which is helpful both for research and for diagnostic purposes [9, 14]. Normally teachers would use this information as a basis for teaching decisions, but in the independent study situation it would be equally possible for the computer to suggest the next step. It would have to be given a list of alternative assignments and a set of decision rules for linking its analysis of the student's progress to the appropriate assignment. It would also have the theoretical capacity to evaluate the decision rules and improve them in the light of evidence from subsequent student performance. This capacity for self-improvement may not be realized in practice for some time yet, but CML is still a realistic proposition without it. It provides a framework within which the computer can take certain routine responsibilities from the teacher and give some guidance to the student when he is studying independently. This could lead to a more effective use of teacher time without needing inordinate amounts of computer time or terminal time. Though our lack of knowledge about how to make appropriate assignments is clearly a handicap, the greatest problem in CML is probably the evaluation problem. The set of objectives which we can easily evaluate with computer markable tests is still very limited, especially in arts subjects.

PROGRAMMED LEARNING

Programmed learning is potentially one of the most confusing of recent innovations because it is difficult to define. Early definitions divided programmes into linear programmes and branching programmes and listed the salient characteristics of each. Schramm in 1962, for example, wrote as follows (with a footnote to the effect that it only applied to linear programmes) [47]: 'To sum up, the, these are essential elements of programmed instruction: (a) an ordered sequence of stimulus items, (b) to each of which a student responds in some specified way, (c) his responses being reinforced by immediate knowledge of results, (d) so that he moves by small steps, (e) therefore making few errors and practicing mostly correct responses, (f) from what he knows, by a process of successively closer approxamation, toward what he is supposed to learn from the program.' One by one these characteristics have been shown to be inessential and [30, 35] the problem of the distinction between programmes and other kinds of learning materials has become acute.

This confusion over the definition of programmed learning has arisen from a failure to distinguish the process, i.e. programming, from the products i.e. programmes. It was not until 1964 that several people independently realized that it was possible to define the process of programming but impossible to describe the nature of its products. By 1967 when the United States National Society for the Study of Education published a yearbook on programmed instruction [29], there was general agreement among the experts that the process could be defined by the following steps: (a) formulation of objectives; (b) design and testing of appropriate criterion measures to determine when the objectives have been achieved; (c) definition of the target population; (d) analysis of learning tasks; (e) preparation of prototype programme; (f) developmental testing of programme; (g) validation of programme. In developmental testing the purpose is to improve the programme and in validation it is to obtain data to demonstrate the effectiveness of the programme.

This process-based definition of programmed learning has not yet been understood by the public at large who, naturally enough, want to recognize a programme when they see one and to refer to any work published with the label 'programme' as a genuine programme. But the implication of the definition in terms of process is that learning materials can only be defined as programmed if accompanied by evidence that they have been systematically developed, i.e. by statements of objectives, criterion measures descriptions of the target population and validation data. Many of the early 'programmes' met this definition and are known to be effective, though they were not usually very efficient. Techniques have improved since then and some recent programmes have achieved similar results without taking so long. But the greatest problem has been the large number of 'pseudo-programmes' which have been published. These pseudo-programmes copied the superficial characteristics of the early programmes in that they contained the first four of Schramm's 'essential elements' but were not carefully developed by the process outlined above. In 1965, Komoski concluded from a survey of 291 programmes that no evidence of testing was available for 40 per cent

64

of them [27]; and the situation appears to be getting worse because in 1967 a survey of 707 programmes by Northeastern University found that 70 per cent had no validation data [40]. Many others are suspect because the tests used to validate them are inadequate samples of the stated objectives. The conclusion can be drawn, though it is rarely heeded, that it is exceedingly dangerous to make general statements about the class of published materials which bear the label 'programme'.

The increasingly divergent activities of programmers have also led to programmes which retain none of the distinguishing characteristics outlined by Schramm. No one in 1962, for example, would have recognized a television presentation as a programme; or a film, or a textbook, or a game, or a set of procedures to be followed by a teacher. As Markle has concluded [34]: 'With the increasing eclecticism in design illustrated above, it is not possible to look at a set of materials and insist that they *are not* programed. On the other hand, because of the ease with which the superficial characteristics of programmed materials can be mimicked without going through even an approximation to the total process as described here, it is equally impossible to look at a set of materials and say that they *are* programed. The only observable distinguishing characteristic is a product description, providing the consumer with the complete set of objectives, matching criterion measures, and data, drawn from research with students, which support the claims for the teaching effectiveness of the materials.'

Selecting a programme has become a sophisticated problem and we have no space to discuss all the issues in detail. We are therefore confining our comments to a list of questions which we have found useful in arriving at decisions on whether to adopt a programme.

QUESTIONS RELATING TO DECISIONS ABOUT ADOPTING A PROGRAMME

Do the objectives of the programme coincide with your own?
Is the population for whom the programme was developed sufficiently similar to your own?
Are there any assumptions about the learner which are not included in the statement of prerequisites?
Is the Final Test an adequate measure of achievement on the objectives of the programme?
Was the general performance of the test population satisfactory?
Did any students in the test population perform badly?
Would you expect to have similar students, and would you be able to give them special attention?
Do you have students who lack the prerequisites for the programme and could you remedy this?
How can the programme be integrated into the curriculum?
Could or should the programme be supplemented by discussion sessions?

Is there a need for tutorial help by students working through the programme and can it be met?

Have you time to plan further activities for students who finish early or students who are already proficient on the material in the programme?

Does the programme contain good subject-matter (i.e. is it accurate, are its assumptions and explanations valid)?

Is the approach of the programme compatible with your approach to teaching?

How does the programme affect pupil's attitudes, (a) towards the subject (b) towards programmes?

Does the programme give weaker pupils confidence?

Predicting the nature of programmed resources in the next decade is difficult because techniques are changing so fast. It is probably safe, however, to predict three trends. Firstly, there will be an increasing tendency to use media other than print, especially when devices like EVR become available for use as multi-media teaching machines. Secondly, there will be a tendency to adapt much more to individual differences, both because usable research findings are now beginning to emerge (see Chapter X) and because the computer will provide a means of handling it. Thirdly, that Green's comment in 1967 will continue to be true: 'The most stultifying programmes seem to be those most carefully modelled on their predecessors' [21].

REFERENCES

1. * BALANOFF, Neal. New dimensions in instructional media. In: P. H. Rossi and B. J. Biddle (eds.), *The new media and education: their impact on society.* Chicago, Aldine, 1966.

2. BARKER, R. E. Copyright at the crossroads. *Bookseller* (London), 1 February 1969.

3. * BENNETT, W. A. The language laboratory in higher education. In: D. Unwin (ed.), *Media and methods: instructional technology in higher education.* London, McGraw-Hill, 1969.

4. BIRKMAIER, Emma; LANGE, Dale. Foreign language instruction. *Review of educational research* (Washington), vol. 37, April 1967.

5. * BROWN, James W.; LEWIS, Richard B.; HARCLEROAD, Fred F. *AV instruction: media and methods.* 3rd ed. New York, McGraw-Hill, 1969.

6. * BROWN, James W.; NORBERG, Kenneth O. *Administering educational media.* New York, McGraw-Hill, 1965.

7. * BROWN, James W.; THORNTON, James W. Jr. (eds.). *New media and college teaching.* Washington, D.C., National Educational Association, 1968.

8. BROWN, Robert M. The learning center. *AV communication review* (Washington), vol. 16, no. 3, Fall 1968.

9. * BUSHNELL, Don D.; ALLEN, Dwight W. (eds.). *The computer in American education.* New York, Wiley, 1967.

10. CAFFREY, John; MOSSMAN, Charles J. *Computers on campus.* Washington, D.C., American Council on Education, 1967.

11.   CARTER-RUCK, P. F. *et al. Copyright.* London, Faber & Faber, 1965.

12.   DARLING, Richard L. Media centers. In: R. V. Wiman and W. C. Meierhenry (eds.), *Educational Media: theory into practice.* Columbus, Ohio, Charles Merrill, 1969.

13.   DEPARTMENT OF EDUCATION AND SCIENCE. *Language laboratories.* London, HMSO, 1968. (Education survey no. 3.)

14.   * DIAMOND, Robert M. *Guide to instructional television.* New York, McGraw-Hill, 1964.

15.   ———. Instructional television in perspective. In: R. A. Weisgerber (ed.), *Instructional process and media innovation.* Chicago, Rand McNally, 1968.

16.   * DUNCAN C. J. A survey of audiovisual equipment and methods. In: Derek Unwin (ed.), *Media and methods: instructional technology in higher education.* London, McGraw-Hill, 1969.

17.   GILBERT, John. Competitor to EVR. *The Times educational supplement* (London), no. 2841, 31 October 1969, p. 54.

18.   * GOODLAD, John J.; O'TOOLE, John F.; TYLER, Louise L. *Computers and information systems in education.* New York, Harcourt, Brace, 1966.

19.   GOTKIN, L. G.; MCSWEENEY, J. F. Learning from teaching machines. In: P. Lange (ed.), *Programmed Instruction.* University of Chicago Press, 1967.

20.   GRAVES, P. D. (ed.). *Film in higher education and research.* Oxford, Pergamon, 1966.

21.   GREENE, Edward J. The process of instructional programming. In: P. Lange (ed.), *Programmed instruction.* University of Chicago Press, 1967.

22.   HANSEN, Duncan N. Computer assistance in the educational process. In: R. A. Weisgerber (ed.), *Instructional process and media innovation.* Chicago, Rand McNally, 1968.

23.   HAWKIN, William R. *Copying methods manual.* Chicago, American Library Association, 1966.

24.   HEPWORTH, J. B. *The language laboratory: a bibliography.* Manchester Libraries Committee, 1966.

25.   HOLLING, K. The Feedback Classroom. In: D. Unwin (ed.), *Media and methods: instructional technology in higher education.* London, McGraw-Hill, 1969.

26.   JANOWITZ, Morris; STREET, David. The social organisation of education. In: P. H. Rossi and B. J. Biddle (eds.), *The new media and education: their impact on society.* Chicago, Aldine, 1966.

27.   KOMOSKI, P. Kenneth. Introduction. *Programmed instruction materials 1964-65.* New York, Teachers College, Columbia University, 1965.

28.   KOPSTEIN, Felix F.; SEIDEL, Robert J. Computer assisted instruction versus traditionally administered instruction: economics. *AV communication review* (Washington), vol. 16, 1968.

29.   * LANGE, Phil (ed.). *Programmed instruction. Sixty-sixth yearbook of the National Society for the Study of Education.* University of Chicago Press, 1967.

30.   LEITH, G. O. M. *Second thoughts on programmed learning.* London, Councils and Education Press, 1969. (National Council for Educational Technology occasional paper 1.)

31. * Loughary, John W. (ed.). *Man-machine systems in education*. New York, Harper & Row, 1966.

32. * MacLean, Roderick. *Television in education*. London, Methuen, 1968.

33. * ——. Television in higher education. In: D. Unwin (ed.), *Media and methods: instructional technology in higher education*. London, McGraw-Hill, 1969.

34. Markle, Susan M. Programming and programmed instruction. Prepublication draft for: *Encyclopedia of Education*. New York, Macmillan. (In press.)

35. ——. *Good frames and bad*. 2nd ed. New York, Wiley, 1969.

36. * National Council for Educational Technology. *Computer-based learning systems: a programme for research and development*. London, Councils and Education Press, 1969. (National Council for Educational Technology workins paper 1.)

37. ——. *Computer-based learning in the U.S.A.* London, 1969. (Report of a study team.)

38. ——. *Proceedings of the Conference on Computer-Based Learning, Leeds, October 1969*. London, 1970.

39. National Council of Teachers of Mathematics. *Computer-assisted instruction and the teaching of mathematics*. Washington, D.C., 1969.

40. Northeastern University. Office of Instructional Resources. *Programmed instruction guide*. Newburyport, Mass., Entelek, 1967.

41. Oettinger, Anthony G. *Run, computer, run: the mythology of educational innovation*. Chicago, Rand McNally, 1968.

42. * Potter, George. Dial-remote resources. In: R. A. Weisgerber (ed.), *Instructional process and media innovation*. Chicago, Rand McNally, 1968.

43. President's Science Advisory Committee. *Computers in higher education* Washington, D.C., Government Printing Office, 1967. (Report.)

44. Robinson, James A. Simulation and Games. In: P. H. Rossi and B. J Biddle, *The new media and education: their impact on society*. Chicago Aldine, 1966.

45. Saettler, Paul. *History of instructional technology*. New York, McGraw-Hill 1968.

46. Sanderson, Richard A. The motion picture: communication channel fo information, concepts, skills, attitudes. In: R. A. Weisgerber (ed.), *Instructional process and media innovation*. Chicago, Rand McNally, 1968.

47. Schramm, Wilbur. *Programmed instruction today and tomorrow*. New York Fund for the Advancement of Education, 1962.

48. —— (ed.). *Television, the next ten years*. Stanford, Calif., Institute for Communication Research, 1962.

49. Smith, Karl U; Smith, Margaret F. *Cybernetic principles of learning and educational design*. New York, Holt, Rinehart & Winston, 1966.

50. Stolurow, Lawrence M.; Davis, Daniel. Teaching machines and computer based systems. In: R. Glaser (ed.), *Teaching machines and programmed learning II*. Washington, D.C., National Educational Association, 1965.

51. * Tansey, P. J.; Unwin, D. *Simulation and gaming in education*. London Methuen, 1969.

52. Taplin, G. The Cosford cube: a simplified form of student feedback. *Industrial training international* (Oxford), vol. 4, no. 5, 1969.

53. Verny, H. R. *Document copying and reproduction processes*. London

Fountain Press, 1960.

54.   WEISGERBER, R. A.; RAHMLOW, Harold F. Individually managed learning. *Audiovisual instruction* (Washington), vol. 13, October 1968.

55.   * ZINN, Karl L. Computer technology for teaching and research on instruction. *Review of educational research* (Washington), vol. 37, no. 5, 1967.

56.   ——. *A basic reference shelf on interactive use of computers for instruction.* Stanford, Calif., Stanford University, ERIC Clearinghouse, 1968.

57.   UNITED STATES GOVERNMENT PRINTING OFFICE. *Copyright law revision.* Washington, D.C., 1967.

58.   EVR revolution. *Economist* (London), vol. 231, no. 6554, 5 April 1969.

59.   * Information. *Scientific American* (New York), vol. 215, no. 3, September 1966. (Reprinted by W. H. Freeman, San Francisco.)

60.   Mediated self-instruction. *Audiovisual instruction* (Washington), vol. 12, no. 5, May 1967.

61.   *Television in the university.* Manchester, Granada TV, 1965. (Report of a seminar on closed-circuit television in the university.)

V. The uses of media

We have just described the repertoire of resources now potentially available to any college or university which seeks to innovate in its teaching and learning methods. The basic question, however, is this: what are the purposes for which they are actually being used and the scale on which they are currently deployed? We cannot provide a comprehensive answer to this question, partly because their use in most universities so far is sporadic and limited, and partly because surveys are only now being made of their deployment, let alone their actual use, at the national or international level. The pace of development is so rapid that the available material cannot be more than indicative of the present situation.

The only medium which has been reported at all comprehensively at the university level is instructional television [6, 7]. In this case, sufficient data are available to give some idea, in quantitative terms, of its scale of development. For instance, the *Compendium of Television Instruction* (of which Michigan State University had published fourteen large volumes up to the end of 1967) requires several hundred pages to list the institutions and courses where television has been employed in schools and colleges [11]. From this compendium it appears that in 1958, out of more than 2,000 American institutions of higher education, only 53 universities and 34 colleges were offering courses in which television was used regularly as part of their instructional process. By 1965 these totals had risen to 166 universities and 524 colleges; by 1967 there were 277 universities, 836 colleges and 91 other institutions of higher education, plus 46 educational television stations, offering regular televised courses with a total enrolment close to 500,000. In some of these cases the installations concerned were quite small. Others, like the University of California at Berkeley, were large multi-channel systems—though even in this case the enrolments for particular courses were often not very great. A typical example of a medium-sized system would be that at Ohio University at Athens, Ohio, which in 1967 was offering its three-channel television service to twenty-six class-rooms plus a broadcast television service to five associated campuses. In the academic year 1966/67, this system had transmitted 1,282 play-backs, serving a total student enrolment of 17,244 in some 56 courses. It is clearly impossible to report in detail a development of this kind. Even on the smaller scales of the United Kingdom [3, 18], the Netherlands [5, 19] and Sweden [4], a mere summary of the departments using television and the programmes made available to specific courses would require greater space than can be devoted to it here. We have therefore given a number of the characteristics of educational television installations at the level of higher education.

The problems which inhibit a descriptive and analytical account of the use of television—which has been the most widespread, eye—catching and discussed development in new media in the last decade—apply even more forcefully to other media. We addressed inquiries to over 500 institutions and government agencies concerned with higher education throughout the world: this was a representative selection ranging from large United States universities to those of Latin America and developing countries in Africa and Asia.

Many of the replies were negative in tone. A striking example came from Japan, where a research institute reported that, even in a society where the technical base is very well developed, there are substantial difficulties in persuading university faculty or administrators to make use of it. The report states that little information is available about 'newly-developed devices applied to the field of higher education in Japan'. It is said that 'the teaching method in the universities and the colleges as yet remains unchanged and very traditional, depending generally upon formal lectures, discussion classes, tutoring and seminars, although there is a tendency for more and more rather simple and primitive audio-visual instruments such as cameras, film projectors, tape-recorders etc. to be commonly used. In addition it can be found that most departments of most foreign languages or linguistic studies at the university level are being equipped with language laboratories. The application of television and teaching machines is still very poor in Japan.' The Central Office of the Swiss Universities briefly reported in a similar vein: 'The means of modern teaching in the universities are not yet very developed or common in our universities.'

A reply from the University of the West Indies stated: 'Overall I would say that we do not at present make a great deal of use of educational technology in our teaching at this University. I gather that in the Faculty of Natural Sciences some use is made of programmed learning and films and other audio-visual media. We occasionally use films for teaching in the Department of Education. There is a computer centre, which is located in the Mathematics Department. Efforts have been made to use it for examining but not for teaching.' Makerere University College of Uganda reported that three programmed courses (each equivalent to ten weeks of full-time work) have been developed for use in the Mathematics Department. The University of Zambia states that it is establishing a closed-circuit television unit in its School of Education, and that it has set up a visual aids centre.

The Norges Tekniske/Høgskole, in Trondheim, reported that it had used television to offer a course on studying techniques for 700 new students and to provide a short course on teaching methods for its own staff; the University of Oslo has begun a systematic study of ways in which new methods can be applied to its work by the establishment of a special audio-visual development centre. Denmark reported a growing number of studies in the field of programmed instruction. Dutch universities, such as Utrecht, Nijmegen, Leyden and Groningen, have for some time been employing films, television, sound tapes and programmed materials in such fields as medical diagnosis, surgery, anatomy, dentistry, biology and child psychology.

A report from the Technion-Israel Institute of Technology shows what may be achieved by a medium-sized institution with a fairly small commitment of resources:

As to the application of educational technology to our undergraduate and postgraduate teaching, the following information might be of interest:
(a) For the past seven years there has been a Teaching Aids Centre active at the Technion. It is headed by a senior member of the academic staff and staffed by qualified technicians in various fields. The centre purchases, maintains and furnishes to interested parties basic teaching aid equipment, such as slide and filmstrip projectors, overhead projectors, opaque projectors and optical sound film projectors (8 and 16 mm), tape recorders, record players, a small unit of closed-circuit television (one camera, two monitors, one video-amplifier).

Also attached to the centre is a photography and cinematography branch with equipment for technical and scientific photography and cinematography for normal and up to high speed (8,000 frames per second). This branch of the centre is also active in the preparation of audio-visual material for use at our institute, and extends assistance for scientific and research workers. The technicians of the unit are qualified to maintain and repair its equipment and other equipment located in various scientific and academic departments of the Technion.

In addition to the equipment concentrated in the Teaching Aids Centre, there is also related equipment in various departments under the supervision of the unit.

The unit's technical services have been instrumental in the development of an audio-visual centre for teaching Hebrew to newcomers and foreign languages to staff and students.
(b) Several experiments have been performed in the field of programmed learning. The results have, in most cases, not been very promising and the method is at present not being further developed.
(c) Closed-circuit television (CCTV) has not been very widely used, mainly because of the relatively low adequacy of the equipment at our disposal.

(d) The facilities of our computer centre have for the time being not yet been utilised for straightforward learning purposes, though the students of all departments are taught computer programming.

(e) At the beginning of each new academic year, all new junior academic staff members (postgraduate assistants and instructors) are invited to attend a one-week seminar (approximately 30 hours) on the methodology of teaching. There, the Vice-President for Academic Affairs, experienced senior staff members of our department for secondary teacher training and the Head of the Teaching Aids Unit, lecture on various aspects of the teaching activities of the junior staff. In addition, various departments, through the initiative of the Deans, organise seminars, discussion groups and actual courses for the improvement of teaching in order to make the teaching process more effective, and to enable the teachers to devote more time to their research work without adversely affecting the quality of instruction.

(f) A number of staff members have conducted research in various aspects of teaching methods and on the comparative value of teaching aids.

We also quote a reply from Potchefstroom University in South Africa, where there appears to be a keen sense of need for new techniques, and a desire to introduce them when resources are available:

We are also confronted with the mounting problems of steeply increasing enrolment of students with varying needs, backgrounds, interests and abilities; of coping with the vast mass of new knowledge in practically every sphere; of finding the answer to the problem of general education with the necessary specialisation, of meeting the diversifying needs of a growing and ever-changing national and international community; of raising funds for a never-ending stream of requests for buildings, equipment, staff, research facilities and the introduction of new courses of study; of finding sufficient properly equipped staff—often even having to train staff for new specialisations—to educate in the fullest sense of the word; of reconciling vocational and academic needs; of continually adapting syllabuses, teaching methods and materials, evaluation techniques, organisation and administration to new circumstances; of finding the happy medium for research and teaching responsibilities of staff; of finding a rational staffing scale; and of defining objectives.

This university has also begun to consider the operational implications of making new approaches to their problems:

The university greatly values personal contact between teacher and student, and all possible steps are taken to improve this contact in order to enable the teacher to educate the student in the widest—sense—as well as to teach in the narrower sense. For this reason the size of classes is limited as far as possible, and in larger groups frequent use is made of tutorials. The stress on personal contact in an effective educational situation does not, however, preclude the university from applying modern technological aids. Some departments are experimenting with programmes and teaching machines (Commerce), some actively use a language laboratory and tape recorders (Arts and others), films, filmstrips, epidiascopes, micro- and overhead projectors are used extensively (Natural Sciences and others), a computer (Statistics) is used in the training of programmers and operators in research (all departments) and in processing administrative data, in common with other South African universities, wide use is made of micro-film in the library, 3M Reader Printers (and other varieties being used), Xerox 914s are frequently encountered and some universities are at present fully computerising their library administration.

Apart from the cost factor, programmed teaching is limited by a scarcity of programmes suited to our syllabuses, by a lack of programmes in the language of our institution (Afrikaans) and mainly by the fact that we do not really, at this stage, deem it necessary to use this aid. Post-graduate students are, however, being trained in programme writing. On the whole, there are few signs of programmed teaching in South African universities, although a weather eye is kept on the subject.

The advantages and limitations of TV in education are fully realised but, at present, for various valid reasons, our country is still without television. The current financial commitments of this university precludes the early introduction of closed-circuit TV (although basic facilities are planned in proposed buildings). Some universities, and teachers' colleges, e.g. Pretoria, Cape Town, Natal and the Johannesburg College of Education use closed-circuit TV on a limited scale and others—the Rand Afrikaans University—are planning extensive introduction.

This university in particular (and all South African universities in general) is fully alive to the uses of the various technological aids and is prepared to introduce them in lecture room, laboratory, library and hostel, should the necessity arise and the funds be available.

An excellent digest of the American situation has recently been provided by James W. Thornton and James W. Brown in *New, Media and College Teaching* to which reference may be made [2]. Part of its value lies in the fact that it is a revised version of a work first produced four years earlier and incorporates a comparison of the activities undertaken in 1963 and 1967. On this the authors comment: 'The evidence reviewed indicates clearly that it is no longer true that college instruction is the most conservative aspect of American civilisation. In a period of only four years, during which problems of rapid growth in numbers of institutions and in numbers of students have had to be accommodated, there is undeniable expansion in the thoughtful application of previously reported new media to instruction. No innovative practice of promise at that time is now reported to have been abandoned for reasons of cost or of faculty inertia; rather there is evidence of careful evaluation of results of experimental instruction and of rapid development of more sophisticated and effective applications of practices that were at first adopted only tentatively and unpretentiously.'

Progress in the U.S.S.R. has also been considerable [17].

But in most cases institutions found themselves unable to describe in detail what was happening within their own walls except in the most general terms, and no clear general picture emerged from the replies as a whole except the general impression (to which we have referred) that it is only in a few countries, and even in relatively few institutions within them, that the first steps are now being taken to move beyond the very elementary provision of simple audio-visual equipment. We have therefore chosen to summarize the purposes for which the new media are being employed.

Firstly, new media can be used as aids to the presentation process. This has hitherto been the usual point of entry for new devices and techniques into the process of teaching and learning. It is significant that they have made their appearance in the majority of institutions on an *ad hoc* basis without much prior consideration of research findings on their utility (see Chapters VI and X) or systematic evaluation of their impact where they are employed. A lecturer using slides in a geography class, for instance, is unlikely to consider their role much more critically than that of the maps or blackboard diagrams that he normally employs. He will simply decide heuristically that they add some extra dimension to his teaching, and will judge their value by the rule-of-thumb methods (such as his impressions of student reaction) that he habitually employs in his work. It can nevertheless be said, as a matter of common observation, that the use of audio-visual materials in a whole range of teaching seems to add clarity and precision to the way the content of a particular lecture or teaching session is presented. The mere discipline of seeking out, or preparing for oneself, materials that are suitable for one's course probably adds a great deal to its educational effectiveness, just as a selection of appropriate readings, rather than a rambling series of bibliographic references, makes it easier for students to comprehend the learning tasks in which they are involved.

Two other closely related results of audio-visual procedure are associated with clarity. One of these is accuracy. A carefully drawn diagram using colour (and possibly, in the case of overhead projector transparencies, several overlays) is usually preferable to a hastily drawn and sometimes inaccurate blackboard sketch; the presentation of mathematical formulae or tables (by slides or overhead projection) will certainly make it easier for a class to take notes and to follow the lecturer's commentary than is the case if he is simultaneously speaking and writing such tables by hand upon his blackboard. This is particularly important in scientific, medical, mathematical and social-science subject areas. It is not only the efficient presentation of the material to the student that is involved here; provided that the lecturer does not have to spend inordinate amounts of time on preparing material and operating the equipment to present it, he himself derives considerable convenience from having high-quality materials at his fingertips. He saves time in the class and, if the materials can be used over a period of years, he undoubtedly saves preparation time in the end. All three of these points, it should be stressed, apply across quite a wide spectrum of presentation and are not confined merely to projected or recorded materials. The use of modern printing, reprographic and duplicating facilities is increasing fast as a means of providing students with essential working materials, and the convenience factor is certainly enhanced when new courses are being offered—especially those of an interdisciplinary character—in which the essential teaching and learning materials cannot easily be found in existing textbooks or other conventional sources.

Secondly, media can be used as aids to demonstration. Leaving on one side the complex issue of improved activation—and there is some evidence that interest is aroused and that learning is enhanced by new methods of presentation—there is a whole series of teaching objectives which can be better achieved by new media. This is because they can actually transmit reality or simulations of reality in a manner superior to that available to the solitary lecturer addressing a class. For example, the demonstration of motion by film or television is usually superior to a verbal description of it. Cases in point range from animation or models which show movement to motion pictures of machinery in operation. There are many occasions, moreover, when it is desired to show a large class a scientific demonstration or a surgical operation which would normally be visible only to a few at close range. A micro-projector may be used to show microscope slides; closed-circuit television may give a whole class access to a mass spectrometer or an example of dental surgery or simply a close-up of instrument readings or a particular piece of apparatus. Though many university teachers are beginning to realize the potential of the new media in this respect, an enormous range of possibilities is now opening up which we have only just begun to explore—many of which, it must be said, do not require either elaborate equipment or complicated procedures to make them viable.

There is another aspect to improved demonstration: that is, access to materials which otherwise would be quite inaccessible. The outstanding recent example familiar to everyone was the first television transmission from the surface of the moon, and the subsequent film and photographs that have been made available. Without these means, needless to say, both the impact and the knowledge of the Apollo missions would have been much less. There are many lesser examples of the same point which either can be found in university teaching already or can be suitably developed in it. The most familiar exemplifications are films relevant to geography and anthropology, which are capable of conveying basic information of a different order from that achievable by print or even still pictures. The same can be said of many types of sound recording, not merely those used for language teaching. Sound remains a cheap and relatively unexploited medium in higher education, and probably offers one of the most convenient lines of development in this field. It can bring a wealth of easily used and original materials into any claas-room, just as various forms of still and motion pictures can be used to demonstrate what otherwise cannot be seen by the student for himself. Techniques have been developing in the use of film and television in such subjects as surgery, engineering and biology which demonstrate what previously could only be conjectured or described; in this category, broadly speaking, we must include situations that are theoretically accessible but may not prove to be so in practice. Certain types of experimental observation fall into this group: the observation of animal behaviour under experimental conditions, where the whole process may take place under conditions in which no human observer can easily be present; even more, one finds the increasing use, in teacher training, of recorded observation of teacher and pupil behaviour where particular attitudes, skills or responses may be monitored and subsequently used as a reference source to demonstrate situations that cannot be readily repeated, or at will; and there are examples in psychiatry and social work where recorded observation of patients or clients is possible but where the presence of an observing group of students would seriously interfere with the work that is being carried out.

Thirdly, media are used as aids to the solution of logistic problems. The arguments for using media as aids to presentation depend upon the hypothesis that they 'improve' teaching and learning within the existing framework. Virtually all the early work in the field of audio-visual aids really related to this hypothesis; and it is true that a widespread development of aids can occur, where there is interest and money, without going beyond that framework. Gradually, however, the newer media have been breaking out of it; they have been increasingly applied to problems created by the inability of the older system to cope with changes coming both from within education and from social pressures.

One of the major characteristics of the newer technology is that it transcends many of the limitations hitherto imposed upon education by the traditional pattern of the teacher in the class-room. As long as the process of educational communication depended upon the range of the human voice and eye, and upon the custodial and organizational constraints which brought a limited number of students together in a room with a teacher, a great many limits were placed on flexibility. The staff structure, the teaching method and even the building plans of most educational institutions reflect these limitations because, apart from the book and other printed matter, educational communication had no viable means of breaking out of the parameters imposed by requirements of time and place. The essence of the newer media, as we pointed out in the previous chapter, is that they are not necessarily limited in this way. The use of broadcast television and radio is the most obvious and dramatic of the changes which are occurring, but many of the other devices now available offer the opportunity for the student to enter a learning situation more or less at will at the time and place he chooses. The essence of this situation is that the software which can be presented by new devices is the visual or auditory counterpart of the printed word and can have much the same permanency and transportability.

In this sense Marshall McLuhan's arguments have some force. The very nature of the new technology offers the potential of an instructional change, irrespective of the messages the media carry. Once it is possible to use television, radio and recordings, some of the need to achieve large concentrations of pupils or students has been removed, though there are other educational and social reasons for maintaining such concentrations in schools and colleges where group personal contact, group interaction and access to library and laboratory facilities are available. Equally, once educational materials are available in a recorded form, it is possible not only to permit repetition and frequent access within an institution; we can also see that high-quality learning materials can be deployed throughout an educational system, whether at the school or university level, to give students opportunities which previously did not exist. It can be seen, therefore, that the concept of 'access' leads to many new ways in which universities might organize learning situations; an examination of the uses to which colleges and universities are putting newer media clearly reveals that this seems to them one promising line of development. It bears a very direct relationship to one of the major and growing problems: organizing the increasingly large numbers which are entering higher education throughout the world.

Instructional television (and also radio), as we indicated above, provides the most obvious demonstration of this fact. The Chicago College of the Air [8], which broadcast courses for credit and associated them with other instructional activities, was an early example of this phenomenon which has now been carried forward by a number of university-based situations in the United States. Similar activities have been undertaken in the U.S.S.R., linked to extensive correspondence-course facilities, and in the Republic of South Africa through the medium of radio, based on the University of Pretoria [12, 20]. Both the Swedish TRU and the Open University project in the United Kingdom are significant steps in the same direction. It seems very likely that the next decade will see a very large increase in the use of broadcasting at the level of higher education which will be directed primarily at students who are not enrolled full-time in institutions of higher education; the materials produced for this purpose may well begin to penetrate even those colleges and universities which have more traditional teaching systems.

The question of numbers, however, applies within institutions as well as generally within the university system and it manifests itself in a variety of forms. Large universities in Europe and Latin America, as well as in the United States, have often to cope with very large classes, especially in the first two years of higher education; they offer introductory courses which may run to totals of a thousand or more enrolments. It is a common sight in an American university or college to see such classes broken into groups of

200 or 300 for lectures, many of which are delivered by relatively young and inexperienced faculty members. As Pennsylvania State University demonstrated at an early stage in the development of television at university level, it was possible to use senior staff to present the main lecture live or in recorded form and to transmit this to many groups of students, using the supporting faculty to cope more directly with student questions and problems.

There are many variations upon this central theme. We find television being used to overcome accommodation problems: where an institution does not have sufficient lecture theatre space to permit the simultaneous housing of all the students in a course, a recorded presentation is used to repeat the same lecture to different sections of the same course at different times of the day. In a similar fashion time-table problems can be overcome. The course offerings and options in some institutions make it extremely difficult to ensure that all students taking a major course are so time-tabled as to be free at the same moment. Where a lecture or programme can be repeated at different hours or even on different days, it is possible to remove some of the constraints upon time-tabling.

It must be said that though considerable progress has been made in these directions in the last few years, most of the developments are still at a comparatively early stage and serve more to demonstrate potential than to provide evidence in strict cost-benefit terms that they have justified themselves. Many institutions now possess quite elaborate television systems which are used well below capacity.

One reason for this lies in the nature of any television system, which requires a minimum level of plant, staff and facilities to reach reasonable professional standards and may not, therefore, in its early stages have the capability to display its special production ability or to meet the demands which faculty are prepared to make upon it. Frequently it costs relatively little more to provide a six-channel distribution system in an institution than to install one-channel capacity; but it costs a great deal more to provide studio space and, even more, the professional staff and the faculty time needed to produce a software output commensurate with the display capability. A further explanation lies in the resistance to innovation of this kind on the part of faculty and others, who feel that this method of teaching is not yet proven, is too expensive, too time-consuming or simply too much bother. A third reason derives from the problem of size. A television installation in an institution enrolling relatively few students (about 3,000 students or below seems to be the cut-off point) is unlikely to find that an elaborate television service will make much immediate impact on its logistic problems, since the numbers of students enrolled in any given course may not be very large. The full operational benefits of television at least are unlikely to be reaped in institutions which are so small, and in which the unit cost of the television installation is unlikely to be competitive with traditional methods [9].

The value of television begins to emerge when programmes can be either used for large classes within an institution or, preferably, provided for students in a number of institutions or in their homes.

Merely to look at media from the standpoint of numbers, nevertheless, is to overlook the contribution they can make to the solution of other operational problems. So far as developing countries are concerned, one of the more serious problems, apart from numbers, is the shortage of highly qualified specialist teachers in subjects such as medicine, applied sciences, agriculture and para-professional courses. This shortage does impose constraints, not merely upon the numbers of students who can be taught effectively but also upon the range of subjects and the levels to which they can be taught. There is no doubt that television particularly can offer a way in which scarce teaching resources can be brought to bear more effectively, whether the medium is used live (from broadcasting stations) or in recorded form through devices such as VTR and EVR. What is true of television and radio in this context applies also to other media-based learning materials which serve as carriers for complete learning sequences. The more such media combinations as audio-tape/slide, or audio-tape and programmed text, are developed to cover fairly substantial units of instruction, the greater the use that can be made of scarce, high-quality instructional resources.

We referred earlier to the failure so far to make adequate use of audio inputs in teaching, even though these are relatively cheap and easy to produce. This may be understood in part by a prestige factor: television has more obvious appeal and attracts professional staff who develop their own innovatory momentum, whereas radio and, even more, audio-recording, have less prestige. It may also be explained by cultural factors that have been insufficiently explored. (In some societies with a strong oral tradition, the use of audio tapes may be more effective than in countries where students are conditioned by long exposure to film, television and other visual information carriers.) Normally, the addition of either still or motion pictures to a sound track seems to add a dimension of involvement for students that has very little obvious relationship to the visual component of the combination. Students offered a choice between a television programme which is no more than a 'talking head' and the sound track of the same lecture, appear to prefer the former; it is significant that the greatest use of sound in higher education has occurred in language teaching, where the audio facilities are used either with teacher-mediation or by the student who is making active responses in language-laboratory conditions. We regard this as a matter that merits a good deal of further inquiry in order to establish more precisely the obstacles to an extended use of sound, since the operational attractiveness of sound (lower cost and effort involved in preparation, easy distribution through radio and wired circuits, tape recorders and discs, and flexibility in use) is great, and the widespread use of sound recording should not encounter certain of the barriers to innovation which affect, let us say, television, film and even programmed instruction. For one thing, materials prepared for audio tape use, separately or in association with print and/or slides, are much more easily translated or cheaply modified for use in different contexts than is the case with expensive films or television productions. It has also been shown by the experience of the language laboratory that audio facilities are among the most easy to adapt to programming which involves an active verbal response by the student.

One of the reasons why this field of investigation merits more attention is that it potentially lends itself to independent study more easily than systems which require elaborate display facilities or the mediation of the teacher. One of the more interesting trends in the United States in recent years has been the establishment of independent study facilities, where students under library-type conditions can get access to recorded programmes, either for original instruction or for review and remedial teaching. In March 1968, the Center for Educational Technology at the Catholic University of America in Washington conducted a study of dial-access facilities in American education. This showed that at the time there were 120 dial-access systems operational in the United States, half of which were in colleges and universities. These installations varied in cost between $ 10,000 and $ 100,000, most of them being audio only, but of the twelve systems with video capability, five were at the college level.

This admirable survey, which included technical specifications as well as operational details, indicated that independent access to recorded media may very well become one of the most valuable and flexible innovations at the higher educational level, for it shifts learning into a library or personal mode of study and away from the class-room or group presentation. It also has the merit that it can be used for long periods of the day (some American systems have terminals located in dormitories which are accessible through internal telephone systems and are on-line from 6.00 a.m. till midnight). There is no technical reason, moreover, why college or university facilities of this kind could not be made available for access from outside a campus through public telephone systems. Such facilities can easily be automated; their capacity is limited only by the size of the recording bank and the available amount of relevant software [15].

They do not require the same staffing or operational commitment that is needed to regulate regular television transmissions or to provide a planned service to specific class-rooms. They begin to approach the ideal of random access, and can be employed either for teachers to secure material for presentation at will or to enable individual students to do so.

There is a further advantage in that such systems can eventually be linked to a variety of information storage and presentation devices. Even before computer-based facilities become widely available (though these can clearly be linked to similar student terminals) there are a variety of retrieval techniques which can be employed to service students with information on request, as well as to present organized learning sequences.

It may very well be that in these early dial-access systems we have, in embryonic form, a much more promising model for media use at the university level than the models which relate to group presentation and are derived originally from a combination of traditional teaching methods and mass media. It is their development potential that attracts: they seem likely to overcome so many of the constraints that other teaching methods encounter and, possibly, to offer ways in the long run of reconciling the paradox that while educational practice is facing more and more the problems of large numbers, educational theory is increasingly indicating the desirability of independent and even individualized learning processes. The experience gained in operating such systems will also be an invaluable preparation for the design and management of computerized learning systems, since many of the procedures, not least the preparation of suitable software and the management of complex combinations of material, anticipate those involved in computer-based learning. Computerization, amongst other things, will add the possibility of assessment and diagnosis of the learning behaviour of students working under these conditions.

Fourthly, media can be used to promote interaction in the teaching and learning process. We have so far been considering the uses to which media are put for presentation, for demonstration and for logistic reasons. As this development occurs, a change in emphasis emerges. The new resources cease to be mere aids to an existing teaching pattern; by a reciprocal process they become more integral to the teaching and learning process [21]. There are now a number of new techniques which are dependent for their existence upon the use of new equipment and methods. That is to say, a particular teaching or learning activity is actually dependent upon one or more media and if the media resources involved were removed, the technique itself would not be viable.

The most obvious example of this kind is the language laboratory, though it still remains a matter of controversy among teachers of languages and linguistics whether language-laboratory facilities are desirable or, if desirable, whether they are being used in the best ways. Serious criticisms have been made in the United States in the last two or three years of the provision of language laboratories on a very large scale in colleges and schools. These criticisms rest both on academic grounds and in terms of relative cost and under-utilization. Some of these strictures appear to be justified but it must be said that where this new technique has been well used, both the teacher and students consider it a valuable innovation.

The opportunity for students to listen, and to respond themselves, to systematic oral instruction in a language undoubtedly contributes to facility in its use. The need for such provision increases to the degree that there is a shortage of competent instructors with a comprehensive knowledge of the language and the capacity to speak it with acceptable idiom and accent. The literature in this field is extensive, and more has probably been done to develop satisfactory methods for this new media-based method than for any other, since language teaching already had developed methodological sophistication and is based upon a cadre of teachers with professional training and interest in teaching. When language teachers were offered a new tool which could be assimilated in the existing methodology and practices, yet still permitted them to play a creative role in relation to their students, through supervision and the production of their own software, many of them were eager to accept it. It seems unlikely that the criticisms now being directed at language laboratories will seriously inhibit their increase, though it may usefully direct attention at shortcomings in the way they are currently used. (It should be noted also that considerable success has been achieved with both radio and television programmes for language teaching, even though these lack the 'active response' capability of the language laboratory.)

The language laboratory is positioned at the bridge point between group and individual instruction. Much the same may be said of the much newer technique of micro-teaching or micro-counselling [1, 13]. In this case various media—primarily television but also audio tapes and slides—are being employed to modify the behaviour of individuals as part of a training process. It has been made possible by the facility offered by video- and audio-tape recorders, which permit an instructor to record a student activity and to play it back immediately, or on a later occasion, for discussion either with the student concerned or a group of students. The technique was first developed for use in the training of teachers but it has subsequently been extended to the retraining of existing teachers (including those at university level) and to assist all those preparing for professional careers in medicine, psychiatry and social work [16].

The principle on which the technique rests is that of systematic feedback and revision. It has been found that if a student teacher performs in front of a real or simulated class, this performance is susceptible to critical assessment with beneficial results. It is possible for the student both to witness his or her performance, observe the pupil or client response, and receive the comments both of the instructor and of other students; the student can then repeat the presentation with modifications. There is accumulating evidence which bears witness to the effectiveness of this process, both in eliminating bad habits and in guiding the student (or university teacher) to more effective and creative activity in the class-room. Micro-teaching can focus upon specific skills, such as cueing and prompting, upon techniques for organizing work, for controlling the discipline of a class or upon the capacity to evoke response from pupils. It is, that is to say, corrective, therapeutic and dynamic. Here again is a promising line of development which integrally depends upon the use of new facilities and it is fortunate that the equipment which it requires is relatively cheap and can be used in most cases with minimal support from professional or technical staff. At its simplest it can be done with audio tapes and slides; a great deal more is possible with a cheap and portable video recording chain, costing about $ 1,500; and where more elaborate television facilities exist, these can be used to achieve higher levels of sophistication in the process [9].

The shift towards more independent and even individualized methods of study and away from large-group presentation also involves the use of new presentation media and promotes interaction in the teaching-learning process [22]. The development of programmed learning, whether it takes the form of printed texts or materials presented through teaching machines or other audio-visual media is a case in point. While programming is a principle which can be applied in any media and is done most cheaply and expediously through print. In recent years new devices and new materials have been developed to present multi-media learning sequences to students working as individuals at times convenient to them or appropriate to the point in the curriculum that they have reached. One of the earliest and most influential of these projects was that undertaken in the biology department at Purdue University, Indiana, by Professor S. N. Postlethwait [14]. His aim was to establish a basic laboratory situation in which students could work through a learning sequence at times and at a pace that suited them. A laboratory was established consisting entirely of individual study places, each equipped with an audio-recorder, slide and, later, 8 mm film loop-projectors together with the necessary instruments and biological materials. This laboratory, open at all times of the working day, enabled students to come and go as they chose, to take their own time on working through any dissections and experiments, to repeat parts of the learning sequence as often as they wished, to go back and review units in the course as they pleased and to have access for questions and problems to one of the graduate students who monitored the work in the lab. The success of the Purdue project has led to its imitation elsewhere, not merely in biology but in other fields.

It has been found that this method is highly suitable for introductory courses, that it relieves pressure upon normal laboratory space, that it adds flexibility of timing and learning pace for the students, and that it opens up new possibilities for assessment and diagnosis. It has the further advantage that it can be used for remedial purposes without requiring the whole class to go back over certain aspects of the course, or to offer elements in a course for which time and facilities are lacking when conventional means are used.

The experience deriving from all these innovations in which the media are integral to the teaching-learning process will prove invaluable as learning systems become more elaborate. We discuss elsewhere some of the implications which follow from the application of computers, not all of which necessarily involve a direct interface between the computer and the student. But to the extent that a direct computer interface is employed either in a tutorial mode where the student engages in a direct activity such as typing or the use of a light pen, or where the computer is organizing and sequencing the presentation of learning materials, the computer must be regarded as an example of a communications medium which is directly integrated in the teaching and learning process. It thereby, like other media, begins to transform the learning situation itself and consequently both the organizational structure and the physical circumstances of learning.

In all the examples we have just been discussing, such a transformation is occurring and creating quite new perspectives for higher education. Once we reach this stage, we are no longer talking about media as agents for reinforcing the conventional pattern; we are beginning to achieve a break-out from the modes of instruction that have done duty for so long and still provide the main learning situations for the majority of students.

Fifthly, new devices and techniques can be used as aids to the assessment process. Any serious study of the wide variety of ways in which media can now be used in teaching and learning suggests that they may also have considerable significance in the processes of diagnosis and assessment. Very little progress has so far been made in this direction, partly because the new media have been entering education in the first instance as presentation devices operating within a system which has employed conventional methods of assessment, partly because no one has been quite sure how to identify and assess what may be different types of learning that are occurring as a result, and partly because very little attention has been paid to the use of electro-mechanical equipment for assessment. It has been argued, for instance, that conventional written tests are not the most appropriate way to assess what has been learnt from visual stimuli, though so little is yet known about the transfer of learning from one type of stimulus to a different type of response that no clear conclusion can be reached on this point. One of the obvious attractions of the language laboratory is that the response mode is congruent with the stimulus mode, and with the objective; a student learns to speak a language he wishes to speak. A television demonstration of a scientific experiment, however, is not necessarily congruent with the development of laboratory skills, though it may well permit a cognitive gain which enables a student accurately to describe an experiment in a written examination answer.

We should expect, as the use of many different new types of equipment develops, many more experiments to be undertaken to establish how they can contribute to effective assessment. We are not merely thinking, for example, of such projects as the use by Duke University in North Carolina of video-tape presentations of dissections for the purposes of examinations in anatomy. We are also considering that forms of concurrent assessment may be devised using the recording capacity of many of the new devices. A development of this kind would fit very well into the need which we have already discussed for learning systems to be revised in the light of the student responses that they evoke, since in this case assessment of student activity is not regarded as the terminal point of an instructional sequence but as something which is crucial to the design and revision of the sequence and to alternative learning paths within it.

Automated marking equipment has also been employed in a number of institutions [10]. This equipment uses standardized answer forms for objective testing, which are afterwards automatically processed by feed-scanning and print-out equipment. Such a method has been in use for some years at Pennsylvania State University, for instance, where it forms part of a testing service which offers individual teachers assistance in the design of objective tests and the randomization of their questions and undertakes the necessary data processing. Where large numbers of students are involved, say in first-year classes, there is no doubt that automated marking can remove a great burden of routine grading of objective tests from junior academic staff who normally spend many hours a week on such tasks. It may very well be that as remote study (of the type envisaged for the Open University in the United Kingdom) develops, forms of automated marking may very well prove a useful means of providing a running check upon certain types of student achievement [12, 20].

Media may also be used for assessing performance skills. We have referred above to the use of television in the context of micro-teaching: there is no doubt that recording of student performance (in the form of video and audio tapes) could provide a rather more reliable indicator of the levels of skill acquired than, let us say, the impressions carried away by supervisors who make infrequent visits to student teachers in class-room practice. Such a technique might very well be extended to a number of fields, particularly those where manipulative or behavioural skills are highly relevant, such as certain branches of medicine, dental surgery, applied sciences, fine arts and physical education.

A much greater level of integration with the assessment process is likely to occur eventually as computers are employed. There are signs, as we show later, that computers may come into use for management and assessment purposes sooner than what may be called 'direct tutorial' activities. Computers can easily hold records of student performance and it would be relatively simple to analyse such records diagnostically and to use the diagnosis to determine what the next set of learning tasks or materials set for the student should be. Though such a development depends upon the devising of suitable diagnostic methods and on the availability of the necessary bank of software, there is no conceptual or operational obstacle to be overcome in this respect. Indeed, what is known as computer-managed learning, employs precisely this principle, which demands only limited access to terminals for the teacher or individual students. There are several American projects of this kind now in operation.

It is implicit in the adoption of media as operational aids that they should help to make higher education more efficient. The difficulty in justifying this proposition is that the criteria of 'efficiency' are difficult to define. Much discussion is now proceeding about the definition of productivity in education and the question of new media is clearly germane to it. As long as educational objectives are not specified in operational and measurable terms (or cannot be) the criteria employed are bound either to be very general and subjective or else quantified into relatively crude critical indicators such as staff-student ratios, the proportion of entrants ultimately graduating, the use of such physical plant as lecture theatres, libraries and laboratories, the cost per student place or per graduate in recurrent or capital expenditure, the division of funds between administration, teaching and research and the like. It is extremely difficult to compare one mode of teaching to another, let alone one department or one university to another in terms of quality, attitudes, skills and long-term professional capacity of university graduates.

In this situation, the ways in which new media can be used to promote efficiency are hard to estimate precisely. Attempts have been made to evaluate them in cost-benefit terms, though few of them have produced significant results, and the ratio of serious evaluative projects to innovations is surprisingly low. (For example, the dial-access survey mentioned earlier reported that only a quarter of the responding institutions were engaged in any type of evaluation of their dial-access systems and only 5 per cent were actively engaged in research into the educational efficiency of dial-access.) Much the same could be said of the great majority of media innovations. We are now approaching a point in time where much more onerous demands for such evaluation will be made upon media innovators. The greater the financial stringency suffered by higher education, the more rigorously will innovatory expenditure be scrutinized. It is also true that such stringency, combined with large numbers, may make academic administrations more anxious to consider innovations in the light of the contribution they may make to efficient use of scarce resources than to judge them by their role in 'improving' learning. It is hard to see the way forward in this respect. Certainly, 'efficiency' has been part of the general rationale for media innovation, but most of those involved have been too concerned with the early problems of setting up operating media systems to devote much time to their evaluation: those with an interest in evaluation have usually found it hard to devise suitable instruments for measurement.

While other aspects of the total system lack systematic evaluation, moreover, it is difficult to know how media innovations can be related to them in comparable terms even where some aspects of these innovations can be precisely measured. For this reason it seems that more progress may at present be made by approaching the cost problem by looking at input rather than output characteristics. Such an approach at least has the advantage that the relative costs of inputs can be estimated more nearly than aspects of ouput which involve judgements about learning effectiveness as well as quantitative features. For example, the role that media can play in promoting the more efficient use of lecture theatres and laboratories or in processing large numbers of students can be determined. Similarly, it would be possible to note where subjects or topics are being covered with the aid of media that could not otherwise have been offered at all or at the necessary level by conventional means. If the introduction of media on any large scale is to continue, for motives other than faith or fashion, it seems necessary for much more serious work to be done to investigate their contribution in cost-benefit terms, though with the proviso that this will only reveal significant results if this is undertaken as part of a general review of an institution's operations, rather than in isolation. Here again, all the evidence points to the need to regard a university as a system, rather than an aggregation of discrete activities.

REFERENCES

1. * ALLEN, D. W.; RYAN, K. A. *Microteaching*. Reading, Mass., Addison Wesley, 1969.
2. * BROWN, James W.; THORNTON, James W. Jr. (eds.). *New media and college teaching*. Washington, D.C., National Educational Association, 1968.
3. JONES, Sir Brynmor (chairman). *Audio-visual aids in higher scientific education*. London, HMSO, 1965. (Committee Report.)
4. COMMITTEE FOR TELEVISION AND RADIO IN EDUCATION (TRU). *Television and radio in Swedish education*. Stockholm, 1969.
5. DE VOGEL, W. *Thinking about university video centres in the Netherlands*. Utrecht, Scientific Film Institute, 1969.
6. DIAMOND, Robert M. *Guide to instructional television*. New York, McGraw-Hill, 1964.
7. ——. Instructional television in perspective. In: R. A. Weisgerber (ed.), *Instructional process and media innovation*. Chicago, Rand McNally, 1968.
8. ERICKSON, Clifford G.; CHAUSOW, Hyman. *Chicago's TV College. Final report of a three-year experiment of the Chicago City Junior College in offering college courses for credit via open-circuit television*. Chicago, 1960.
9. GIBSON, Tony. *Multi-purpose ETV on a budget. A guide to television in education and training*. London, British Association for Commercial and Industrial Education, 1968.
10. LINDQUIST, E. F. The impact of machines on educational measurement. In: R. W. Tyler (ed.), *Educational evaluation: new roles, new means*. University of Chicago Press, 1969.
11. McKUNE, Lawrence E. *Compendium of television instruction*. Vol. 14. Michigan State University, 1967.
12. OPEN UNIVERSITY. *First prospectus*. Milton Keynes, England, 1969.
13. PERLBERG, Arye. Microteaching: a new procedure to improve teaching and training. *Journal of educational technology* (London), January 1970.
14. POSTLETHWAIT, S. N.; NOVAK, J.; MURRAY, H. *An integrated experience approach to learning*. Minneapolis, Burgess, 1964.
15. POTTER, George. Dial-remote resources. In: R. A. Weisgerber (ed.), *Instruc-*

tional process and media innovation. Chicago, Rand McNally, 1968.

16. SCHUELER, H.; LESSER, G. S.; DOBBINS, A. L. *Teacher education and the new media.* Washington, D.C., American Association of Colleges for Teacher Education, 1967.

17. SHAKMAEV, N.; ZILKIN, N.; PETRUSHKIN, S. Studies in the U.S.S.R. on the use of technical media in education. *New methods and techniques in education,* Paris, Unesco, 1963.

18. * UNWIN, D. (ed.). *Media and methods: instructional technology in higher education.* London, McGraw-Hill, 1969.

19. VAROSSIEAU, Jan W. The use of closed-circuit television and scientific films for university teaching in the Netherlands. *Impact of science on society* (Paris), vol. 18, no. 1, 1968.

20. VENABLES, Sir Peter (chairman). *The Open University. Report of the Planning Committee.* London, HMSO, 1969.

21. WEISGERBER, Robert A. (ed.). *Instructional process and media innovation.* Chicago, Rand McNally, 1968.

22. * WIMAN, Raymond V.; MEIERHENRY, W. C. *Educational media: theory into practice.* Columbus, Charles Merrill, 1969.

VI. The ideology of media

Many arguments are used to support the introduction of new media into education, to suggest that these new devices can extend the scale and improve the quality of learning. Clearly, some of these arguments have proved persuasive, since considerable sums of money and effort are already being devoted to these innovations in the hope that they will soon begin to pay dividends in the form of more extensive and more effective learning. As a group they may be described as the ideology of media: that is, the system of attitudes, beliefs and hopes which sustain those who are attempting to introduce new media into education, expressed in its most extreme form by Marshall McLuhan [6].

The first of the arguments is not even based on educational experience at all: it is essentially an argument based upon analogy. It has been noted that education—variously called 'a cottage industry' and 'the last of the manual trades'—has so far failed to profit from the revolution in communications technology (notably in electronics) which is transforming so many other aspects of work and leisure. It is further suggested that it is time for education to change from being a labour-intensive to a capital-intensive occupation: a shift that modern technology has accomplished in so many industries in this century. The point has often been made at length, but it has been well put briefly by Dr. Philip H. Coombs, lately director of the International Institute for Educational Planning, who has written that [2]: 'Education's technology, by and large, has made surprisingly little progress beyond the handicraft stage, whereas remarkable strides have been made in the technology and productivity of many other sectors of human activity, such as medicine, transportation, mining, communications and manufacturing.'

There are, of course, special difficulties to be overcome in the case of education, even though its especially heavy demands on the scarce supply of skilled personnel—and the high proportion (between 60 and 80 per cent) of educational budgets spent on the salaries of teachers—make the idea of lower labour-intensity most attractive. The underlying fear that mechanization and automation will devitalize what is essentially a humanist enterprise underlies many expressed doubts about the effectiveness and cost of the new technology. Some critics have suggested that all it may accomplish is to substitute a passive class sitting before a television set for a passive class sitting in front of a teacher. Yet despite such anxieties, there already appears to be sufficient promise in the new media, even at this early stage in their development, to justify the pilot ventures that are now being made in universities round the world.

The problem here is not lack of evidence about the impact of this revolution on other sectors of society, but the difficulty of transferring conclusions based on advertising or leisure activities to the special conditions of education. For a number of reasons (which include the structure of an educational system, the rationale of the teaching profession, and the peculiar difficulty of measuring both the inputs and outputs of the educational process), there is an unavoidable cultural lag. In fact, it is proving extremely hard to progress from the general hypothesis that modern concepts of communication must somehow be applicable to education to the particular evidence that this is operationally possible—especially in higher education. The critical shortage of serious and large-scale research on educational innovation reduces most such attempts to pragmatic projects that are not easily susceptible to meaningful research. What is true, moreover, of loose analogies between education and other large social enterprises, applies (though less forcefully) to analogies between one educational system and another, and between different levels of education. The further one moves along a spectrum of innovation, from mechanical and electronic devices to changes in learning environments, in teaching methods, in the curriculum and in the materials used for teaching and learning, the more innovations become culturally and educationally specific, and the harder it becomes to translate evidence of their effectiveness into other contexts. The difficulty is that the demand for helpful innovation tends to be made in general terms, whereas the response is most likely to be helpful if it is particular to a given teaching problem or learning situation and is couched in practical terms.

The temptation to use analogies, however, is very great, despite their obvious shortcomings, for such arguments are not only persuasive in themselves but the case for technological potential fits neatly into its counterpart: the argument based on need. In previous chapters we considered the emerging needs of higher education and showed why it has been widely assumed— though the case is still far from proven—that the new media may help to meet them. This dovetailing between potential solutions and problems to which they may be applicable—for that is the way many people approach this question—is all the more attractive since other educational changes in the past have exemplified the same principle: that is, an innovation originates outside the educational system, and is imported into it because it appears relevant to a given problem. There is nothing wrong with such a process. It is, indeed, one of the mechanisms whereby educational systems adapt to changes in social structure, technology and ideas. Yet it leads inevitably to one of the characteristic biases of contemporary research on the uses of new media—those who are preoccupied with means rather than with problems naturally attempt to make problems match means rather than the converse.

The point was made by Professor Wilbur Schramm, writing in 1963, who pointed out that the case for developing a new technology in education was a strong one. Arguing that students could learn through new instructional media, and that in some circumstances they might well learn better, he remarked that it is [7]: '. . . a fortuitous coincidence that at the time when so many countries are endeavouring to speed their rate of development, and are desperately short of technical skills, basic education, teachers and schools, so many devices should become available to share teaching over a wide area and to encourage efficient individual study.'

The second line of argument stresses intrinsic merits of the new media which appear to be relevant both to the quantity and quality of teaching. They are, after all, instruments of communication, and communication is a vital part of the teaching-learning process; some of them, such as television, radio and film, are also means of mass communication and therefore seem to be especially appropriate to the age of mass education [5, 8, 9]. Broadcasting, for instance, offers a way of communicating with more people simultaneously; it therefore holds out the hope that teaching may be liberated from the traditional limitations upon the range of the human ear and eye, and the class-room format which such limitations impose. The ability to record information in a variety of forms (such as video and sound tapes, or on films, slides, transparencies and other graphic materials) permits repetition whenever it is desirable. It thus liberates the teacher and the student from the need to march in the lock step of a formal time-table and opens the road to more independent patterns of learning. By means of these new media, therefore, it is possible in principle to overcome the constraints of time and space which have hitherto geared student numbers to the totals which could conveniently be taught in person by a teacher in a class-room or laboratory. What is more, some of these new communication techniques (e.g. broadcasting, recording, etc.) have one special characteristic which commends them: unlike the conventional pattern of teaching, where the ratio of teachers to pupils is high, these techniques become cheaper the more they are used, for reaching larger numbers means falling unit costs. They are thus peculiarly suitable for mass education.

We can judge the importance of this characteristic—which we agree is potentially so significant as to encourage every effort to overcome the pedagogic and practical problems involved in taking advantage of it—by comparing it with the known virtues of the book. In terms of freedom of use, the book is a superb means of learning, for it stores a mass of ideas and information in compact and portable form and it can be used whenever and wherever the reader chooses, and read at whatever pace is suitable. Professor Morris Janowitz, in fact, has argued that the paperback revolution in recent years has been the single most valuable contribution to improved learning in higher education. True, the new media do not have the same flexibility as the book. Although broadcasts can reach large numbers of people, they have to be transmitted at fixed hours, and broadcast channel capacity is severely limited; recordings usually require fixed installations for listening or viewing or, at the minimum, they need play-back devices that are costly and bulky. But they do have advantages that the book lacks. They can offer a much wider range of learning experiences, presenting reality or simulations of reality, in audio and visual modes, in motion, colour, magnification, reduction and animation. Unlike the book, moreover, some of the devices now available can accept, record and play back student responses, and more sophisticated versions based on computer technology can monitor, analyse and modify these responses. In short, even in their present infant form, new media appear to bear precisely upon four key objectives—the need to reach more students, to reach them with an improved range of learning materials, to offer greater opportunities for independent study and to permit at least a limited student response.

Almost all the innovations in the use of media have been prompted initially by arguments which fall into these first two categories—even though experimental evidence may have been sought subsequently to justify them. Once universities begin to use new media seriously, however, a third and important argument emerges, i.e. the argument from existing practice. The original innovations themselves now provide some sort of evidence to support imitations. At worst, this is a matter of fashion, but at best it is a matter of fact. Once a few institutions try out an innovation, others come to study their experience and to ask how it is relevant to their own circumstances. It would be fascinating, for instance, to devise case studies of specific innovations to demonstrate the manner and pace in which they have been diffused. Whether one takes an example of a particular device, such as a language laboratory or a closed-circuit television system; a method, such as programmed instruction, or an organizational pattern, such as the creation of a learning-resource unit in a college or university, it is clear that they have moved outwards from a few innovatory centres along certain fairly well-defined routes. A valuable but hitherto neglected field of research in educational sociology would be the mapping of these routes, and an evaluation of the way in which ideas or experience have been modified as they have moved along them. In the absence of such research it is not possible to discern with any accuracy the means whereby a particular institution learns of innovations elsewhere, or to know just how it weighed the evidence before deciding whether to reject, adopt or modify the innovation.

It is important to note here the dangers of an uncritical and 'promotional' approach to the use of media. It avoids the most critical issue of all. How does one decide when an innovation has been successful? Much of the general debate about new methods in teaching and learning has been utterly confused by a failure to distinguish between disputes about evidence and disputes about the appropriate criteria for judging the evidence. This confusion is even more marked in most controversies about the value of media; many articles and books discussing new media seem to proceed on the assumption that the introduction of media into an educational institution is a success in itself. It may be so regarded by the innovators whose promotional activities have been successful, just as they may feel that the continuing use of the media (and of their own services) is sufficient proof that they remain successful. But we have virtually no satisfactory means of judging from most reports whether the experiment is truly successful because no one bothers to define the criteria whereby it is to be judged.

An administrator, for example, may adopt any combination of the following success criteria: decreased cost, better use of space, saving of scarce personnel, increased range of courses offered, improvements in teacher morale, improvements in student attitude, decreased failure rate, improved quality or even the improved reputation of his institution. He will presumably try and combine these in some form of cost-benefit analysis in spite of the difficulty of quantifying many of these benefits. One thing, however, is certain: the relative emphasis on these different criteria will vary from one institution to another, and the extent to which a given innovation satisfies each of these criteria will also vary from one institution to another. For these reasons no innovation is completely transportable, and it becomes important for the evaluation of an innovation to build up a profile of evidence which enables discussions to be based on several different sets of criteria.

A teacher's judgment of the success of an innovation may differ from that of an administrator, because he will certainly use a very different set of criteria. Given the priorities accorded to teaching in most institutions of higher education, decreased preparation time and decreased contact time would figure prominently in a teacher's set of criteria, though decreased cost would also be an acceptable criterion if it was linked to an increase in salaries. Improvements in their professional status and greater job-satisfaction in their teaching role are also important for many teachers and they would attach equal importance to demonstrated improvements in the quality of learning or in student attitudes. Teachers place different emphases on these aspects of their job and differ widely in their approaches to any one aspect. There is certainly no consensus on what kind of teaching role gives the most satisfaction or on what constitutes quality in learning.

Student opinion is often equally divided. There are those who want to be entertained, there are those who want an easy pass, there are those who want to cover as much vocationally relevant material as possible, there are those who want to think deeply and there are those who want to browse and explore. It is becoming quite common to use questionnaires to sample student opinions on courses. But how much weight should one attach to them and is it always the opinions of the average student that are wanted?

Perhaps the most important point to note is the fact that innovations may have done well by one set of criteria that, judged by other criteria, have appeared disastrous failures. The classic example is summed up in the phrase: 'The operation was successful but the patient died.'

A fourth argument for the introduction of new media is derived from the research literature. This is now increasing rapidly but much of it is fragmentary or not particularly conclusive [3]. It is necessary to use its findings with caution and not to treat them as inspirational texts upon which policy decisions can confidently be based. We return below, in Chapter X, to the question of research in educational technology. At this stage we merely wish to consider the role that such research plays in the ideology of media.

For research on the use of new methods and media is seriously handicapped, like all educational research, by certain inherent constraints. The greatest and most obvious of these is the fact that so many variables are involved in human learning that it is seldom clear (even in experimental conditions) which of them have been responsible for a given result. This situation raises serious methodological problems in small-scale projects, but these are compounded rapidly as the scale of a project increases and is extended over time [12]. It is unlikely that any innovation which is sufficiently comprehensive in scope and lasts long enough to make a significant impact on the knowledge or skills of the learner can at present be evaluated in precise or wholly convincing terms. It is not possible to control sufficient variables for enough time to permit more than general conclusions, and the data that emerge are usually susceptible to a number of conflicting interpretations.

All those who attempt educational research are painfully aware of this constraint, and of the limitations it imposes upon their work. At one extreme it leads to a concern with laboratory-type experiments that are restricted to testing one or two effects—possibly minor ones; at the other extreme, it produces innovatory schemes of such grandeur, looseness and complexity that their results are evaluated as much 'by-guess-and-by-God' as by any rigorously defined or generally accepted criteria. Between these extremes, regrettably, lies precisely the area in which educators need more definite guidance from research in order to make up their minds about the utility of new methods. The lack of such guidance on many crucial points is one of the reasons why education decision-making is often so muddled and ineffective, and why decision-makers themselves often dismiss research as pettifogging or irrelevant.

It is sometimes suggested that this situation has arisen because educational research has not been sufficiently supported with funds, and because it has failed to attract professional staff of high quality. Both comments are valid. The proportion of any educational budget devoted to research is derisory when compared to the research and development allocations of any occupations of comparable scale and social significance; this applies particularly to higher education. (A simple comparison of the money spent on media research, as against equipment and staff for media in education, would underline this point dramatically.) The status of educational research in most universities, moreover, has traditionally been at the bottom of the research hierarchy. But funds and research workers have also not been forthcoming because the prospects of useful progress—or of research findings actually being applied on any scale—have hitherto seemed fairly poor.

There have been some other important constraints. There is the understandable reluctance of teachers to put any large group of pupils or students at risk for any substantial period merely to provide a constituency for experiment. There is an accompanying hesitation about disrupting long-established procedures, simply because innovations demand extra training, preparation and organization, as well as a willingness to challenge existing assumptions about the curriculum and the way it is taught. There is resistance to spending scarce funds on untried schemes, when there is insufficient money to support existing practices properly. And, finally, there is a deep-rooted belief that education is so qualitatively different from other enterprises that it is not amenable to research processes in the same way.

It is in this context that research on new teaching methods, and particularly on the application of new media, has had to proceed. It is not surprising that the findings so far are hedged by uncertainties and riddled by unanswered questions. For media research not only suffers from the general constraint we have indicated: it has special problems of its own.

We review some of these problems and give additional references in Chapter X. For the present it is sufficient to note that while earlier media research projects were primarily concerned to demonstrate that media could be used successfully for teaching purposes and to compare one method of presentation with another, there has recently been a significant shift of emphasis. If we consider the bulk of the research work done in the period after 1960 (a decade in which instructional technology has been developing rapidly) we find the major concern is increasingly with the design of instructional systems, or learning sequences [1, 11]. Much of the long tradition of specific media research is only marginally relevant to this development, because many experiments which varied the medium through which educational information is transmitted grossly neglected the message variable itself. At the same time it has been increasingly realized that more may be gained by seeking ways in which new learning resources can be more effectively organized, managed and utilized than by laboratory demonstrations that one means of presentation is fractionally more effective than another.

Our concern here is to warn against misunderstandings about media research (or even misrepresentations of what it implies) that arise when its findings are summarized to form part of the media ideology.

Professor Richard E. Spencer has rightly criticized what he has called the 'religiosity' of instructional technology projects [10]: 'those that are in the field seem to believe that the potential is just lying there waiting to be tapped. . . . Faith is built into many research designs but satisfaction occurs with no significant regularity. An evident assumption appears to be that the media are in fact the message.'

Professor Spencer's comments admirably summarize the ideological aspects of media promotion. His criticisms do not imply that all research in this field is valueless, poor or unhelpful—any more than the argument based upon analogy or the potential of new media are necessarily invalidated because they cannot be substantiated as yet with detailed evidence. It is necessary in many educational innovations to proceed by trial and error; otherwise no progress at all might be made. But even though it is essential to make some decisions in the absence of conclusive evidence, it is as well to know the limitations of the arguments employed. Those limitations explain why it is preferable to speak of 'the state of the art' than to claim much more for our present knowledge of the uses of media. Modesty in this respect will do no harm, because the case for new media is only one element of the larger case for the introduction of new methods in teaching and learning. The initiative for new methods is coming as much from other sources of innovation as from the much-publicized media-innovations themselves [4]. As a change in concepts and methods of learning occurs, media will prove to be its servants—just as they can, when desired, extend and improve the conventional pattern of teaching in higher education.

REFERENCES

1. Briggs, Leslie J.; Campeau, Peggie L.; Gagné, Robert M.; May, Mark A. *Instructional media: a procedure for the design of multi-media instruction. A critical review of research, and suggestions for future research.* Palo Alto, American Institutes for Research, 1967.
2. Coombs, Philip H. *The world educational crisis: A systems analysis.* New York, Oxford University Press, 1968.
3. Edling, Jack (ed.). *The contribution of behavioral science to instructional technology: a resource book for media specialists.* Oregon, Division of Teaching Research, Oregon State System of Higher Education, 1968.
4. Finn, James D. The emerging technology of education. In: Robert A. Weisgerber (ed.), *Instructional process and media innovation.* Chicago, Rand McNally, 1968.
5. Hovland, C. I.; Lumsdaine, A. A.; Sheffield, F. D. *Experiments in mass communication.* Princeton University Press, 1949.
6. McLuhan, Marshall. *Understanding media: the extensions of man.* New York, McGraw-Hill, 1964.

7. SCHRAMM, Wilbur. The newer educational media in the United States. *New methods and techniques in education.* Paris, Unesco, 1963.
8. ——. *The process and effects of mass communication.* Urbana, University of Illinois Press, 1954.
9. * SCUPHAM, John. *Broadcasting and the community.* London, Watts, 1967.
10. SPENCER, Richard E. *The role of measurement and evaluation in instructional technology.* Urbana, Ill., University of Illinois, 1968.
11. TOSTI, Donald T.; BALL, John R. A behavior al approach to instructional design and media selection. *AV Communication Review* (Washington), vol. 17, no. 1, 1969.
12. WALLEN, Norman E.; TRAVERS, Robert M. W. Analysis and investigation of teaching methods. In: N. L. Gage (ed.), *Handbook of research on teaching.* Chicago, Rand McNally, 1963.

Part three

Systematic
approaches to
teaching and learning

VII. The clarification of objectives

Most of the problems that must be faced in developing a course of learning are familiar to university teachers, because they arise from any attempt to prepare a course for students. But they are rarely considered systematically and the implications of them are often not understood. Chapters VII to XI are therefore devoted to a discussion of these problems. This chapter on the clarification of objectives is followed by chapters on evaluation, on teaching methods and on research in educational technology, i.e. into the design and development of learning situations. Then Chapter XI outlines a general procedure for developing courses and discusses its implications.

The 'clarification of objectives' is not a phrase that will be familiar to most teachers in higher education and many will be tempted to dismiss it as meaningless pedagese. Yet it describes a process for making explicit a problem which is normally implicit: the problem of deciding what to teach. It has been traditional to list topics in the form of a syllabus, to make general declarations of intent such as 'we try to teach our students to think' or 'we want our students to be good engineers', and to leave the rest to the individual teacher. The teacher then has to decide how much of a topic to include and to what level to take it, and at the same time somehow to relate his decision to his 'inspirational' aims of 'teaching his students to think', 'developing good engineers', etc. The relationship between the syllabus and its aims remains implicit and individual. But this relationship is the cause of the problem. The difference between an aim and an objective can be expressed in a number of ways. For example, we may consider an aim as a general declaration of intent which gives direction to a teaching programme, and an objective as a particular point in that direction. To use a motoring analogy, we may aim to drive north and have London as our objective. Alternatively, an aim can be defined as an answer to the question of why a topic is taught, and an objective as an answer to the question of what will have been achieved when it has been taught. For this reason instruments of assessment can only be derived from objectives; they cannot be directly derived from aims.

One of the strongest arguments for giving greater attention to objectives has come from those concerned with problems of assessment [5]. There is now an increasing desire in higher education to design more valid instruments of assessment which attempt to measure what the teacher wishes to teach, but this can only be done once the teacher has specified his objectives. Psychologists studying teaching and learning have also found a need for clearer statements of objectives, since it is becoming apparent that some methods of teaching and learning are better for some objectives, and other methods are better for other objectives. Then there is the further problem of communication. Even though a senior professor's closest colleagues may know exactly what he is teaching when he lectures on a given topic, his junior colleagues may be less certain, and his students will sometimes have very little idea of what is coming. It is difficult for them to focus their attention if they do not know what is to be learnt and the syllabus gives them little guidance. Thus the problem of evaluation, the problem of selection of teaching methods and the problem of communication are all dependent upon the clarification of objectives [2].

The seriousness of the problem becomes apparent if one analyses the earlier chapters of this book. We have had to describe innovations in teaching and learning without more than vague references to what was being taught or learnt. This is inevitable when there has been so much emphasis on the quantitative aspects of new methods, and when there is so little published evidence on the qualitative aspects of the innovation concerned. But when one is seriously concerned with the quality of learning this question of objectives is of prime importance. This is not entirely the fault of those responsible for reporting the innovations, because there is as yet no common language in which teachers can communicate with one another about objectives with any degree of precision. Though teachers are prepared to discuss their aims in general terms and indicate what they are trying to teach, it is rare to find the objectives of any course stated clearly—certainly not with sufficient clarity for it to be possible to judge the success of the teaching by comparing its outcomes with the original objectives. While this is partly due to the professional status of teachers in higher education, which makes it difficult to challenge either the aims or the effectiveness of a teacher, it is also due to the difficulty of the task of describing objectives with adequate precision. A further difficulty arises from the fact that the curriculum is based primarily upon tradition; and what seems to the participants like a genuine discussion of aims will often seem to the outsider to refer only to the icing on the cake, with the marginal modifications that faculty make to a traditional curriculum they take for granted. Often 'aims' mean no more than normative statements by teachers about the 'nature' of university education.

Perhaps the most useful way to approach a discussion of the problem of objectives is to list a number of general statements of aims and to attempt to specify some of the possible interpretations. Some of the most frequently suggested aims are: to make good chemists, historians, etc.; to teach students to think; to give students a fundamental understanding of physics, sociology, etc.; to train students for work as a doctor, engineer, lawyer, teacher, etc.; to encourage a rational approach to controversial problems and issues; to develop a spirit of criticism; to produce good citizens; to get students to think imaginatively; to develop the student's creative talent; and to acquaint the student with the great ideas of mankind.

Most of the aims listed above involve three distinct kinds of objectives: (a) objectives related to knowledge and comprehension of content; (b) objectives related to the development of intellectual abilities; and (c) objectives relating to the inculcation of attitudes. Although all three types of objectives are involved in any given teaching-learning situation the relative emphasis placed upon them varies considerably. These emphases differ not only between courses but also between teachers giving the same course and between students taking the same course from the same teacher.

Content objectives usually receive the greatest emphasis, because courses are normally described and discussed in terms of their syllabi. The weakness of this technique, so widely employed in universities, is that it lists the topics to be covered but gives little indication of the level at which any particular piece of content is expected to be understood or even applied. For this reason decisions which are regarded as content decisions may in reality be decisions about the balance between content objectives and other kinds of objective. Consider the breadth-depth controversy, for example. Those pressing for treatment of a narrower range of content at a greater depth may be wanting their students to accumulate more information in certain areas so as to acquire 'a critical mass'; but more often they are wanting to place a greater emphasis on the development of intellectual abilities by giving the student more independent work and including special projects.

There have been a number of attempts to try and set out classification schemes for intellectual abilities or levels of understanding. None of them are ideal and they certainly do not have the status of theories of knowledge [13] but many are of considerable practical use in clarifying ideas about objectives. In particular they can be used to build profiles of a curriculum in terms of the different kinds of objectives and to guide decisions about the relative emphases to be placed on them.

The scheme which has received the greatest attention has been the Taxonomy of Educational Objectives compiled by Bloom and his co-workers [4, 8, 9]. This recognizes three major classes of objectives—cognitive, affective and psychomotor—and has developed classification schemes for the cognitive and affective domains. The cognitive domain is set out in terms of levels of understanding and proceeds from the simplest to the most complex.

1.0 Knowledge
    1.1 Knowledge of specifics
    1.2 Knowledge of ways and means of dealing with specifics
    1.3 Knowledge of universals and abstractions in a field
2.0 Comprehension
    2.1 Translation
    2.2 Interpretation
    2.3 Extrapolation
3.0 Application
4.0 Analysis
    4.1 Analysis of elements
    4.2 Analysis of relationships
    4.3 Analysis of organizational principles
5.0 Synthesis
    5.1 Production of unique communication
    5.2 Production of a plan or a proposed set of operations
    5.3 Derivation of a set of abstract relations
6.0 Evaluation
    6.1 Judgement in terms of internal evidence
    6.2 Judgement in terms of external criteria

Levels 1 and 2 of Bloom's cognitive domain further subdivide the first kind of objective we outlined earlier, that is the knowledge and comprehension of content; and levels 3 to 6 classify the second kind of objective, the development of intellectual abilities. Our third kind of objective, the inculcation of attitudes, is covered by Bloom's affective domain which we discuss later. In order to illustrate the way in which Bloom's taxonomy can function, we shall take one of the general aims we listed above, 'to encourage a rational approach to controversial problems and issues', and derive objectives from it to fit each of the major categories of the cognitive domain. Suppose, for example, we consider the problem of race relations. At level 1.1 we may want our students to know facts relating to the distribution of different races in our country; and at level 2.3 to be able to predict changes in population on the basis of data about birth rates, death rates, and immigration rates. At level 3 there is 'the ability to relate principles of civil liberties and civil rights to current events' and at level 4 'the ability to recognize the point of view or bias of a writer in a newspaper account'. At level 5 we might be interested in a student's description of the attempts of a member of a racial minority to find housing in an 'upper class' area or in a proposed plan for the improvement of race relations in a given area. And at level 6 we might hope for 'the ability to identify and appraise the judgements and values involved in the choice of a particular course of action by a local or national government'.

The taxonomy does not provide us with any criteria for selecting objectives, but it does provide a useful language for discussing the problem. Certainly its hierarchical nature suggests that performance at the higher level is dependent upon appropriate performance at lower levels and hence that some kind of pyramidal structure is needed with level 1 at the base and level 6 at the peak; but no guidance is given as to the slope of the pyramid. There is a strong movement in favour of making it as steep as possible and two main types of argument have supported this. The first is essentially an argument about 'ends' and the second an argument about 'means'. The ends argument focuses on the changing nature of society, the rapidity with which knowledge becomes out of date, the coming revolution in information retrieval and the need for continuing re-education. All these factors are making learning at levels 4, 5 and 6 indispensable because learning at levels 1 and 2 and possibly even 3 is useful only in the short term. Against this runs the counter-argument about the need for skilled professionals rather than ever-increasing numbers of 'researchers'. These are partly questions of national policy and of short-term versus long-term pay-off. But they are complicated by related arguments about means. Some would claim that many students are incapable of performing above level 3 in many subjects, and that in any case a very broad knowledge base is necessary for an understanding of the important generalizations. But others, notably Bruner, are asserting the exact opposite [6, 7]. Bruner argues that nothing is learnt without it being linked to some kind of cognitive structure and that the best means of teaching objectives at levels 1 and 2 is to provide such a structure by also teaching objectives at levels 4, 5 and 6.

There is good evidence to support Bruner's argument for a concentration on higher order objectives when there are able students but no general agreement on how able the students need to be. The initial variables probably include the teacher and the teaching materials as well. Indeed some would claim that the ends argument is so strong that a major attempt should be made to maximize both the range and the effectiveness of the Brunerian strategy by concentrating on the continuing education of teachers and the development of appropriate teaching materials. Since practically no resources have yet been allocated in higher education either to teacher training or to course development, the potentialities of this approach are still largely unexplored. The situation in higher education stands in marked contrast to that in secondary education where innovations of this kind have caused sweeping changes over the last decade [10, 11, 12, 15, 16, 20].

Related uses of Bloom's taxonomy at the strategic level include its use in analysing and comparing alternative curricula and in matching examinations to the objectives of the courses they are intended to assess. Then at a more detailed level, it can be used to suggest categories of objective which have been unintentionally omitted; or to help investigate situations where unsatisfactory performance on higher-level objectives is clearly related to lack of sufficient emphasis on certain lower-level objectives of initial importance. In the social sciences, for example, it is not uncommon to find sophisticated performances being required at level 6 when level 4 has been almost totally neglected. This is one of the common consequences of the content-oriented curriculum which we shall discuss in greater detail later on.

Though Bloom's cognitive domain has been widely acknowledged, his affective domain is less well known [14].

The affective domain is concerned with objectives related to interests, appreciations, attitudes and values and is organized round the concept of 'internalization'. The lowest degree of internalization is simply a state of awareness that something exists, and the highest degree is shown by an attitude which forms an essential part of someone's character.

BLOOM'S TAXONOMY: AFFECTIVE DOMAIN

1.0 Receiving (attending)
    1.1 Awareness
    1.2 Willingness to receive
    1.3 Controlled or selected attention
2.0 Responding
    2.1 Acquiescence in responding
    2.2 Willingness to respond
    2.3 Satisfaction in response
3.0 Valuing
    3.1 Acceptance of a value
    3.2 Preference for a value
    3.3 Commitment
4.0 Organization
    4.1 Conceptualization of a value
    4.2 Organization of a value system
5.0 Characterization by a value or value complex
    5.1 Generalized set
    5.2 Characterization

To illustrate the affective domain, we shall again take one of our general aims listed above, 'to produce good citizens', and devise relevant objectives at each level of the taxonomy. At level 1.3 we have 'sensitive to the importance of keeping informed on current political and social matters' and at level 2.2 'interests himself in social problems broader than those of the local community'. 'Deliberately examines a variety of viewpoints on controversial issues with a view to forming opinions about them' is at level 3.2. Then at level 4.1 we have 'forms judgements as to the responsibility of society for conserving human and material resources' and at level 4.2 'weighs alternative social policies and practices against the standards of the public welfare rather than the advantage of specialized and narrow interest groups'. At level 5.1 there is 'changes his opinion on controversial issues when an examination of the evidence and the arguments call for revision of opinions previously held', and at level 5.2 'develops for regulation of one's personal and civic life a code of behaviour based on ethical principles consistent with democratic ideals'.

These examples also show the interrelationship between the cognitive and affective domains. The example we gave of level 3.2 on the affective domain, 'deliberately examines a variety of viewpoints on controversial issues . . .', clearly requires at least performance at the analysis level, 4.1, on the cognitive domain. Other objectives at this affective level may have much weaker cognitive components, but by the time one has reached level 4 on the affective domain, one must surely also be at level 4 on the cognitive domain. It is also probably true that any objective in higher education is expected to be at the 2.2 (willingness to respond) level on the affective domain and probably at the 2.3 (satisfaction in response) level. But even this may be inadequate as has been convincingly argued by Bruner [6]:Mastery of the fundamental ideas of a field involves not only the grasping of general principles, but also the development of an attitude toward learning and inquiry, toward guessing and hunches, toward the possibility of solving problems on one's own. Just a physicist has certain attitudes about the ultimate orderliness of nature and a conviction that order can be discovered, so a young physics student needs some working version of these attitudes if he is to organize his learning in such a way as to make what he learns usable and meaningful in his thinking.'

This confidence is surely an important component of aims which are concerned with developing a student's ability to think critically and imaginatively. It probably requires attainment of at least level 3 or 4 on Bloom's affective domain. But the student attitude questionnaires now increasingly being used to 'evaluate' courses in higher education are normally focussed at level 1 or 2. Perhaps this is why many sceptics still regard good results on these questionnaires as better evidence of good entertainment than of good teaching.

Many classification schemes which are essentially modified versions of Bloom's have been developed in the last decade. We shall just quote one of them which was drawn up by The School Mathematics Study Group to classify cognitive behaviour in mathematics: there is no indication as to whether it is meant to have taxonomic structure. Although intended for the school level, it is still relevant to higher education and the subject matter, mathematics, is one for which Bloom's classification is particularly difficult to apply [19].

SMSG CLASSIFICATION OF MATHEMATICAL OBJECTIVES

Knowing:	Knowing terminology, facts, and rules.
Translating:	Changing from one language to another; expressing ideas in verbal, symbolic, or geometric form; codifying patterns.

Manipulating:	Carrying out algorithms; using techniques.
Choosing:	Making comparisons; selecting appropriate facts and techniques; guessing; estimating; changing one's approach; selecting new symbolism.
Analysing:	Analysing data; finding differences; recognizing relevant and irrelevant information; seeing patterns, isomorphisms, and symmetries; analysing proofs; recognizing need for additional information; recognizing need for proof or counter example.
Synthesizing:	Specializing and generalizing; conjecturing; formulating problems; constructing a proof or a problem.
Evaluating:	Validating answers; judging reasonableness of answers; validating the solution process; criticizing proofs ; judging the significance of a problem.

Scriven has also suggested a classification scheme which owes much to Bloom but he adds one important dimension by identifying three levels of description for educational objectives [21]: (a) the conceptual level which is relatively abstract is the level at which discussions of 'breadth *v.* depth' and 'knowledge *v.* comprehension' are carried out and the 'structure' of the course is outlined; (b) the manifestational level which is concerned with ways in which a student's achievement of an objective can be demonstrated; and (c) the operational level which defines an objective in terms of the precise means by which it is to be assessed.

Scriven's classification of the conceptual and manifestational levels is outlined below. The operational level was not treated by him in any detail but we shall discuss it later.

CONCEPTUAL DESCRIPTION OF EDUCATIONAL OBJECTIVES

1. Knowledge of:
   (a) Items of specific information including definitions of terms in the field.
   (b) Sequences or patterns of items of information including sets of rules, procedures or classifications for handling or evaluating items of information (we are here talking about mere knowledge of the rule or classification and not the capacity to apply it).
2. Comprehension or understanding of:
   (a) Internal relationships in the field, i.e. the way in which some of the knowledge claims are consequences of others and imply yet others, the way in which the terminology applies within the field; in short what might be called understanding of the intrafield syntax of the field or subfield.
   (b) Interfield relations, i.e. relations between the knowledge claims in this field and those in other fields; what we might call the interfield syntax.
   (c) Application of the field or the rules, procedures, and concepts of the field to appropriate examples, where the field is one that has such applications;

this might be called the semantics of the field.
3. Motivation (attitude/values/affect):
   (a) Attitudes toward the course, e.g. acoustics.
   (b) Attitudes toward the subject, e.g. physics.
   (c) Attitudes toward the field, e.g. science.
   (d) Attitudes toward material to which the field is relevant, e.g. increased scepticism about usual advertising claims about 'high fidelity' from miniature radios (connection with 2 (c) above).
   (e) Attitudes toward learning, reading, discussing, inquiring in general, etc.
   (f) Attitudes toward the school.
   (g) Attitudes toward teaching as a career, teacher status, etc.
   (h) Attitudes toward (feeling about, etc.) the teacher as a person.
   (i) Attitude toward class-mates, attitude toward society (obvious further subheadings).
   (j) Attitude toward self, e.g. increase of realistic self-appraisal (which also involves cognitive domain).
4. Non-mental abilities:
   (a) Perceptual.
   (b) Psycho-motor.
   (c) Motor, including, e.g. some sculpting skills.
   (d) Social skills.
5. Non-educational variables: There are a number of non-educational goals, usually implicit, which are served by many existing courses and even by new courses, and some of them are even justifiable in special circumstances as, e.g. in a prison.

MANIFESTATION DIMENSIONS OF CRITERIAL VARIABLES

1. Knowledge: In the sense described above, this is evinced by:
   (a) Recital skills.
   (b) Discrimination skills.
   (c) Completion skills.
   (d) Labelling skills.
   Note: Where immediate performance changes are not discernible, there may still be some subliminal capacity, manifesting itself in a reduction in re-learning time, i.e., time for future learning to criterion.
2. Comprehension: This is manifested on some of the above types of performance and also on:
   (a) Analysing skills, including laboratory analysis skills, other than motor, as well as the verbal analytic skills exhibited in criticism, précis, etc.
   (b) Synthesizing skills.
   (c) Evaluation skills, including self-appraisal.
   (d) Problem-solving skills (speed-dependent and speed-independent).
3. Attitude: Manifestations usually involve simultaneous demonstration of some cognitive acquisition. The kinds of instrument involved are questionnaires, projective tests, Q-sorts, experimental choice situations, and normal lifetime choice situations (choice of college major, career, spouse, friends, etc.). Each of the attitudes mentioned is characteristically identifiable on a passive to

active dimension (related to the distinctions expounded on in Bloom, but disregarding extent of systematization of value system which can be treated as a (meta-) cognitive skill).

4. The non-mental abilities: All are exhibited in performances of various kinds, which again can be either artificially elicited or extracted from life-history. Typical examples are the capacity to speak in an organized way in front of an audience, to criticize a point of view (not previously heard) in an effective way, etc. (This again connects with the ability conceptually described under 2 (c).)

Scriven's three levels of description can be used as a basis for the first three stages in a systematic approach to course design, and we return to this in Chapter XI. But Bloom's scheme, which roughly corresponds to Scriven's manifestational level, is less readily applicable. This is probably because Bloom's taxonomy was originally intended for the analysis of examinations rather than for the formulation of objectives *ab initio*. If in designing a course one tries to go straight to the manifestational level, one is liable to arrive at rather segmented and unrelated groups of objectives and to have no clear guide-lines for deciding upon priorities. But if one begins at the conceptual level one is primarily concerned with the structure of the subject, interrelationships between principles are important, and it is possible to make decisions about what is central and what is peripheral. One is constructing some kind of cognitive map of what one wants the student's eye view of the subject to be, and deciding which intellectual skills one wants him to have mastered and what attitudes one hopes he will have acquired. Then at the manifestational level one has to specify how one is to probe the student's actual conceptual map and find out what his intellectual skills and attitudes really are. Finally at the operational level, one decides what one will accept as evidence of success or failure. What was originally implicit has now become totally explicit.

Objectives at this operational level are often referred to as 'behavioural objectives', because ultimately objectives can only be assessed by observing some aspect of a student's behaviour. Whether the student's behaviour is observed in the formal context of a test or not, it is the only available indication of his unobservable thought processes and cognitive structure. According to Mager, the characteristics of a behavioural objective are as follows [17]: (a) specification of the kind of behaviour which will be accepted as evidence that the learner has achieved the objective; (b) description of the important conditions under which the behaviour will be expected to occur; and (c) description of how well the learner must perform to have his behaviour considered acceptable.

To illustrate the difference between a manifestational objective and an operational objective let us take one of the objectives we used in our discussion of Bloom's taxonomy, 'ability to recognize the point of view or bias of a writer in a newspaper account', and attempt to operationalize it. One possible operational objective might be as follows: 'given a non-technical report (i.e. not science, business or sport) from a popular newspaper the student will list the facts reported, the inferences made from the facts, the additional assumptions introduced and the arguments based primarily on the additional assumptions. He will be expected to include at least 50 per cent of the teacher's list and to make no more than one mistake in his classification.' Another possible objective might require the student to: 'list 80 per cent of the adjectives which were value-loaded.' Other relevant operational objectives could also be devised from the same objective at the manifestational level and a list of all the relevant operational objectives could be very lengthy indeed. In developing a course one has to make some decision about which of these objectives is to be given priority and about what assessment gives adequate information on whether one's objectives have been successfully achieved. Usually it will be best to go straight from the manifestational level to the actual instruments of assessment without trying to set out the whole universe of relevant operational objectives. But in certain circumstances, especially when an objective is both important and difficult to achieve, a thorough analysis of the possible operational objectives can be extremely helpful.

It is important in this context to emphasize the dangers of over-operationalizing objectives. We have already pointed out that initiating the development of a course at the manifestational level can lead to difficulty, but initiating it at the operational level can lead to disaster. The tendency to confine a course to those objectives which are easy to measure can be difficult to resist. If, however, one has already developed formulated objectives at the manifestational level one can avoid the danger of lowering the level of one's objectives, which is inherent in the process of trying to operationalize them, by checking one's operational objectives back against one's original list of manifestational objectives. Any course that is assessed must have operational objectives even though they are not recognized as such; and the best way to ensure that these operational objectives are the right objectives is to compare them with the manifestational objectives. The criticisms that have been directed against those who attempt to clarify objectives have been that they make educational aims trivial, but this criticism is only valid for those who try going straight to the operational level. As Wood has commented [22]: 'The complaint that teaching concentrates far too much on exercising the pupil's memory was heard long before objectives were invented. A pledge to nurture more exalted talents, which is what stating objectives implies, can hardly fail to make some improvement.'

Scriven uses a classification scheme rather than a taxonomy and thus avoids the content v. process controversy over whether a curriculum should be based on using intellectual skills to build up an increasing understanding of the content of a discipline, or whether it should concentrate on developing the intellectual skills or processes of a discipline and use the content

111

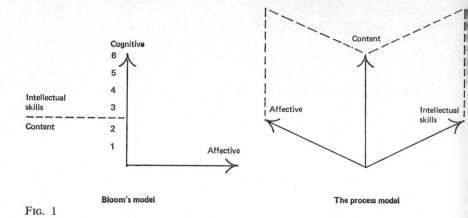

FIG. 1

merely as illustrative material or data to be manipulated. Bloom, by developing a taxonomy, emphasizes the build-up of intellectual skills upon appropriate knowledge in a given content area. It is a content-based model but nevertheless one which assigns considerable importance to process objectives. Some recent curricula, however, have considered it more important to emphasize the transfer of intellectual skills from one content area to another within a given field and have developed a process model which places these skills on a separate dimension orthogonal to the content dimension. Both models include an attitudinal dimension (see Fig. 1).

Naturally the process model is not lacking in content but it treats content as data to be manipulated rather than as facts to be learnt. This is well illustrated by the set of inquiry skills used by Fenton as the basis of his social studies curriculum [10]:

Recognizing a problem from data.

Formulating a hypothesis: asking analytical questions; stating a hypothesis; and remaining aware that a hypothesis is tentative.

Recognizing the logical implications of a hypothesis.

Gathering data: deciding what data will be needed to test a hypothesis; selecting or rejecting sources on the basis of their relevance to the hypothesis.

Analysing, evaluating, and interpreting data: selecting relevant data from the sources; evaluating the sources by (a) determining the frame of reference of the author of a source, (b) determining the accuracy of statements of fact and interpreting the data.

Evaluating the hypothesis in light of the data: modifying the hypothesis, if necessary by (a) rejecting a logical implication unsupported by data, (b) restating the hypothesis; stating a generalization.

Many scientists have adopted a similar approach and even an elementary science curriculum has been based on process objectives.

112

Clearly the appropriateness of any given classification scheme will depend on one's aims and priorities, and many people will not wish to use any of them. Our purpose in discussing them has been as much to illustrate the difficulties of formulating objectives as it has been to recommend specific procedures, though we have ourselves found it useful to use such schemes. It is our conviction that even when classification schemes are ultimately rejected the attempt to use them leads to a deeper understanding of the problems involved.

This brings us back to the question with which this chapter began. Why are objectives important? There are three main arguments: (a) objectives aid communication; (b) objectives are essential for evaluation; and (c) objectives aid a rational and efficient selection of teaching and learning activities. Let us examine each argument in turn.

Explicit objectives may improve communication between teacher and student, between students and between teachers. The student usually gets three conflicting views of the objectives of a course: one from the syllabus; one from his teacher(s); and one from the examination. Objectives which are unnecessarily imprecise can increase this conflict and lead to anxiety, lower performance and a bad self-image. Yet if teaching and learning are to form part of a single co-operative process the teacher and his students will need to share a common statement of objectives. In some cases this statement may be all the teaching that is required; because, given adequate resources, a student, as an intelligent being, can achieve them alone [18]. In others it will help to increase student initiative, to develop student capacity for self-evaluation and to encourage co-operation between students.

The importance of objectives for co-operation between teachers should also be noted. The increasing emphasis being placed on the interrelationships between different areas of knowledge needs to be translated into the curriculum; and this has to mean more than expecting students to derive integrated patterns while their teachers preserve a segmented course structure. Yet courses cannot easily be linked together to form a coherent curriculum if their objectives are undefined.

Evaluation in higher education tends to be associated with grading or discriminating between students, and it can fulfil this function irrespective of whether or not there is a mis-match between the objectives of the course and the methods of evaluation employed. Such a mis-match, however, militates against improvement in the quality of teaching and learning. It is not uncommon for faculty to complain that their students learn everything by rote and do not think for themselves, although the examinations set by the same teachers encourage precisely this kind of behaviour [3]. The student is left to try and guess what is really required; and without any adequate feedback in the form of objective-linked evaluation to guide him as he learns. The most neglected aspect of evaluation, however, is its role in providing information about the quality of teaching. We have already emphasized the need

113

for improvements in the quality of teaching without increases in cost. Ye
no one can even tell if any improvement has taken place unless it is possibl
to compare a statement of objectives with some form of assessment of hov
adequately they have been achieved. Increased scores on a test are of littl
use if the test does not measure the appropriate objectives. It cannot be to
strongly emphasized that if evaluation is to contribute to problems c
teaching and learning and not to remain merely an administrative con
venience for disciplining and grading students it will have to be based o
precisely formulated statements of objectives.

Our third and final argument concerns the role of objectives in the selectio
of teaching and learning activities. A traditional educational research stud
compares two methods of teaching physics to college freshmen and generalize
about the teaching of physics. The critical variable that is neglected is th
precise nature of the objectives. In view of the wide range of possible type
of objective it is unlikely that changes in method will have the same effect c
all of them. A traditional psychological research study goes to the opposit
extreme when it totally ignores the subject matter, compares two methods c
teaching problem solving and generalizes about the teaching of proble
solving. Once again the missing variable is the precise nature of the objective
Given that knowledge is structured differently in different disciplines an
that students are known to have differential aptitudes, it again seem
naïve to assume that conclusions about problem solving will necessaril
transfer from one discipline to another. These two areas of research, th
educational and the psychological, will only be brought together to solv
important problems at the higher education level when educators and psychc
logists are able to describe objectives with a common language.

REFERENCES

1. AXELROD, Joseph. *Model building for Undergraduate colleges: A theoretic*
   framework for studying and reforming the curricular instruction subsyster
   in American colleges. Washington, D.C., U.S. Dept. of Health, Educatio
   and Welfare, 1969.
2. BEARD, R. M.; HEALEY, F. G.; HOLLOWAY, P. J. *Objectives in higher Educa*
   tion. London, Society for Research in Higher Education, 1968.
3. BLACK, P. J. University examinations. *Physics education*, vol. 3, no. 2, 196
4. * BLOOM, Benjamin S. *et al. Taxonomy of educational objectives handbook*
   Cognitive domain. New York, Longmans Green, 1956.
5. * BLOOM, Benjamin S. Some theoretical issues relating to evaluation. In: R. V
   Tyler (ed.), *Educational evaluation: new roles, new means.* University c
   Chicago Press, 1969.
6. BRUNER, Jerome S. *The process of education.* Cambridge, Mass., Harvar
   University Press, 1960.
7. * ———. *Towards a theory of instruction.* Harvard University Press, 1966.

8.   Cox, Richard C.; Unks, Nancy Jordan. *A selected and annotated bibliography of studies concerning the taxonomy of educational objectives: cognitive domain.* University of Pittsburg, 1967.

9.   Eggleston, J. F. Bloom's cognitive domain revisited. *Journal of Curriculum Studies* (London), vol. 1, no. 1, November 1968.

10.   Fenton, Edwin. *The new social studies.* New York, Holt, Rinehart & Winston, 1967.

11.   Goodlad, John I. *School curriculum reform in the United States.* New York, Fund for the Advancement of Education, 1964.

12.   Heath, R. W. *New curricula.* New York, Harper & Row, 1964.

13.   Hirst, Paul H. The contribution of philosophy to the study of the curriculum. In: J. Kerr (ed.), *Changing the curriculum.* University of London Press, 1968.

14. * Krathwohl, David R.; Bloom, Benjamin S.; Masia, Bertram, B. *Taxonomy of educational objectives handbook II: affective domain.* New York, David McKay, 1964.

15.   Lockard, J. David (ed.). *Report of the International Clearinghouse on Science and Mathematics Curricular Developments.* University of Maryland, 1967.

16.   MacLure, J. Stuart (ed.). *Curriculum innovation in practice.* London, HMSO, 1968.

17. * Mager, R. F. *Preparing instructional objectives.* Palo Alto, Calif., Fearon, 1962.

18.   ——; McCann, John. *Learner controlled instruction.* Palo Alto, Calif., Varian Associates, 1962.

19.   Romberg, T. A.; Wilson, J. W. *The development of mathematics achievement tests for the national longitudinal study of mathematical studies.* Stanford, Calif., School Mathematics Study Group, Cedar Hall, 1966.

20.   Schools Council. *The Schools Council report 1968-9.* London, Methuen, 1969.

21. * Scriven, Michael. The methodology of evaluation. In: R. Stake (ed.), *Perspectives of curriculum evaluation.* Chicago, Rand McNally, 1967.

22.   Wood, R. Objectives in the teaching of mathematics. *Educational research,* vol. 10, no. 2, February 1968.

VIII. The role of evaluation

It seems natural to follow a chapter on objectives (that is, the problem of deciding what one wants to teach) with a chapter on evaluation, for that is concerned with finding what one has actually taught. Yet in higher education this is not the context in which evaluation is normally conceived. Evaluation is invariably associated with examinations, with the labelling, grading, and failing of students. This traditional role of evaluation may provide information to guide selection decisions; but selection decisions, after all, are not the only decisions with which higher education is concerned.

We define evaluation as the assembling and analysis of evidence prior to decision-making; and in any particular instance the nature of evaluation will depend on the kind of decision then being made. Therefore discussion of the role of evaluation in higher education needs to consider the whole range of decisions and not just selection decisions. In this chapter, however, we shall be concerned primarily with educational decisions and not with purely administrative decisions; and these educational decisions can be divided into four main categories:

Selection decisions: selection for higher education; selection for graduate work; selection for employment; and placement decisions.

Curriculum decisions: decisions about what to teach; decisions about how to teach.

Guidance decisions: student decisions about what subjects to take; what career to choose; etc.

Short-term decisions: decisions made by teacher and students during teaching and learning; diagnostic decisions.

Selection decisions have such important consequences for the individual pupil that 'equality of treatment' has always been the predominant consideration [3, 11]. The validity of selection decisions (that is, the extent to which they select the right people and emphasize the right characteristics) has received much less emphasis [8, 14]. One remarkable feature of the present system in most countries is the extent to which evaluation for selection is oriented towards the production of a single indicator, whether it be the grade-point-average or the class of degree. Such indicators have been shown to be exceedingly poor predictors of subsequent performance on most types of job, including even advanced academic research [9]. This is not surprising in view of the wide range of objectives being evaluated, the great differences between students, and the variation in marking standards between examiners, or even between the same examiner's performance on different days. Yet it imposes restrictions on evaluation practices which are scarcely tolerable. In what other context could it be considered meaningful to attach similar numerical values to historical judgement, the application of statistical techniques, the analysis of mechanical structures and a knowledge of the metabolism of glucose monophosphate?

Curriculum decisions are based on two kinds of evaluation, intrinsic evaluation and performance evaluation. Intrinsic evaluation, which is essentially an armchair activity, is concerned with the analysis of an existing or proposed curriculum in order to discern its likely effects. These may be planned effects related to either stated or implied objectives or they may be unplanned effects. Performance evaluation is concerned with finding out to what extent these effects are realized in practice. It includes both an assessment of the extent to which intended objectives have been achieved and an attempt to detect whether there have been any unintended outcomes. Clearly the ideal situation is one in which the standard of performance on intended objectives is high and there are no undesirable side-effects; though even in this situation the decision could be to go for a more ambitious set of objectives rather than maintain the *status quo*. When, however, there is a mis-match between intended objectives and actual outcomes there are two alternative lines of action. One can either modify the objectives or attempt to change the curriculum.

Changing the curriculum can be said to involve either changes in what is taught or changes in how it is taught, but in practice it will involve both. This is why we refer to curriculum decisions rather than to content decisions or method decisions. This interdependence of content and method stems from the complex nature of the learning process. Any learning situation is relevant to a number of objectives. At the very least it is likely to affect a student's knowledge of specifics, his understanding of the field in general and his attitudes towards it. For example, the way in which we teach a student to apply Newton's Second Law will affect other objectives besides that of being able to apply Newton's Second Law. It affects the student's understanding of the law and its relationship with other generalizations about bodies in motion, it affects his attitudes towards the subject of physics, and probably a number of other objectives as well. If then we change the way we teach in the hope of improving the student's ability to apply Newton's Second Law, we are

117

likely at the same time to affect his performance on these other objectives; and the change may not necessarily be beneficial. Unless all these different outcomes are affected in the same way and to precisely the same extent, the student performance profile along these different dimensions will be altered. Changes in method will not only cause changes in the level of performance but changes in the kind of performance. What is taught and how it is taught are inevitably interdependent.

Clearly curriculum decisions need evidence from performance that can be related to all the likely outcomes and not just the intended outcomes. One of the purposes of intrinsic evaluation is to ensure that performance evaluation meets this need, i.e. that the methods being used to assess performance provide the right kind of evidence. Otherwise, unintended outcomes will fail to be detected. More seriously still there could be a gross mis-match between the instruments used for assessment and the outcomes they are supposed to assess. This mis-match is particularly common when the main purpose of the assessment is to provide information for selection decisions rather than information for curriculum decisions; which can easily lead to an over-emphasis on reliability at the expense of validity. For example, a set of short-answer questions or a three-hour examination may be more reliable than a project or a dissertation, but they may not measure qualities of persistence initiative and originality which might be considered more important.

Guidance decisions need yet another set of evidence, though naturally there is some overlap with the information requirements of selection decisions and curriculum decisions [1]. Much of the evidence, particularly that relating to aptitudes and achievement, has to be obtained from assessments which are primarily designed for other purposes, usually for categorizing students as a basis for selection decisions. This information usually comes in the form of single scores rather than in the form of student profiles which show differential performance on different kinds of objective. But in guidance decisions it may be more important to know whether a student has a particular kind of mathematical ability than to know how he scored on a mathematics examination which measured several different types of mathematical attainment.

The most critical factor of all in guidance, however, is self-evaluation. For someone wishing to improve guidance decisions the extent to which evaluation procedures facilitate or inhibit self-evaluation will always be at least as important as the usefulness of the information provided. We shall return to this problem later. Meanwhile it is important to note that each use of evaluation we have considered so far has served a different decision-making agency. Selection decisions are made by employers or by university administrators, curriculum decisions are made by teachers and guidance decisions are made by students. Hence the importance of providing information to students to guide their self-evaluation.

If curriculum decisions are fundamentally teacher decisions and guidance decisions are fundamentally student decisions, the short-term decisions which constitute the framework of the teaching-learning process fall into both categories. The teacher continually makes decisions as he teaches, the student continually makes decisions as he learns. Ideally many of these decisions are co-operative; in practice many of them are not even compatible. The student, for example, may decide not to attend. The teacher may decide to teach something already understood by the student or something beyond his comprehension. The process which guides both sets of decisions is evaluation and the extent to which teacher and student make the same evaluations determines whether their decisions are co-operative or the converse.

In discussing evaluation it is easy to concentrate on the formal aspects and forget that informal and subjective evaluation is a normal and essential part of one's daily life. One is always making decisions about what one is doing; and these decisions are usually based on a constant flow of information about what is going on and how one's plans are working. Each decision can be said to be based on an evaluation which compares one's assessment of the situation with one's objectives; and this basic pattern applies both to semi-conscious minute-by-minute decisions and to critical decisions which require weeks of deliberation. Life in the class-room or lecture-hall is no exception; for there decisions are also constantly being made by both students and teachers. The question of whether to evaluate is meaningless because evaluation is always going on. The key questions are how to bring some of the evaluations that are already taking place to the conscious level and how to find means of improving them. Semi-conscious evaluation cannot itself be evaluated.

While teaching and learning is proceeding the student will be continually making decisions. Some will be decisions of attention (to his work, to his teacher, to his neighbour, to his private thoughts, etc.); some will be decisions of action (to talk, to write, to move, etc.); some will involve judgement (is this valid, is it meaningful, is it important, is it interesting?). All these decisions will be guided by the student's own evaluation, based on the student's own objectives and the student's assessment of whether he has achieved them or is likely to achieve them. Effective communication between student and teacher will need to be based on common views about objectives and common views about the assessment of performance related to those objectives.

In the last chapter we discussed the selection of teacher objectives. The selection of student objectives proceeds along rather different lines. Four important factors affect the student's choice:

The extent to which the teacher's objectives are clearly perceived. This depends partly on the extent to which the teacher has clarified and communicated his objectives and partly on the extent to which the teacher is consistent about his objectives in describing them, teaching them and assessing them.

The intrinsic interest or value of a piece of work which makes him want to

119

pursue it for its own sake. This can be influenced though obviously not totally determined by the nature of the teaching.

The extent to which he sees an objective as part of some larger and highly valued objective. This also can be influenced by the teaching.

The estimated probability of success. This depends partly on the success of the teaching and partly on the student's self-evaluation.

Only when all these factors are favourable will teacher objectives and student objectives be likely to coincide. Otherwise there will be a conflict of interests.

The student's assessment of his performance on these objectives will also be critical; and one of the most important functions of teacher assessment will be to support the student's gradual acquisition of standards of judgement and to serve as a final check against which the student can match his own assessment. Teacher assessment will also be the main vehicle for the communication of objectives, because it is in the assessment situation that objectives become most precise and are taken most seriously. Thus teacher assessment can help the student in three important ways: it can help clarify the teacher's objectives, it can inform him how successful he has been in achieving those objectives and it can communicate the teacher's standards of judgement.

Assessment can also help the teacher by providing information about how much his students have learnt and by detecting important deficiencies in their performance. This contrasts with the traditional use of assessment as a motivational device. There is no need to neglect this motivational aspect of assessment but it can be dangerous if it is allowed to become predominant. Tests or assignments given primarily to get the students to work may have deleterious effects by giving the student a false conception of the teacher's objectives or by giving inadequate feedback about his performance. Moreover the stick-and-carrot concept contradicts what many people consider to be a major aim of higher education—that is to create independent self-motivating, self-evaluating learners. The main factors which determine the form of assessment used during teaching and learning should therefore be: (a) the need to include all the important objectives; (b) the need to provide the learner with adequate information about the nature and level of his performance; and (c) the need to provide the teacher with information to help him fit his teaching to the needs of his students.

In structured subjects there is also a need for special purpose diagnostic tests which can be given to students in difficulty to diagnose the nature of their conceptual misunderstandings and trace them back to as elementary level as possible. These could be self-tests which would give the student the responsibility for diagnosing his own strengths and weaknesses [6]. If he can successfully locate his main areas of misunderstanding, then he can seek help on his own initiative either from a book or from his peers or from his teacher.

Clearly assessments of the kind we have been discussing are an integral part of the teaching-learning process. They guide the short-term decisions of teachers and students; and also provide some evidence for curriculum decisions and guidance decisions. But the assessments which come at the ends of courses and are used primarily for selection purposes are not often perceived as part of the teaching-learning process in spite of their considerable effects upon it [2]. These end of course assessments, usually referred to as examinations, affect the general pattern of teaching and learning in a number of ways:

Examined objectives tend to assume priority over non-examined objectives. This follows from the recognition by teachers, administrators, employers and students of the importance of examination results for a student's career. It leads to conflict whenever there is a mis-match between the objectives which are examined and the objectives which arc communicated before or during teaching [13]. It also gives rise to the not unusual situation where faculty complain that their students cram for examinations instead of trying to understand the subject. Short cuts to higher performances such as question-spotting and over-reliance on a few key books defeat their teaching objectives. The fault lies not with the students but with the examinations.

The conditions of performance in many examinations can distort the intended objectives. Even when the objectives which the examination is intended to measure are perfectly matched with those of the course being examined, they are liable to be distorted by the nature of the examining procedure. By restricting access to reference material, by imposing severe limitations of time and by creating conditions of anxiety, the traditional examination procedures are likely to promote memorization and regurgitation at the expense of comprehension and understanding.

Examinations can inhibit self-evaluation. If the critical test of a student's performance is impersonal and apparently arbitrary and, as is usually the case, the student receives little feedback about the nature of his performance, he will be more inclined to perceive himself as a pawn in the system than as a self-motivating self-evaluating individual. This feeling of inadequacy is enhanced by the fact that most students think that they have not had a chance in an examination to show their best performance. So even if the examination does provide a realistic assessment, the student will be less likely to accept it as such.

There is no useful purpose in reviewing methods of examining in this chapter when several excellent reviews are already available [3, 4, 5, 10, 12, 15]. But it is worth summarizing the three main criteria by which examination methods should be chosen: (a) their predictive validity, i.e. the usefulness of the evidence they provide for selection decisions; (b) the extent to which they also provide useful information for curriculum decisions and guidance decisions; and (c) their effect on the teaching-learning process.

The discussion on the use of evaluation to support curriculum decisions and short-term decisions during teaching and learning will be continued in the next three chapters, and will perhaps help to dispel the inevitable association of evaluation with examinations and with selection decisions. This partly arises from the fact that selection decisions are unavoidable and therefore assume priority over curriculum decisions which are avoidable. Yet, if the fundamental aims of higher education as it plans for the future are to predominate over the exigencies of keeping the system running, the Parkinsonian principle that unavoidable decisions take priority over avoidable decisions regardless of their respective importance will need to be replaced by the principle that the total cost (including time) of making a decision should be commensurate with the importance of the decision [7]. Such a change would enable us to regard evaluation with a proper perspective as serving all kinds of decisions and not just selection decisions. For the administrator, evaluation is the key to the optimum use of teaching resources. For the student, evaluation is the key to self-evaluation. For the teacher, evaluation is the key to professionalism, for applying the same intellectual standards to his teaching as he applies to his research.

REFERENCES

1. BERDIE, Ralph F. The uses of evaluation in guidance. In: R. W. Tyler (ed.), *Educational evaluation: new roles, new means.* University of Chicago Press, 1969.

2. BLOOM, Benjamin S. *et al. Taxonomy of educational objectives handbook I: cognitive domain.* New York, Longmans Green, 1956.

3. * Cox, Roy. Examinations and higher education. *Universities quarterly* (London), vol. 21, no. 3, June 1967.

4. DRESSEL, P. *et al. Evaluation in higher education.* New York, Houghton Mifflin, 1961.

5. DREVER, James (chairman). *Assessment of undergraduate performance.* Report of Conference convened by the Committee of Vice-Chancellors and Principals and the Association of University Teachers, London, 1969.

6. ERAUT, Michael R. The design of variable input learning systems. In: W. R. Dunn and C. Holroyd (eds.), *Aspects of educational technology.* Vol. 2. London, Methuen, 1969.

7. ——. The role of evaluation. In: George Taylor (ed.), *The teacher as manager.* London, Councils and Education Press, 1970.

8. FURNEAUX, W. P. The psychologist and the university. *Universities quarterly* (London), vol. 17, 1962.

9. HUDSON, Liam. Degree class and attainment in scientific research. *British Journal of Psychology* (London), vol. 51, no. 1, 1960.

10. LINDQUIST, E. F. (ed.). *Educational measurement.* Washington, D.C., American Council on Education, 1951.

11. * OPPENHEIM, A. N.; JAHODA, Marie; JAMES, R. L. Assumptions underlying the use of university examinations. *Universities quarterly* (London), vol. 21, no. 3, June 1967.

12. PIGEON, Douglas; YATES, Alfred. *An introduction to educational measurement.* London, Routledge & Kegan Paul, 1968.
13. SPENCER, Richard E. *The role of measurement and evaluation in instructional technology.* Urbana, Ill., University of Illinois, 1968.
14. WHITTA, Dean K. Research in college admissions. In: R. W. Tyler (ed.), *Educational evaluation: new roles, new means.* University of Chicago Press, 1969.
15. WOOD, Dorothy Adkins. *Test construction.* Columbus, Ohio, Charles Merrill, 1961.

IX. Teaching methods

Discussions on teaching methods tend to be plagued by overgeneralizations both with respect to the way they are classified and with respect to the way they are evaluated. It is normal, for example, for teaching methods to be classified into four, five or even six categories on the basis of the size of the group and the presence or absence of dramatic instrumentation such as television. These categories are then compared on the assumption that the variation between categories is much more important than the variation within categories. This assumption is rarely justified by the evidence. Evaluation of teaching methods also tends to be confined to one or two dimensions, usually the score on a single test and sometimes the student's rating on an attitude questionnaire. Yet this assumes that there is no significant relationship between how you teach and what wou teach, i.e. that the method which proves best for one kind of objective will also be best for all other kinds of objective, which is another unlikely assumption [13, 20, 29]. The question of cost also affects judgements about teaching methods. Though in practice it often determines which method is selected, in theory it tends to be totally ignored and many research studies are more concerned with comparisons on the basis of equal contact time than they are with comparisons based on equal cost.

The purpose of this chapter is to create a framework for discussion which avoids these often unjustified assumptions and generalizations. It therefore attempts to characterize teaching methods along a number of different dimensions, quoting research findings where it is considered necessary to demonstrate the importance of a dimension which might otherwise be ignored. A brief discussion of criteria for evaluating teaching methods will then be followed by a summary of the research evidence. Finally, we add our own recommendations: these go beyond the very limited research evidence but are nevertheless reasonable extrapolations from what is now known about teaching and learning.

The following six dimensions are considered to be important for the description and classification of teaching methods: the composition of the group; characteristics of group members; modes of interaction between members of the group; the nature of the material resources available; the modes of use of those resources; time factors, i.e. preparation time, contact time, follow-up time, etc. These dimensions are not entirely independent and there is no suggestion that all combinations are possible. In the group consisting of a single student, for example, the third dimension relating to modes of interaction between members of the group would obviously be irrelevant.

COMPOSITION OF THE GROUP

The group usually contains two teachers, one teacher or no teacher and it may contain any number of students. The teacherless situations most commonly found are the large group watching television and the student working by himself. The use of teaching assistants when classes are watching television has been shown to have no effect, so this appears to be a genuinely teacherless situation. Learning also takes place in informal meetings between small groups of students and the use of planned teacherless groups has also been reported. These groups appear to have been useful when planned into a course and we believe that more use of them will be made in the future. A student's colleagues often represent the least recognized, least used and possibly the most important of all the resources available to him. Until student unrest forced a fresh look at this matter, very few teachers ever considered the student as a resource; a search for ways of tapping that potential could be the most significant consequence of the current debate on student roles.

When one teacher is present the possible modes of interaction (described in further detail below) are limited by the size of the group. It is therefore useful to classify groups into four types and to name them accordingly:

Number of students	Type of group	Number of students	Type of group
1-3	Tutorial	15-32	Class
4-14	Discussion group	Over 32	Audience

These names are often used to refer to groups which are slightly smaller or larger, but for the purposes of this chapter they will be used as defined above.

Situations in which more than one teacher is present are rare but should not be neglected. Possibilities include discussion groups in which teachers with different backgrounds and perspectives participate, practical classes in which senior and junior teachers both advise, and lectures to which more than one lecturer contributes.

CHARACTERISTICS OF GROUP MEMBERS

One of the major sources of variation in teaching method is the teacher. Distinguishable factors affecting teacher behaviour include the knowledge he brings to the situation, the extent and nature of his teaching experience, certain personality factors and certain teaching skills [3, 10, 36]. Some of these can be significantly changed by training, others cannot. Selection of teaching methods cannot therefore be separated from questions such as 'Do we need a training programme for college teachers?' and 'If different teaching skills are needed, can we allocate teachers in a way that builds on each teacher's individual strengths rather than plays upon his weaknesses?' Experiences with team teaching in secondary schools have given strong support for the view that different teachers do have strength in different aspects of the teaching process and that responsibilities can be at least partially allocated on this basis [34]. But the university situation is rather different because professionalization is associated with research skills rather than teaching skills.

Student characteristics are also important. The knowledge students bring to the situation may have serious gaps, they may or may not have a mental map of the subject before they begin, they may or may not be motivated to learn [43]. Not only are these attributes important for each student but the extent to which they are shared is equally important. However, even if the group is relatively homogeneous on cognitive dimensions, there are likely to be important differences in the personalities and learning styles of the students involved, and there is much research to suggest that these factors affect the teaching method which suits each student best [8, 45]. Too many discussions of 'teaching' have been conducted on the assumption that the teacher sets a reasonable norm (reasonable, that is, for 'normal' students) and those who have difficulty learning according to the norm are regarded as difficult deviants. The dimensions of convergent—divergent, anxious—non-anxious, and extrovert—introvert all affect the degree of uncertainly and the degree of structuring which individual students prefer; and there is good evidence relating these factors to student performance as well as to student attitudes [15, 38]. The extent to which individual differences of this kind can be catered for will depend both on the constraints of the system and on the resourcefulness of the teachers concerned. It could even be an institutional objective to help students to learn in both structured and unstructured situations. We return to these questions in the next chapter where we also discuss situations where heterogeneity has been shown to be advantageous.

MODES OF INTERACTION BETWEEN MEMBERS OF THE GROUP

Interaction between members of the group is most constricted in an audience group (over thirty-two students). Such a group is too large for a single teacher to maintain effective contact by any means other than lecturing, and its size is relatively unimportant [19]. Practical classes of this size either have more than one teacher present or are effectively teacherless for most of the time. In the typical lecture situation verbal communication is entirely one-way and teaching skills such as voice projection and dramatization are at a premium. This pattern can be varied by having a second lecturer or a member of the audience ask questions to high-light conceptual difficulties or by stopping and setting questions for the audience to answer or discuss, either individually or in 'buzz' groups. If immediate feedback to the lecturer is considered important, these questions can be put into multiple-choice format and the results transmitted back to the lecturer by means of coloured cardboard discs or electronic feedback devices (see Chapter IV).

The lecture pattern can also be used with smaller groups and is not unknown even in the tutorial situation. But with numbers below thirty-two it becomes possible for students to question the teacher on a regular basis and for the teacher to question individual students. The group is still too large for students to question one another but it can be split into subgroups for the purposes of discussion or working with resources or both. If the group remains undivided the mode of interaction can be quite complicated to define. Relevant factors include the time spent by each participant in speaking, the extent to which students follow up each other's questions or refer back to their teacher each time, the extent to which teacher questions elicit one word or extended answers and the general level of questions (i.e. factual, conceptual, evaluative, etc.). Activities such as role-playing, simulation and gaming are also possible with groups of this size [24, 39]. Many teachers are restricted in their ability to interact with classes in different ways, but their repertoire can be extended by appropriate training. This problem has been tackled at Stanford University where they have made considerable use of television [2, 30, 37]. They record short segments of teaching and play it back to the teacher, who then reteaches a topic with different students and sees himself in action once more. Using this technique of micro-teaching (described in Chapter V) they have been able to improve teaching skills such as 'using questions effectively, recognising and obtaining attending behaviour, control of participation and providing feedback'.

With numbers of fourteen or less it becomes possible to have a discussion group in which members sit in a circle or round a table. When this replaces an arrangement with the teacher up front and students facing the front, it becomes much easier for students to interact with one another; and the teacher can if desired assume the humbler position of *primus inter pares*. Student-student interactions now become as important as teacher-student interactions and the level and number of them can differ greatly [35, 44]. Particularly important is the extent to which students genuinely listen to each other and follow up each other's points rather than strive for their personal share of the limelight without regard for the progress of the group as a whole. Research in the general area of group dynamics [11, 14, 24] has contributed greatly to our understanding of the interaction possibilities of discussion groups but its findings have only been applied by a few enthusiasts [1, 5, 9]. Most teachers in higher education do not possess group management skills appropriate to the discussion group situation, though there is considerable scope for training in this area. In the meantime they tend to treat a discussion group as a small class or lecture audience because this is the way they are used to teaching, and also, because if they do attempt to break the pattern the students are unlikely to co-operate since student expectations of teacher dominance will have been determined by previous experience.

The tutorial situation allows the greatest flexibility in student-teacher interaction, though this is not always realized in practice. Both the extent to which the teacher lectures and the extent to which his questioning gets the student involved in genuine explanation and discussion rather than just assenting are clearly important. Again, the student may come with expectations of a passive role.

The advantage of teacherless groups is that there is no longer any danger of the teacher monopolizing the conversation, anxiety is reduced and students are free to interact with one another. However, it is also important for the groups to be well briefed and carefully prepared, and it may take some time for students to learn to work effectively in this way [11, 24]. Some knowledge of group dynamics, for example, might be helpful to them. Leaderless groups have also proved useful in programmed learning situations which we discuss more fully in the next chapter.

NATURE OF THE MATERIAL RESOURCES AVAILABLE

The use and misuse of resources for teaching and learning was discussed in Chapters IV, V and VI but in this section we wish to make one further point. If we disregard resources for practical work such as scientific equipment and materials, and computers in their role as calculating tools for the student, and concentrate on resources for communication, it becomes useful to distinguish between the functions of structured, unstructured and structuring resources. Structured materials include workbooks, programmes and the expository kind of film. They are primarily concerned with communicating a body of content (though not necessarily at a low conceptual level). Unstructured materials include all forms of source material, printed, audio and visual, which can be considered to be information presenting; and theory-presenting materials such as scholarly treatises. Structuring materials may be information-structuring as in an annotated bibliography or a transparency summarizing the possible areas on which a discussion might concentrate, question-provoking as in a list of questions or an anomalous film, or assignment-setting as in a set of problems or even the statement of objectives for a course.

Some resources, such as textbooks, may serve more than one of these functions but this is not necessarily very efficient, as Lumsdaine pointed out [25]: 'Despite the venerability of the textbook as a medium of instruction, a case may be made for the position that it actually has two quite distinct functions—that of a reference source of information and that of a sequenced medium of instruction or learning. The basic requirements for these two functions differ fundamentally, as, for instance, in the need for sequencing and redundancy of information. With the development of programmed self-instructional media and concomitant improvement in the information-retrieval utility of handbooks, and similar reference sources, it seems possible that the next decade or so may witness the decline, if not the demise, of the textbook, as now conceived, in favour of programmed instructional material on the one hand and of the well-designed reference handbook or source book on the other.'

MODES OF USE OF EDUCATIONAL MATERIALS

The ways in which materials are used in the teaching-learning situation can be categorized according to who selects the materials and who controls the materials [21]. Materials may be selected by the student, by the teacher or by some external producer, perhaps a television producer or a curriculum development team, and either the student or the teacher can control the materials by deciding when and where to start and stop and by determining the pace. Five of the six selector-controller combinations are outlined below. The sixth is only found in unusual political circumstances.

Materials controlled by	Materials selected by		
	Learner	Teacher	Producer
Learner	Project mode	Assignment mode	Learning package mode
Teacher		Teacher presentation mode	Mediated teaching mode

The *project mode* is the situation where the student selects his own materials and uses them for some special project, task or essay; in the *assignment mode,* on the other hand, the selection is made by the teacher. Clearly there is no sharp division between the two and often a teacher will recommend rather than assign materials to a student or at least narrow his choice considerably by providing appropriate guidance. The *learning package mode,* where the materials have been selected by some outside producer but are controlled by the learner, is typified by correspondence courses and teach-yourself language packs. Though Oakland Community College and a few other United States colleges have made considerable use of this mode, it has until now been extremely rare in higher education. The advent of teleplayers which present motion pictures and can be used like audio tapes (see Chapter IV), combined with radical new ventures like the Open University in the United Kingdom, may well increase the use of this mode significantly. The *teacher presentation mode* uses materials such as slides, chalk, overhead transparencies and short films to present visual information, to clarify points or to emphasize the main headings. The *mediated teaching mode,* in which the teacher is on film or on television, is a remote version of the same thing. It has the disadvantages of inflexibility and lack of human contact, but the advantages of being more ambitious in its use of resource materials, of being able to use an exceptionally talented presenter and of being better prepared, possibly even tried out and revised.

TIME FACTORS

For the teacher, time is spent in contact with students and in preparation; and his preparation time can be divided into immediate preparation which is necessary each time he teaches the course and long-term preparation which does not have to be repeated until he wishes to revise that part of the course. This long-term preparation can involve preparing lecture notes, inspecting other people's teaching materials, making television programmes, preparing student assignment sheets, etc. Its distinguishing feature is that it results in some kind of re-usable resource material (even if the notes are only legible to their creator!). When this long-term preparation is pursued systematically, we call it course development, and this is discussed in some detail in Chapter XI.

Time factors obviously affect the cost of teaching but in this section we are only concerned with pointing out that within any given teaching situation the time factor is an important variable. A well-prepared lecture and a badly prepared lecture cannot always be regarded as equivalent examples of the same teaching method. Indeed the general problem of the optimum allocation of teacher time between contact time and preparation time is a critical one which will be treated at length in later chapters.

From the student viewpoint it is almost meaningless to consider time factors at the teaching-method level. He is always involved in a combination of methods, e.g. lectures and independent work, and one cannot usefully distinguish time spent writing up lecture notes from independent work. For the student time has to be considered at the course level both in terms of the total time he spends and of his allocation of this time to different learning activities. It is not unusual for him to be overtaught in terms of quantity and undertaught in terms of quality; changing the first might help to correct the second.

EVALUATION OF TEACHING METHODS

Teaching methods can be evaluated in terms of outcomes, (i.e. changes in student behaviour) or in terms of inputs (i.e. costs), or by some combination of the two using cost-benefit analysis. Evaluation of outcomes has already been discussed in Chapters VII and VIII, which emphasized the wide range of outcomes which were both possible and desirable. These chapters also stressed the disadvantages of using a single index of performance to assess outcomes and suggested that an outcome profile was more likely to be meaningful. Unfortunately, much research on teaching methods has ignored this need and used a single performance measure; and it often gives very little indication of the nature of that measure. Since there is evidence to suggest that some methods are more appropriate for one kind of outcome and other methods more appropriate for another kind of outcome, research which fails to specify the learning outcomes in sufficient detail is virtually useless [27].

Costing methods are equally primitive. Time costs are usually limited to estimates of the proportion of a teacher's teaching load allocated to a given course on the assumption that he is paid only for teaching and not for research. This gives different costs from those obtained from costing the time that he actually spends in teaching (preparation time included) and ignores factors such as the cost of student time. As mentioned earlier, little research has been devoted to comparisons of teaching methods on an equal-cost basis and this makes institutional decisions about teaching particularly difficult.

Although the cost-benefit approach is beginning to be applied to education at the macro-economic level, it is extremely difficult to apply at a micro-economic level within a given institution because both the total cost of a course and its total benefits are difficult to quantify. It is, however, possible to compare marginal changes in cost with marginal changes in benefit, though academic decision-making rarely proceeds in this way, perhaps because benefit is often conceived in terms of benefit to an 'academic empire' rather than in terms of benefit to the institution.

EVIDENCE FROM RESEARCH

Before proceeding to outline the evidence available from research on teaching methods in higher education, it is worth emphasizing the primitive state of our knowledge in this area. The position has not noticeably altered since 1963 when Wallen and Travers commented that [42]:

'Studies which supposedly compare the effectiveness of two teaching methods are generally studies which compare two largely unknown conditions. It is hardly surprising that most such studies cannot be considered to be a major contribution to scientific knowledge, for they compare the effect of one vaguely defined condition with that of another. . . .

'Too often the designer of a teaching method has based an entire method on a single appealing principle. Such behaviour is analogous to that of the engineer who, in designing a machine, attended only to the laws of friction and neglected all other established laws of physics. The faults of design make it futile to conduct studies comparing them with other teaching methods which are just as poorly designed. Such research merely reveals that all the methods compared are approximately equal in their ineffectiveness.'

From this viewpoint it is only natural that most prescribed teaching patterns should have been influenced much more by philosophical traditions, cultural traditions and the needs of teachers than they have been influenced by research on learning.

We have already discussed research relating to improvements obtainable by marginal changes in method, e.g. the use of questions during lectures, training teachers to run discussion groups, etc., and research specifically relating to educational technology will be summarized in the next chapter. This section concentrates on research bearing on the selection of teaching methods. This does provide some useful evidence in spite of the methodological weaknesses already discussed. Most of the research of this type in higher education has concentrated on comparing the use of lectures with the use of classes or discussion groups. The American literature usually refers to a group of fifteen to thirty-two students, which we have defined as a 'class', as a discussion group, but we will persist with our definition as it is more consistent with the interactions which can take place in groups of this size. Most of these comparisons give no significant differences on tests of knowledge, though a couple of studies have favoured the lecture. Several comparisons, however, have detected significant differences in favour of the class on measures of critical thinking and attitude change [4, 17, 41]. There is also good evidence from a number of studies that student-centred discussions are superior to teacher-centred discussions on measures of motivation, attitude change and conceptual learning [26, 40]. This suggests that it is the mode of interaction which is the critical factor and that the size of the group is only important in so far as it sets a limit on the possible modes of interaction. This would be supported by the evidence of Bloom who found that students in lecture classes as opposed to students in discussion classes reported significantly more thoughts classified as 'irrelevant' and 'simple comprehension' and significantly less thoughts classified as relating to 'self', 'other persons' and 'problem solving' [12].

A further set of research studies relate to the use of 'independent study', which is even less well-defined in the literature than 'discussion group'. We take independent study to be a teacherless situation, though the American literature usually refers to an 'independent study programme' which includes contact with teachers in tutorials and small discussion groups [18, 22]. Baskin concluded from several experiments with such independent study programmes at Antioch that [7]: (a) there were no significant differences in learning or retention after two years; (b) independent study need not be restricted to superior students; (c) achievement may depend on personality factors as much as on academic ability; (d) students were initially dissatisfied with independent study but became increasingly satisfied as they became accustomed to the technique; and (e) no real saving of instructor time was evident even though class-room time was significantly reduced in the experimental courses.

Experiments at Colorado, however, showed that students on independent study with freedom to consult their teacher learned fewer facts and simple applications (no difference after three months) but were superior to students in conventional classes in making difficult applications and in learning new material [23]. At Michigan students learnt less facts after independent study but were more motivated towards further learning, as shown by a questionnaire and by their electing for more advanced courses in the same subject (psychology) [28]. Some short-term experiments have shown that students learn more facts from reading than attending lectures, but in general independent-study experiments have only been successful when considerable teacher support was given [6]. This suggests that it might well be more profitable to investigate means of training students for independent study and guiding their independent study experience than to continue with comparative research in situations where students and faculty are both unused to the problems of an independent study emphasis.

In some English universities independent study with tutorial support is the main teaching method and the Oxbridge system is often admired. But there has been little research to determine its comparative effectiveness, mainly because those institutions using it are so committed to it that their faculty would be most reluctant to deny it to any group of students for experimental purposes. However, it is clear that at least some English tutorials fail to take advantage of the special modes of interaction that become possible in the tutorial situation. Many teachers have not yet learnt to get their students to make critical contributions and some tutorials approximate to mini-lectures. Moreover there has been little systematic exploration of the use of resource materials for independent study.

TEACHING METHODS AS AIDS TO INDEPENDENT STUDY

It has become a truism to say that attention should be focused on learning rather than on teaching but the implications are usually ignored. It is rare, for example, to find a course in higher education in which students do not spend considerably more time in independent study than in contact with a teacher. Yet a combination of lectures and independent study is invariably called the 'lecture method' and a combination of discussion groups and independent study is called the 'discussion method'. There is no ambiguity in this nomenclature as the independent-study element is taken for granted, but it does support the tendency of teachers to define a course solely in terms of its contact hours. We consider, however, that it is more logical to reverse the conventional view and thus to define a course largely in terms of its independent-study element. When this is done it becomes possible to define teaching methods in higher education as aids to independent study. This position is consistent with an emphasis on learning rather than teaching and it recognizes that the greater part of a student's time is actually spent in independent study, and that when he leaves it will often be the only method available to him.

In defining teaching methods as aids to independent study we have to make the distinction between material aids to independent study and teaching aids to independent study. We have already discussed material aids and it was pointed out that they can be broadly divided into three categories, structured materials, unstructured materials and structuring materials. The relative importance of these different kinds of material aids and of teaching aids such as lectures, tutorials, etc., will depend on the objectives of the course, and it is from this viewpoint that our final section on the selection of teaching methods and learning materials will be written. Many of the recommendations will not be fully supported by research evidence as this is scanty and unreliable, but in our view they are reasonable extrapolations from what is already known about teaching and learning. They could also be construed as hypotheses which future research could aim to support or refute.

SELECTION OF TEACHING METHODS AND LEARNING MATERIALS

The use of material aids to independent study has yet to be fully explored. Considerable use has been made of structured and unstructured materials, but little use of structuring materials. Let us consider a number of cases. If the objectives of a course are knowledge, comprehension and application over a limited range of examples, structured materials are likely to be the most effective. The programmed-learning literature gives good evidence for this. But if, as is not unusual in higher education, no suitable structured materials are available and it is uneconomic to develop one's own, maximum attention needs to be given to the use of structuring materials. Structuring materials such as statements of objectives, conceptual maps and graded assignments with knowledge of results have all been used on occasions; but they have tended to be planned as addenda to lectures or classes rather than as important aids to independent study. For this latter use they have to be more detached, more carefully thought out and revised in the light of student experience.

If, however, we are concerned with a different type of course in which the priority objectives are application of principles and techniques to new kinds of examples and intellectual skills such as analysis, synthesis, evaluation or problem-solving, it becomes important for the student to be able to create his own structure. This does not necessarily mean that he should be left unguided, though many would hold that an important aim of higher education is to develop students who can learn entirely from unstructured materials without additional help. This independence is rarely achieved by throwing students in at the deep end. A carefully planned destructuring, with first-term courses highly structured and final-year courses relatively unstructured, would appear to be the most appropriate way to achieve this objective of 'learning how to learn', and the planned use of structuring materials would undoubtedly assist this phasing-out process.

The selection of teaching methods as aids to independent study also depends on the objectives they are intended to achieve. All of the following functions are sometimes required of teaching: (a) information presenting; (b) communicating objectives; (c) structuring the field; (d) explaining difficult concepts and problems; (e) motivating the student; (f) developing critical thinking; (g) developing alternative frames or reference; (h) changing attitudes; (i) encouraging originality; (j) developing self-evaluation; and (k) developing ability to solve problems.

Of these functions (b) and (c) and possibly (d) and (e) are capable of being met by independent study if appropriate learning materials are provided. The lecture is not a very effective method of transmitting information and the communication of objectives, often cited by students as the main reason for attendance at lectures, can be accomplished by printed handouts [13, 31, 32, 33]. But it can be argued that a lecture or a set of lectures are particularly appropriate for providing a conceptual framework as a basis for independent study. For this purpose the advantages of lectures over a good textbook will clearly depend on the talents of the lecturer. A conceptual map which shows relationships with the field in diagrammatic form can also be helpful.

The function of explaining difficult concepts and problems (d) is traditionally assigned to the class because the teacher can explain slowly and the group is small enough to be able to interrupt and question him where necessary. A smaller group would normally be considered uneconomic for this particular purpose. If however the real purpose is to develop problem-solving techniques (k) in the student rather than just to ensure that he can understand and reproduce the solutions to certain limited types of problems, the small discussion group or tutorial is probably more appropriate because it allows sufficient teacher-student interaction for dissonance techniques to be used and for the process of problem solving to be discussed on an individual basis. It can also be argued that the role of the class as a vehicle for the explanation of given concepts and solutions could be more effectively and efficiently achieved by a programme, particularly if the programme was taken by students in small groups of two or three rather than independently.

The last seven teaching functions on our list undoubtedly require contact with a teacher. For some of them it is clear that the smaller the group the better, for others the optimum size of group is probably the discussion group [16, 35, 44]. The role of motivating the student may be partially achieved by a lecturer with great inspirational qualities who can arouse great interest in his subject. But even with such inspiration the student may need to belong to an identifiable group, to become absorbed in a specific project or to derive motivation from tutorial contact with a motivated teacher.

The discussion group is probably the best method of developing critical thinking as the student is more likely to criticize his peers than his teacher and to justify himself against criticism from his peers. Similarly he is more likely to recognize alternative frames of reference when they become apparent in discussion and to change his attitudes when the group as a whole changes. Some forms of evaluation, particularly those relating to social skills, self-image, etc., may also be most effectively transmitted in discussion groups, but feedback relating to standards of judgement, etc., is likely to be much more meaningful in the tutorial situation. It is also possible for a tutorial to focus on a single student's over-all performance and skills in a way which is never possible in a discussion group. This makes the tutorial the most effective means of evaluating a student's performance and guiding his work. In addition to this the tutorial is the best group for encouraging originality, which may be much more difficult to foster in the critical atmosphere of a discussion group.

The conclusion which follows from this analysis of the functions of teaching in higher education is that quality is at least as important as quantity in assessing the value of teacher-student contact time, and that the use of structuring aids to independent study needs to be further developed. This suggests that the traditional allocation of faculty time may not always be the most appropriate. It may be better to have smaller groups meeting less often. It may pay to devote some faculty time to the development of aids to independent study. It could also be useful to explore further the potentialities of scheduled teacherless groups where students could help one another. When teaching resources are particularly scarce a policy of saving on some courses in order to improve others would seem sensible, though the common pattern of devoting more resources to the final year may not necessarily be the best. An investment in helping students learn to work independently when they first enter higher education could well give a better pay-off in some situations.

REFERENCES

1. ABERCROMBIE, M. L. J. *The anatomy of judgement.* London, Hutchinson, 1960.
2. ALLEN, D. W.; RYAN, K. A. *Microteaching.* Reading, Mass., Addison Wesley, 1969.
3. AXELROD, J. *Model building for undergraduate colleges: a theoretical framework for studying and reforming the curricular-instruction subsystem in American colleges.* Washington, D.C., U.S. Dept. of Health, Education and Welfare, 1969.
4. BARNARD, J. D. The lecture-demonstration versus the problem-solving

method of teaching and college science course. *Science education* (New York), vol. 26, 1942.

5. BARNETT, S. A. An experiment with free group discussions. *Universities quarterly* (London), vol. 12, 1958.

6. BASKIN, Samuel. *Quest for quality: some models and means.* Washington, D.C., U.S. Government Printing Office, 1960. (New Dimensions in Higher Education No. 7.)

7. ——. Experiment in independent study (1956-1960). *Journal of experimental education* (Madison, Wis.), vol. 31, 1962.

8. BEACH, L. R. Sociability and academic achievement in various types of learning situations. *Journal of educational psychology* (Wash.), vol. 51, 1960.

9. BEARD, Ruth M. *Small group discussion in university teaching.* University Teaching Methods Research Unit, Institute of Education, London University, 1967.

10. BENDIG, A. W. Ability and personality characteristics of introductory psychology instructors rated competent and empathic by their students. *Journal of educational research* (Madison, Wis.), vol. 48, 1955.

11. BENNE, K. D.; LEVIT, G. The nature of groups and helping groups improve their operation. *Review of educational research* (Wash.), vol. 23, 1955.

12. BLOOM, B. S. Thought processes in lecture and discussions. *Journal of general education* (University Park, Pa.), vol. 7, 1953.

13. ——. Twenty-five years of educational research. *American educational research journal* (Wash.), vol. 3, no. 3, 1966.

14. * CARTWRIGHT, D.; ZANDER, A. *Group dynamics: research and theory.* New York, Row & Peterson, 1953.

15. CHICKERING, Arthur W. Dimensions of independence. *Journal of experimental education* (Madison, Wis.), vol. 32, 1964.

16. COTTRELL, T. L. The effect of size of tutorial group on teaching efficiency. *University of Edinburgh gazette*, vol. 33, 1962.

17. DAWSON, M. O. Lectures versus problem-solving in teaching elementary soil sections. *Science education* (New York), vol. 40, 1956.

18. DEARING, Bruce. The student on his own: independent study. In: S. Baskin (ed.), *Higher education: some newer developments.* New York, McGraw-Hill, 1965.

19. DE CECCO, J. P. Class size and co-ordinated instruction. *British journal of educational psychology* (London), vol. 34, 1964.

20. DRESSEL, P.; LEHMANN, I. J. The impact of higher education on student attitudes, values and initial thinking abilities. *Educational record* (Washington), summer 1965.

21. ERAUT, Michael R. Educational technology and curriculum development: implications for colleges of education. In: M. R. Bar (ed.), *Curriculum innovation in practice in relation to colleges of education.* Ormskirk, Edge Hill College of Education, 1970.

22. HATCH, W. R.; RICHARDS, Alice (eds.). *Approach to independent study.* Washington, D.C., U.S. Government Printing Office, 1965. (New Dimensions in Higher Education No. 13.)

23. HOVEY, Donald E.; GRUBER, Howard E.; TERRELL, Glenn. Effects of self-directed study on course achievement, retention and curiosity. *Journal of*

Educational Research (Madison, Wis.), vol. 56, 1963.

24. * KLEIN, Josephine. *Working with groups.* London, Routledge, 1965.

25. LUMSDAINE, A. A. Instruments and media of instruction. In: N. L. Gage (ed.), *Handbook of research in teaching.* Chicago, Rand McNally, 1963.

26. * MCKEACHIE, W. J. Teaching at college level. In: N. L. Gage (ed.), *Handbook of research in teaching.* Chicago, Rand McNally, 1963.

27. ———. *The appraisal of teaching in large universities.* Ann Arbor, Mich., University of Michigan, 1959.

28. —— *et al.* Individualised teaching in elementary psychology. *Journal of educational psychology* (Wash.), vol. 51, 1960.

29. * ———. *New developments in teaching.* Washington, D.C., U.S. Government Printing Office, 1967. (New Dimensions in Higher Education No. 16.)

30. MCKNIGHT, Philip C.; BARAL, David P. *Microteaching and the technical skills of teaching: a bibliography of research and development at Stanford University, 1963-69.* Stanford, Calif., School of Education, 1969.

31. * MCLEISH, John. *The lecture method.* Cambridge, England, Cambridge Institute of Education, 1968.

32. MACMANAWAY, L. A. Using lecture scripts. *Universities quarterly* (London), vol. 22, June 1968.

33. MILTON, O. Two-year follow up: objective data after learning without class attendance. *Psychological reports* (Missoula, Mont.), vol. 11, 1962.

34. SHAPLIN, Judson J.; OLDS, Henry F. (eds.). *Team teaching.* New York, Harper & Row, 1964.

35. * SMITH, Peter B. The seminar. In: D. Layton (ed.), *University teaching in transition.* Edinburgh, Oliver & Boyd, 1968.

36. SOLOMON, Daniel; BEZDELL, William F.; ROSENBERG, Larry. *Teaching styles and learning.* Chicago, Center for the Study of Liberal Education for Adults, 1963.

37. STANFORD CENTRE FOR RESEARCH AND DEVELOPMENT IN EDUCATION. *Third Annual Report.* Stanford, Calif., October 1968.

38. STERN, G. G. Environments for learning. In: N. Sanford (ed.). *The American College.* New York, Wiley, 1962.

39. TANSEY, P. J.; UNWIN, P. *Simulation and gaming in education.* London, Methuen, 1969.

40. THISTLEWAITE, P. L. College environments and the development of talent. *Science* (Wash.), vol. 130, 1959.

41. TISTAERT, G. A classroom experiment on lecture and discussion methods. *Paedagogica europaea* (Amsterdam), vol. 1, 1965.

42. WALLEN, Norman E.; TRAVERS, Robert M. W. Analysis and investigation of teaching methods. In: N. L. Gage (ed.), *Handbook of research on teaching.* Chicago, Rand McNally, 1963.

43. WARD, J. Group-study versus lecture-demonstration method in physical science instruction for general education college students. *Journal of experimental education* (Madison, Wis.), vol. 24, 1956.

44. WATT, I. The seminar. *Universities quarterly* (London), vol. 18, 1964.

45. WISPE, L. G. Evaluating section teaching methods in the introductory course. *Journal of educational research* (Madison, Wis.), vol. 45, 1951.

X. Research in educational technology

The term educational technology can be interpreted in two distinct ways: first, to describe the use of technology *in* education or, secondly, to imply the concept of a technology *of* education [16]. The former is concerned with increasing the use of equipment, the latter with improving the effectiveness of learning. In this chapter we are concerned with research relevant to the technology *of* education, of which one aspect is research into the effects on student performance of using technology *in* education.

The concept of a technology of education implies a systematic approach to learning in which one tries to develop means to achieve given ends and persists in one's attempts to find solutions to problems. Often one does not understand how or why a particular approach achieves the effect it does. But a successful method can be used even when it is not understood, and no one is going to wait for the research which explains the whys and wherefores. Take, for example, metallurgy. It was a technology for thousands of years and only recently become a science. A science of learning is now beginning to emerge but as yet it has only a little to offer to the practising teacher. The basic experiment which compares method A with method B takes one little further when neither method is particularly good. If one starts to improve method A then one has to do the comparison all over again, and one could also improve method B and get yet another result. As Wallen and Travers commented [65]: 'These studies . . . are comparable to the effects made by a mediaeval physician to determine which of two herbs had the greater curative value, when he had no knowledge of the chemistry, physiology or pharmacology involved.'

The sceptical teacher has always said that educational research is of little help and that even the best research only confirms what is already known by experience. One way of looking at the technological approach is to consider it as a method of institutionalizing experience by trying to use it more systematically. Experience comes from trying something out, seeing what the problems are, changing it where necessary and trying it again, and it is this process of using information from try-out as a basis for further improvements that characterizes the technology of education. As Leith comments [38]: 'In the absence of scientifically established principles, educational technology implements techniques of empirical testing to improve learning situations.'

This point is perhaps best illustrated by a simple model (Fig. 2) for the development of a teaching topic.

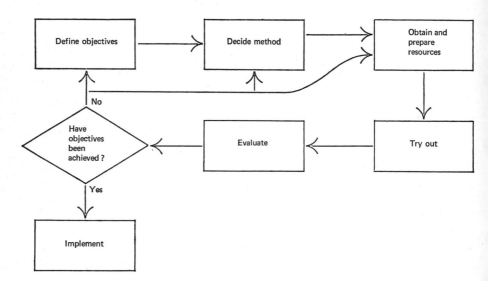

FIG. 2

This development cycle consists of deciding what to teach and how to teach, preparing to teach, trying out one's chosen approach and then evaluating it. Failure to achieve all one's goals leads to a modification of goals, or to a change in method or to further preparation with attention focused on marginal improvements. We develop this model further in the next chapter when we discuss course development in detail.

The emphasis which educational technology places on the development cycle does not however mean that research is unimportant. Development by trial and revision is a lengthy process and any evidence from research which enables us to start with a good design provides a valuable short cut. Educational technology is concerned both with the application of research into the learning process and the conditions of learning to the design of learning situations, and with the use of trial and revision procedures to make further improvements in those learning situations.

There are three main kinds of research studies in educational technology: *comparative effectiveness studies, basic studies* and *process studies*. The comparative effectiveness studies compare alternative methods and provide some evidence relevant to the selection of method. The basic studies are highly analytical and seek to explore learner variables and variables within a given method rather than variables between methods. The evidence from these basic studies relates partly to method selection but mainly to the design of learning situations once the method has been chosen. The process studies, however, relate not to the design of learning situations but to their improvement. It is these studies which must provide the justification for the development cycle and the 'technology of education' approach.

COMPARATIVE EFFECTIVENESS STUDIES

In Chapter X we discussed the comparative effectiveness of teaching methods but postponed discussion of studies on the new media and on programmed learning. Since most of the comparative studies with new media have compared them with the lecture, it was important to examine the lecture in the conventional context first, where it has to compete with other traditional methods. Studies comparing the effectiveness of television with conventional instruction (usually lectures) represent much the largest category and have tended to find no significant differences. Schramm, summarizing 100 studies at the higher education level, found that 84 showed no significant differences in achievement, 3 favoured television and 13 favoured conventional instruction [58]. Attitudes of college students were sometimes negative but depended upon the subject, the teacher and the viewer. Similar results have been obtained when the use of film has been compared with conventional teaching [45, 57] and two studies by Popham in which the lecture element of a course was replaced by sound recordings also gave no significant differences [55, 56].

Most reviewers of these comparative effectiveness studies have concluded that there are usually no significant differences in achievement between the use of television or film and the lecture, but that there are often slight attitudinal preferences for the face-to-face situation [8, 13]. McKeachie however has come to a conclusion less favourable to television and his argument is worth quoting at length [46]: 'Taking the results of all research on television instruction, we feel safe in concluding that television instruction for a complete course is inferior to classroom lectures in communicating information, developing critical thinking, changing attitudes, and arousing interest in a subject but that this inferiority is probably not great. This conclusion may surprise the reader who has seen publicity releases reporting no significant differences between classroom and television instruction. In our consideration of methodological issues, we noted the logical fallacy in concluding that no difference exists because the difference found was not great enough to disprove the null hypothesis. This is particularly pertinent here

141

because a review of a number of studies of television leaves one with quite a different conclusion than he might draw from a review of just one. In 20 of the 26 well-controlled experiments reviewed, conventional classes were superior to television classes in achievement. Although few of the differences were statistically significant by themselves, simple application of the sign-test indicates that the differences were not random. In contrast with research comparing other instructional methods, the consistency of results favoring conventional instruction over television is unusual. When one weighs heavily the necessity for accommodating higher education to large numbers of students, however, the differences between television and conventional instruction seem very small. It may be that researchers are reluctant to report findings contrary to the hypotheses of the foundations that support them, and their reports are thus as gentle as possible.

Studies comparing the effectiveness of programmed learning with conventional teaching have been a little more conclusive. One-third of the college-level comparisons made by Schramm in 1964 favoured programmed learning and none favoured conventional teaching [59]. Hartley's review in 1966 used three measures, time taken, test result, and retest result [27]. Though he criticizes all the studies on methodological grounds, it cannot be denied that taken as a whole the evidence in favour of programmed learning is considerable.

His data for university-level comparison studies are given in Table 2.

TABLE 2

Measure recorded	Number of studies	Programmed learning superior		No significant difference		Programmed learning inferior	
		Number	%	Number	%	Number	%
Time taken	19	11	58	4	21	4	21
Test result	25	11	44	14	56	0	0
Retest result	4	3	75	1	25	0	0

A CRITIQUE OF COMPARATIVE EFFECTIVENESS STUDIES

Most reviews of comparative effectiveness studies have been critical of this type of research but have had little effect on stemming the flow of papers. It is perhaps inevitable that each new device or technique should be subjected to a kind of 'comparison test' as a condition of entry into the educational repertoire, and not even surprising in view of the obvious methodological deficiencies of most of such tests that people should wish to conduct their own comparison test rather than accept the findings of others. But many comparison tests probably have a further purpose which is not even research in the strict sense and explains why so many projects are in essence repeated in situations where it is unlikely that anything significantly new will emerge. What is loosely called 'research' is often a concealed form of innovation:

the term 'research' is used to give protective coloration (and secure funding) for what are actually development projects. We probably have to resign ourselves to many more such studies in the future. But nevertheless we shall continue to emphasize their shortcomings.

Criticisms of comparative effectiveness studies are of two main types, those which criticize them on methodological grounds and those which criticize them on utilitarian grounds for trying to answer the wrong questions. The first and most frequently invoked methodological criticism relates to the Hawthorne effect [54]. McKeachie comments [46]: 'Sometimes students react to a new method with enthusiasm, at other times, with outraged hostility. A hostile reaction seems particularly likely when students taught by a new method know that they are competing on examinations with students taught by traditional methods. In any case, it is difficult to know how much of student improvement (or loss) in learning may be accounted for by emotional reaction to a new and different method and how much we can expect when the new method is routine. This "Hawthorne effect" influences professors as well as students. How many new curricula, new courses, or new teaching methods have flowered briefly and then faded as the innovators' enthusiasm waned or as new staff members replaced the originators?

Other criticisms relate to problems of sampling and of establishing an appropriate control group. Such questions as equal coverage and emphasis of content, adequate sampling of the student population, and sample size are often ignored, and time is another variable that is rarely taken into account.

Then there is the teacher variable: there is usually more variation between teachers than between methods. One way of trying to avoid this source of error is to get the same teacher to use both methods; however, he is still likely to influence the outcome, and getting several teachers to use both methods is an almost impossible task of salesmanship and organization. Even when programmed learning is being used, there is evidence to show that the attitudes of the teachers involved may significantly affect student performance [34, 51, 59]. Much teaching also takes place outside the 'experimental' or 'control' situation and in many comparison studies the methods being compared are only part of the total teaching. Studies on the effectiveness of television for example often compare lecture/discussion/independent study with television/discussion/independent study, and most of the learning may come from the discussion or the independent study with the lecture or television making a relatively minor contribution. McKeachie writes [46]: 'Because passing or excellent grades are so important to students, they may compensate for ineffective teaching by additional study in order to pass the course examination at the level to which they aspire. Thus the effects of ineffective procedures may be masked or even misinterpreted when course examinations are used as criterion measures. Nachman and Opochinsky [53] provided a neat demonstration of this when they found differences between a small and large class on surprise quizzes but no difference on a final examination.

When significant differences in achievement are found in an experiment, the difference may simply reflect the degree to which students in differing classes were able to find out the content of the examination and the degree to which it would determine their course grade.

The criterion problem can also be treated as methodological. Nearly all comparative studies have used a single measure of achievement and, as was discussed in Chapter IX, it is at least as likely that one method will be better for some objectives and worse for others as it is that a single method will prove best for all possible objectives.

Significant interactions have also been shown between teachers and objectives: some teachers are better for some kinds of objective and worse for others. Often the criterion measures used as a basis for the comparison are themselves so unreliable as to mask significant differences between methods that might otherwise become noticeable. Comparative-effectiveness studies rarely publish the measures used and hardly ever give information on their reliability, so it is difficult to check these points.

The second main line of criticism of comparative effectiveness studies is based on utilitarian grounds. It attacks them for claiming a false degree of generalizability and for trying to answer questions of no practical use. As Lumsdaine has repeatedly pointed out, conclusions from an evaluative study of a single set of lectures or films or programmes can only be applied to those particular lectures, films or programmes, and the generalization of the results to other lectures, films or programmes has, at most, the status of an untested hypothesis [43]. Of what use is it to an appointments committee selecting college teachers to receive an extensive series of research reports comparing the effectiveness of men and women teachers? They would only be concerned with the particular teachers who had applied and would know full well that their sample was likely to be atypical. They might even question the criteria of effectiveness. But they probably would not bother because the reports would show no significant differences.

Then there is the danger of generalizing about future forms of a method on the basis of the present forms. Howland, Lumsdaine and Sheffield warned against this when discussing comparison studies on the effectiveness of films on a specific subject such as general science [30]: Even if an adequate sample of existing films of this type were used and compared with an adequate sample of other instructional devices, the conclusion would apply only to *existing* films of this type and would not determine how effective such film *could* be. This point is particularly important in making judgements about programmed learning, whose principles are based on making successive improvements in the light of evidence from performance and whose techniques are changing rapidly (see Chapter IV). Indeed the first reaction of a programmer to a finding of no significant differences between a programme and conventional instruction would be to revise the programme, unless the main objective was one for which he considered the present repertoire of programming techniques to be inadequate. But the programmer also has to select a medium or media of communication and he too tends to look for guidance to media research. All he perceives, however, are findings of no significant differences.

Two explanations for these findings of no significant differences between media of communication have been put forward. The first suggests that significant differences do exist at the atomic level which cancel at the molecular level. This appears to be the view of Briggs, Campeau, Gagné and May [8]: 'When a single medium is used to present an entire lesson, unit, or course, and achievement resulting from this presentation is compared with achievement from essentially the same presentation by an alternative medium, it is quite feasible that each medium alternately succeeds and fails in supplying the (unspecified) array of learning events required for the various elements in the total learning task. Whether comparisons take into account effectiveness of media or methods, or identify special characteristics of learners and media which influence learning, it is furthermore quite feasible that over the duration of a lesson, unit or course, the net result of these alternate successes and failures, when expressed as total criterion test scores, is to conceal real differences which *do* exist. Hence, perhaps, the great preponderance of "no-difference" findings in media research.'

These authors naturally look for research of practical use to basic studies which 'compare alternate media for a single instructional event'.

The second possible explanation is that apart from situations where information can only be transmitted in sound (e.g. music and comprehension of a spoken language) or pictorial form (e.g. art, cell structure, animal behaviour) the medium of communication is unimportant. It is felt, for instance: that the extent to which preparatory effort is required from teaching staff to prepare learning materials is likely to have more result on the effectiveness of teaching than the form in which the materials are communicated; that when time is spent on classifying and defining educational objectives, similar improvements may also occur; and that variation between teachers and between students, changes in methods of assessment and the degree to which student responses are used to modify the course design and materials may all turn out to have more relevance to effective learning than a straightforward concern with media research implies. The proponents of this point of view tend to look partly to basic studies but mainly to process studies for research of practical use.

One further point needs to be made. Student attitudes towards teaching methods appear to be largely determined by social factors and the degree to which they perceive themselves getting personal attention. Research on the effects of group size has always found student preferences for smaller groups even when there is no detectable change in effectiveness [11]. The degree to which television is seen as a personal medium of communication will therefore be attitudinally important. At Miami University [48] students preferred television to lectures and at New York University [32] they preferred lectures, but differences between lectures were probably far more important. New York students, for example, preferred television or a large class to a small class if they could be sure of having a good teacher and not have to take pot luck. These results point to the potential advantages of using television to make outstanding lecturers more readily available and as a method of reallocating teaching resources in order to allow more small-group teaching. Is there not a case for student participation in decisions of this kind? The potential for inter-institutional co-operation is also important and we return to this in Chapter XII. A questionnaire on a series of television lectures by an outstanding professor at Sussex University included the following results [47]:

Q. Would you have preferred to have a live lecture given by another faculty member instead of the television recording?

A. Yes, 11 per cent; no, 75 per cent; no strong opinion, 14 per cent.

Q. Would you be willing to watch more lectures on television if this gave you the opportunity to hear and see outstanding lecturers from other universities?

A. Yes, 94 per cent; no, 6 per cent.

BASIC STUDIES

In discussing basic studies we are primarily concerned with the psychology of human learning, an area in which there has been much more research than any other area covered in this book. Many of our readers, however, will have little background in psychology and it is not our intention to give space to psychological discussions which have been extensively reviewed elsewhere [3, 6, 12, 41]. We wish merely to high-light those aspects of the psychology of human learning which have immediate relevance to the problems we have been discussing in the past few chapters. We shall consider three main areas of research: learner participation; the structuring and sequencing of learning situations; and the adaptation of learning situations to meet individual differences.

In higher education, learning is normally a conscious and deliberate activity and it is not unreasonable to assume that some form of interaction either with a teacher or with a fellow-student or with a learning resource is a necessary condition for learning. At the lowest level of learner participation this interaction can best be described as attention; at the highest level of participation the learner is engaged in a project or dissertation and has only spasmodic interaction with a teacher or with structured learning resources; at medium levels of participation the learner may engage in such activities as taking notes, answering questions, asking questions or making short contributions to a discussion. Most of the research on learner participation has concetrated on impersonal learning situations which can be reliably replicated in order to eliminate irrelevant variables, and the student has either been in an audience watching a film or television programme or in an independent study situation working from a book, workbook or programmed text. Activities such as questioning a teacher or fellow student or making discussion contributions were not possible. Some of these studies have concentrated on response factors, i.e. student activities during learning, while others have concentrated on feedback factors, i.e. with ways in which the resource can help the student to evaluate his response.

Lumsdaine has distinguished three main types of response, implicit, overt and covert, and has defined them as follows [43]: 'In ordinary reading, listening to a lecture, or watching a film, responses are implicit rather than being explicitly evoked by specific questions or gaps which the student is directed to fill in. Explicit responding on cue need not, however, be overt (e.g. written or oral) but can be performed covertly or mentally. In this chapter, the term "covert response" is used to designate response acts which, unlike implicit responding to a text or lecture, are deliberately made as explicit answers to a question or other express invitation for response, but which are not performed overtly. Such responses may serve as active symbolic practice but afford a less clear basis for differential feedback to the student from an instructional program or teacher (and vice versa) than do overt responses.' There has been much research on the optimum type of response, though little of it has been at the higher-education level. But some definite conclusions have emerged:

1. Explicit responding is superior to implicit responding provided that the responses are non-trivial and relevant [29, 33].
2. If the nature of the task is essentially response learning (e.g. learning a new word, a new shape or a new movement) then the responses should not only be explicit but overt: overt responding is preferable to covert responding [44].

If, however, the responses are already in the learner's repertoire, as is usually the case in conceptual learning, the research is less conclusive. Some studies suggest that overt responding is better for difficult material and covert responding for easy material [14, 23], and that overt responding is preferable when the learner is unfamiliar with the subject-matter and covert responding when the learner is relatively familiar with the subject-matter [36, 40].

The problem of whether to provide knowledge of results to student responses to questions is also unresolved. The weight of evidence now seems to support the proposition that knowledge of results is important when it provides corrective feedback but not important as a motivational aid (or 'reinforcer'). Thus if the student is likely to be wrong or to be seriously uncertain about his correctness, knowledge of results is likely to help, but if the student knows he is right there is little point in giving knowledge of results [3]. Student personality is also important: some can tolerate greater ambiguity than others [10] and agressive students perform best when they are not only informed about wrong responses but positively reprimanded [17].

In lectures this need for explicit student responding can be met by asking questions or using special feedback devices (see Chapter IV) and there is evidence to support this practice. But the more usual form of student participation is through note-taking. In spite of the almost universal practice of taking notes during lectures, there has been very little research into its effects. The evidence seems to indicate that taking notes interferes with comprehension as measured by immediate recall and retention, but serves as an important guide to subsequent revision [18]. There is also some evidence that the efficiency of note-taking diminishes fairly rapidly as the lecture proceeds [28]. But most of this research assumes that the main purpose of the lecture is to transmit information, a purpose for which it is manifestly inefficient, as we pointed out in our last chapter. The use of the lecture for structuring information has not been investigated experimentally and it would be difficult to do so, though it is practised with conviction by a number of faculty.

Note-taking during independent study is another universal practice on which no evidence is available.

To conclude our survey of research on student participation in the learning situation we shall briefly summarize findings on teacher-centred and student-centred discussions. Though varying definitions of teacher-centred and student-centred groups have been used, the evidence seems to suggest that teacher-centred methods lead to improved comprehension and more efficient information transmission, but that student-centred methods are better for higher-level outcomes. McKeachie summarizes the research studies thus [46]:

In eleven studies, significant differences in ability to apply concepts, in attitudes, in motivation, or in group membership skills have been found between discussion techniques emphasizing freer student participation compared with discussion with greater instructor dominance. In ten of these the differences favored the more student-centred method. The eleventh had mixed results.

'In short, the choice of instructor-dominated versus student-centred discussion techniques appears to depend upon one's goals. The more highly one values outcomes going beyond acquisition of knowledge, the more likely [it is] that student-centred methods will be preferred.'

As a footnote we might add Thistlewaite's finding of a significant negative correlation between a college's productivity of Ph.D.s in natural science and the directiveness of the teaching methods used [62].

The second set of basic studies we wish to discuss are concerned with the structuring and sequencing of learning situations. This is an area of considerable controversy and little agreement. The problems of structuring and sequencing are different for different kinds of learning task, and there are considerable differences in learning task both between subjects and within subjects. Psychologists concerned with human learning are more familiar with this problem than subject experts and can usually suggest reasonable designs for any given series of learning situations. But there is no simple transformation from the structure of a subject as perceived by its experts into the categories of learning task as perceived by psychologists, and psychologists who think that this transformation can be achieved by a single mapping operation are likely to run into difficulty. Psychologists tend to be more aware of learning-task differences within subjects but less aware of differences between subjects, whereas subject experts tend to be the reverse.

The use of discovery methods in education has recently been re-emphasized by Bruner and others and has had considerable influence on school education but much less on higher education. Bruner defines discovery as 're-arranging or transforming evidence in such a way that one is enabled to go beyond the evidence so assembled to additional new insights' [9]. The types of learning for which it might therefore seem appropriate are the attainment of concepts, the interrelating of concepts and methods of inquiring and problem solving. Discovery learning must be carefully distinguished from independent learning, which involves the assembling of evidence, but does not necessarily lead to new insights above and beyond that evidence, and from inductive learning which leads a student through evidence to a generalization but does not necessarily expect him to discover that generalization for himself. What little research there has been on discovery learning appears to indicate that it is no more effective and often less efficient than giving the answer, when the criterion is the ability to apply the discovered principle to new situations either immediately after learning or several weeks later [3]. Leith, however, has shown that there are important personality effects: extrovert college students perform best with a completely guided approach [39]. Tolerance of uncertainty seems to be essential for benefiting from a discovery approach, but one could regard this as a dependent variable rather than an independent variable. The ability to tolerate uncertainty and learn from unstructured situations can be considered as an educational objective in its own right and it may be of possible relevance to the fostering of fruitful discoverers. This suggests that a careful and gradual destructuring might help some students to gain confidence and take greater intellectual initiative, but no one has studied this. It is not unreasonable however to suggest that the same personality variable is important in independent study, and long-term observations of independent study programmes have shown that it takes many students a considerable period of time (up to two years) to adjust. No one in higher education has attempted to follow discovery-based curricula for a similar length of time.

The lack of evidence in favour of a discovery approach does not necessarily extend to the inductive approach, which can be more effective for some purposes in some circumstances. A good example is quoted by Leith [41] when he discusses an experiment by Szekely [61]:

'Students were given either a set of principles in physics followed by demonstration of a phenomenon covered by the rules, or they witnessed the demonstration as a puzzling phenomenon and read the principles to help them to explain it. Two kinds of test were given: (1) finding the solution to a problem; (2) answering verbal test items. The principles + demonstration group were successful in the latter but most of them failed to solve the problem. The demonstration-as-problem + principles group, however, solved the problem but failed the verbal test. Moreover, they were unaware that the test problem and the demonstration were related. Similar results have been achieved by others.

'In this experiment the content was the same (though ordered differently for each group). The mental activities engaged in by the two groups (*how* they learned) were different and the outcomes (*what* they learned) were also different.'

Another feature of sequencing is that it is possible to create conflict and interference between successive sections. There is both the normal problem of pro-active and retroactive inhibition whereby new information prevents one from remembering what came just before or just after, and the special problem which arises when successive topics require different schemata or learning sets. Ausubel found that these problems could be lessened by providing 'advance organizers' at a more abstract level which help the student to fit the material into his cognitive structure [4]. But Leith has shown that a review between the sections which compares and contrasts them and gives a wider perspective is even more useful, and that, contrary to the usual practice, it could sometimes be beneficial in conflict situations to introduce the less-familiar material first [37, 41].

Two further points need to be made about problems of structuring and sequencing. The first is to emphasize the importance in hierarchically organized subjects of the competencies which the learner brings to the learning situation [19]. There is considerable evidence to show that as learning progresses in such a subject, it depends increasingly on the achievement of subordinate competencies [7, 20, 21]. Thus a student who is not fully proficient on relevant previous topics and therefore lacks the prerequisites for a particular topic is unlikely to succeed in coping. We return to this question below when we discuss the problem of adapting to learner populations with varied competencies. The second point relates to the problem of step size or difficulty level. However this is defined, the only agreement in the literature is almost a truism: that step size should match the capacities of the learners. Again, there are likely to be personality interactions in that extroverts who tolerate uncertainty better and prefer to be challenged are likely to want larger steps than introverts.

The third set of basic studies relates to the problems of adaptation to individual differences. We shall consider these in four separate sections, corresponding to differences in pace, previous knowledge, ability and personality (though many of these factors are interrelated and can be considered as facets of the same over-all problem). Adaptation to individual rates of learning has always been put forward as a traditional advantage of programmed learning, although it also applies to most other forms of independent learning. But Gropper and Kress have presented data to suggest that self-pacing can be non-adaptive to the needs of the learner, that some learners need to be speeded up and others need to be slowed down [24]. It needs a sophisticated device like a computer to present material at the optimum rate for each individual, but in the absence of such adaptive pacing, group-pacing can sometimes prove more efficient than self-pacing [35]. Group-pacing can obviously help to speed up slow learners but is likely to be less successful in slowing down the over-impulsive. Grouping students in pairs or small groups may, however, be a useful way of making the over-impulsive take a second look at a problem. We shall return to the question of grouping later, but meanwhile let us note that the fact that group-pacing is not necessarily less effective implies that group-paced media such as audio tape, film and television may not be any less effective because of their failure to adapt to differences in rate.

One of the main advantages of self-pacing in some situations may well be that it helps students with differences in previous knowledge to accept the same learning sequence. They can move slowly if they are in difficulty because they lack important prerequisites and move fast if they already know half the material. Most of the experimental studies on pacing have been in situations where previous knowledge was only of minor importance and may therefore have neglected this point. It may be better however to make a direct rather than an indirect adaptation to differences in previous knowledge. We have already discussed the importance in a hierarchically organized subject of the competencies which the learner brings to the situation, and it would appear that self-pacing is a crude and relatively inefficient method for catering for differences in learner competencies. Branching programmes attempt to cope with this problem by offering remedial instruction wherever a learner makes a mistake, but experiments have shown that they are not very successful in achieving this [5, 6]. The reasons are probably threefold: (a) the decision to branch is based on a single response from the learner; (b) the competency is often not assessed in a relevant way; and (c) it is difficult to use the same question both as direct teaching for those that do not need to branch and as a test for those that might need remedial work.

A computer can take many more factors into account but one still has to find appropriate decision rules to put into the computer. We believe that this particular problem can be adequately solved without using a computer if learning situations are carefully embedded in a system of diagnostic tests, which ensures that each learner is properly prepared but not already proficient [15].

The problem of adaptation to a student's ability has hardly been studied in higher education. Lewis and Pask have suggested that learning situations might be adapted to a student's preferred error rate, but this has not yet been

tion to ability or previous knowledge achieved at present by placement tests may be sufficient. There is some evidence at the school level that students in mixed-ability pairs perform better than as individuals [1].

We have already discussed the effect of personality on preferred learning style, especially on tolerance for uncertainty. There are four ways of dealing with this. One is by gross adaptation: this involves providing both structured and less structured learning situations and letting the students choose. The second is by fine adaptation: this involves assigning different learning situations on the basis of personality tests and perhaps, when the programming problems have been solved, using a computer to adjust the error rate to an optimum level. The third method uses grouping, possibly the pairing of extrovert and introvert students, though this may be difficult in subjects where particular personality types predominate [2]. The fourth approach does not adapt to these differences but gives students both highly structured and open-ended learning situations on the grounds that an important aim of higher education is that a student should be able to learn from all kinds of learning situations.

A CRITIQUE OF THE BASIC STUDIES

Some of the criticisms of comparative effectiveness studies which we made earlier also apply to many of the basic studies. In particular there is the failure of many basic studies to attend seriously to the criterion problem. Only some of them have taken care to specify the nature of the learning task and to relate their findings to it. There is also a similar tendency to over-generalize their results. But taken together these basic studies do provide some guidance. The problems arise when we try to apply their results to practical problems in the design of learning situations [8, 64]. We know that some student participation is important but not how much; that sequencing is important, but not what the optimum sequence is for any given learning situation; that adaptation to individual differences may be helpful, but not how best to do it. And there is no evidence relevant to media selection at the higher education level. In other words, research findings may help us to design better learning situations, and may help us to locate deficiencies in existing situations; but they cannot remove the need for empirical development to improve learning situations once they have been designed.

PROCESS STUDIES

It is possible to argue an *a priori* case for an empirical development process involving successive try-outs and revisions, but it is also useful to examine whether the application of the method has led in practice to the improvement of learning situations. There is, however, much evidence to support and document the fact that learning situations modified in the light of try-out are accomplished in practice [42]. It may well be, however, that the gross adapta-

significantly improved. Empirical development has been shown to improve programmed texts [60], filmstrips [26], films [22, 49, 52], television programmes [25, 63] and learning systems [50]. Studies by Silberman, Markle Gropper and Lumsdaine, Van der Meer and Tiemann, Paden and McIntyre are particularly well documented. Tiemann's study is particularly interesting because the televised lectures had already been revised several times by conventional intuitive procedures, yet clarification of objectives and preparation of appropriate tests, followed by further try-out and revision, led to an additional improvement of about 15 per cent.

NEEDED RESEARCH

The problems we have been discussing in this chapter have high-lighted the limited nature of our present knowledge and the need for further research. The kinds of research which seem to us to offer the greatest potential are further basic studies clearly focused on specific types of learning task, and long-term studies on the progressive destructuring of the curriculum and its effect on learning styles. To take the basic studies first, what we need for each particular kind of learning task and for each particular type of student are answers to the following questions:

1. What is the optimum degree of student participation in a given learning situation?
2. What is the optimum structure and sequence?
3. What are the most appropriate media of communication?
4. What are the likely side-effects or unintended outcomes?
5. How much is lost by aiming at something less than the optimum which is both cheaper and more convenient?

We also anticipate that the computer will be increasingly important in basic research of this kind, but would not be surprised if it turned out that the much-canvassed capability of the computer to adapt learning situations to individual students proved to be relatively unimportant for most learning tasks.

Though computer-assisted learning may be found only to be economic for certain special kinds of learning task, we suggest that computer-managed learning will become increasingly important and that it will help to create the framework for long-term research studies. In the last two chapters we have repeatedly emphasized the desirability of helping students to learn how to learn by a progressive destructuring of learning situations as they proceed through higher education. A similar argument has been put forward by Jahoda and Thomas as a result of a pilot study of student learning styles [31]. There is some evidence both that flexibility of learning style is important and that changes in learning style require long periods of time. So long-term studies are needed of the interaction between changing learning styles and changing kinds of learning situations. To anyone who regards the development of independent learners as one of the main aims of higher education, such studies must surely be given priority.

REFERENCES

1. AMARIA, R. P.; BIRAN, L. A.; LEITH, G. O. M. Individual versus co-operative learning. I: influence of intelligence and sex. *Educational research*, vol. 11, 1969, p. 95.

2. ———. LEITH, G. O. M. Individual versus co-operative learning. II: the influence of personality. *Educational research*, vol. 11, 1969, p. 193.

3. * ANDERSON, Richard C. Educational psychology. *Annual reviews of psychology*, vol. 18, 1967, p. 129.

4. AUSUBEL, D. P. *The psychology of meaningful verbal learning.* New York, Grune & Stratton, 1963.

5. BIRAN, L. A.; PICKERING, E. Unscrambling a herringbone: an experimental evaluation of branching programming. *British Journal of Medical Education.*

6. * BRIGGS, Leslie J. Learner variables and educational media. *Review of educational research* (Wash.), vol. 38, no. 2, 1968.

7. ———. *Sequencing of instruction in relation to hierarchies of competence.* Pittsburgh, American Institutes of Research in the Behavioral Sciences.

8. * CAMPEAU, Peggie L.; GAGNÉ, Robert M.; MAY, MARK A. *Instructional media: a procedure for the design of multi-media instruction. A critical review of research, and suggestions for future research.* Palo Alto, Calif., American Institutes for Research, 1967.

9. BRUNER, Jerome S. The act of discovery. *Harvard educational review* (Cambridge, Mass.), vol. 31, 1961.

10. CAMPEAU, Peggie L. *Level of anxiety and presence or absence of feedback in programmed instruction.* Palo Alto, Calif., American Institutes for Research, 1965.

11. DE CECCO, John P. Class size and co-ordinated instruction. *British journal of educational psychology* (London), vol. 34, 1964.

12. * ——— (ed.). *Educational technology.* New York, Holt, Rinehart & Winston, 1964.

13. ECKERT, Ruth E.; NEALE, Daniel C. Teachers and teaching. *Review of educational research* (Wash.), vol. 35, no. 4, 1965.

14. EIGEN, L. D.; MARGULIES, S. Response characteristics as a function of information level. *Journal of programmed instruction* (West Nyack, N.Y.), vol. 2, no. 1, 1963.

15. ERAUT, Michael R. The design of variable input learning systems. In: W. R. Dunn and C. Holroyd (eds.), *Aspects of technology.* Vol. 2. London, Methuen, 1969.

16. ———. A critical analysis of educational technology and its implications for the future. In: B. N. Lewis, R. W. Lyne and M. W. Neil (eds.), *New directions in educational technology.* London, Iliffe. (In press.)

17. FRASE, Lawrence T. *The effect of social reinforcers in a programed learning task.* Urbana, Ill., Training Research Laboratory, University of Illinois, 1963. (Technical Report no. 11.)

18. FREYBERG, P. S. The effectiveness of note-taking. *Education for teaching*, no. 17, February 1965.

19. GAGNÉ, R. M. *The conditions of learning*. New York, Holt, Rinehart & Winston, 1965.

20. ——. The acquisition of knowledge. *Psychological reviews*, vol. 69, 1962, p. 355. Reprinted in: J. P. De Cecco (ed.), op. cit. (see no. 12 above).

21. ——; PARADISE, N. E. Abilities and learning sets in knowledge acquisition. *Psychological monographs*, vol. 75, no. 14, 1961.

22. GERLACH, Vernon S. *et al.* Programing the instructional film. *AV communication review* (Washington), vol. 14, fall 1966.

23. GOLDBECK, R. A.; CAMPBELL, V. N. The effects of response mode and response difficulty on programmed learning. *Journal of educational psychology*, vol. 53, 1962, p. 110. Reprinted in: J. P. De Cecco (ed.), op. cit. (see no. 12 above).

24. GROPPER, G. L.; KRESS, Gerard C. Individualising instruction through pacing procedures. *AV communication review* (Wash.), vol. 13, summer 1965.

25. GROPPER, G. L.; LUMSDAINE, A. A. *The use of student response to improve televised instruction: an overview*. Pittsburgh, Pa., American Institutes for Research in the Behavioral Sciences, 1961.

26. HALL, K. A.; JOHNSON, D. W.; VANDERMEER, A. W. *An investigation of programming principles as applied to the production and utilisation of filmstrips and filmstrip type materials in natural science*. Pennsylvania State University, 1964.

27. HARTLEY, J. Effectiveness of programed learning. *New education* (London), vol. 29, January 1966.

28. ——; CAMERON, A. Some observations on the efficiency of lecturing. *Educational review*, vol. 20, no. 1, 1967.

29. HOLLAND, J. G. Research on programming variables. In: R. Glaser (ed.), *Teaching machines and programmed learning. II: Data and directions*. Washington, D.C., National Educational Association, 1965.

30. HOVLAND, C. I.; LUMSDAINE, A. A.; SHEFFIELD, F. D. *Experiments in mass communication*. Princeton, N.J., Princeton University Press, 1949.

31. JAHODA, Marie; THOMAS, Laurie. The mechanics of learning. *New scientist* (London), 14 April 1966.

32. KLAPPER, Hope L. *Closed circuit television as a medium of instruction at New York University*. New York University, 1958.

33. KRUMBOLTZ, J. D. The nature and importance of the required response in programed instruction. *American educational research journal* (Wash.), vol. 1, 1964.

34. LA GAIPA, John J. Programmed instruction, teacher ability and subject matter difficulty. *Journal of psychology* (Provincetown, Mass.), vol. 68, 1968.

35. LEITH, G. O. M. *Second thoughts on programmed learning*. London, Councils and Education Press, 1969. (National Council for Educational Technology occasional paper 1.)

36. ——. *A handbook of programmed learning*. University of Birmingham, 1966.

37. LEITH, G. O. M. *Conflict and interference: a study of the facilitating effects of reviews in learning sequences*. University of Birmingham, 1967.

38. ——. Developments in programmed learning. In: J. Robinson and N.

Barnes (eds.), *New media and methods in industrial training*. London, BBC, 1967.

39. ——. Learning and personality. In: W. R. Dunn and C. Holroyd (eds.), *Aspects of educational technology*. Vol. 2. London, Methuen, 1969.

40. * ——. Programmed learning in higher education. In: D. Unwin (ed.), *Media and methods: instructional technology in higher education*. London, McGraw-Hill, 1969.

41. * ——. Programmed learning: acquisition of knowledge and mental development of students. *Journal of educational technology* (London), vol. 1, no. 2, May 1970.

42. LEWIS, Brian N.; PASK, Gordon. The theory and practice of adaptive teaching systems. In: R. Glaser (ed.), *Teaching machines and programed learning. II: Data and directions*. Washington, D.C., National Educational Association, 1965.

43. LUMSDAINE, A. A. Instruments and media of instruction. In: N. L. Gage (ed.), *Handbook of research in teaching*. Chicago, Rand McNally, 1963.

44. —— (ed.). *Student response in programmed instruction*. Washington, D.C., National Academy of Sciences, 1961.

45. * ——; MAY, M. A. Mass communication and educational media. *Annual review of psychology*, vol. 16, 1965, p. 475.

46. McKEACHIE, Wilbert J. Teaching at college level. In: N. L. Gage (ed.), *Handbook of research in teaching*. Chicago, Rand McNally, 1963.

47. MacKENZIE, Norman; FIELD, John; BLUNDEN, John. *Student reactions to large-screen television*. Centre for Educational Technology, University of Sussex, 1967.

48. MACOMBER, F. G.; SIEGEL, L. *Final report on the experimental study in instructional procedures*. Oxford, Ohio, Miami University, 1960.

49. MARKLE, David G. Empirical film development. *National society for programmed Instruction Journal* (San Antonio, Tex.), vol. 4, no. 6, 1965.

50. * ——. *Final report: the development of the Bell system first aid and personal safety course*. Palo Alto, Calif., American Institutes for Research, 1967.

51. MARKLE, Susan M. Empirical testing of programs. In: P. Lange (ed.), *Programed instruction*. Chicago, University of Chicago Press, 1967.

52. ——; TIEMANN, Philip W. *Programing is a process*. Chicago, University of Illinois, 1967. (Film with technical manual.)

53. NACHMAN, M.; OPOCHINSKY, S. The effects of different teaching methods: a methodological study. *Journal of educational psychology* (Washington), vol. 49, 1958.

54. NEIDT, C. O.; SJOGREN, D. D. Changes in student attitudes during a course in relation to instructional media. *AV communication review* (Wash.), vol. 16, no. 3, fall 1968.

55. POPHAM, W. J. Tape recorded lectures in the college classroom. *AV communication review* (Wash.), vol. 9, no. 2, 1961.

56. ——. Tape recorded lectures in the college classroom II. *AV communication review* (Wash.), vol. 10, no. 2, 1962.

57. REID, J. Christopher; MACLENNAN, Donald W. *Research in instructional television and film. Summaries of studies*. Washington, D.C., Bureau of Research, U.S. Government Printing Office, 1967.

58.   SCHRAMM, Wilbur. Learning from instructional television. *Review of educational research* (Wash.), vol. 32, no. 2, 1962.
59.   ——. *Research on programed instruction: an annotated bibliography*. Washington, D.C., U.S. Government Printing Office, 1964.
60.   SILBERMAN, Harry; COULSON, John. *Use of exploratory research and individual tutoring techniques for the development of programming methods and theory*. Santa Monica, Calif., Systems Development Corporation, 1964.
61.   SZEKELY, L. Productive processes in learning and thinking. *Acta psychologica* (Amsterdam), vol. 7, 1950.
62.   THISTLEWAITE, P. L. College environments and the development of talent. *Science* (Wash.), vol. 130, 1959.
63.   TIEMANN, P. W.; PADEN, D. W.; MCINTYRE, C. J. *An application of the principles of programed instruction to a televised course in college economics*. Urbana, Ill., University of Illinois, 1966.
64.   * TOSTI, Donald T.; BALL, John R. A behavioral approach to instructional design and media selection. *AV communication review* (Wash.), vol. 17, no. 1, 1969.
65.   WALLEN, Norman E.; TRAVERS, Robert M. W. Analysis and investigation of teaching methods. In: N. L. Gage (ed.), *Handbook of research on teaching*. Chicago, Rand McNally, 1963.

XI. Course development

INTRODUCTION

The previous four chapters have all been concerned with different approaches to the improvement of teaching and learning. The first was concerned with the clarification of objectives, the second with evaluation, the third with teaching methods and the last with the design of learning situations. All these approaches, if taken seriously, require a great deal of time, and some of the possible changes involve the development of special learning materials, yet another time-consuming activity. A number of questions arise. How much time should be spent in these kind of activities rather than in getting on with the teaching? What is the best way of tackling decisions about teaching? By what criteria do we allocate our limited teaching resources? What assistance do teachers need in carrying out these improvements?

We believe that these problems can be approached systematically and that the most appropriate unit of teaching to tackle at any one time is the 'course', which we define as 'a separately time-tabled or separately assessed teaching-learning unit occupying from one half to one quarter of a student's time over one, two or three terms'. Hence this chapter, which is intended to bring together the contributions of the previous four chapters, is entitled 'Course Development'. The procedures suggested below have not been invented by the authors, or by anyone else for that matter. They represent the combined work of a number of institutions which have been concerned with these problems over the last decade [2, 3, 8, 9, 15, 16]. The first half of this chapter will be devoted to describing the process of course development and the second half to discussing its implications in terms of allocation of resources, changing roles, needs for specialist personnel, etc. Considerable attention will be given to the question of whether it is worth doing at all and, if so, under what circumstances.

It is useful to consider a course as a system in which students, teachers and learning materials interact; the purpose of course development is to optimize the system [5]. The initial problem is to define the constraints on the system and to define what is to be optimized. The constraints on the system primarily affect its input. The student input, for example, will have certain definite characteristics in terms of knowledge, abilities and attitudes. Some of these can be altered by changing the selection policy or by changing previous courses, but usually the characteristics of the student input are at least temporarily fixed. The input of teachers and materials is often less rigidly determined, though it is rare indeed to find a programme budgeting system which allocates a fixed budget to a course and does not specify how much of it should be spent on teachers. Normally there are constraints on how many teachers should participate and on which teachers should participate, constraints on expenditure on learning materials, and constraints on the availability of learning spaces. None of these factors however is likely to be totally predetermined and there is usually some scope for adjustment.

The problem of optimization is also concerned with the system's output, i.e. with what students can do at the end of the course. In theory a number of alternatives exist. One can aim to improve efficiency by reducing costs and maintaining the same output. One can aim to improve effectiveness by improving the student's performance at the end of the course; or one can aim to improve quality by raising the level of the objectives of the course. In practice, existing measures of performance at the end of a course are likely to be inadequate and it will therefore be difficult to measure changes in output. Moreover, it could be dangerous to make decisions about the optimum mix of objectives for a course before the total range of objectives has been outlined. The best policy is usually to set general guide-lines for optimization at the beginning but not to make irrevocable decisions on these until after work on the clarification of objectives has been completed. Even then the decisions may have to be altered if the selection of objectives is later shown to be over-ambitious. But one constraint on the objectives of a course cannot be ignored, that is, the requirements of the following course and of potential employers, etc., though this is not always as rigid as is sometimes assumed.

Our discussions in the last two chapters have been conclusive on one point: they have emphasized that we know very little about teaching and learning, and the implication of this is that any course we design will be far from the optimum in its effectiveness. Nor will any further consultation with experts or searching of the research literature be likely to result in significant improvements. If due attention has been paid to what little is known about teaching and learning, trial and error becomes the only remaining method of improvement. Further information about how to improve a 'prototype' course can best be obtained from trying it out and evaluating it. Moreover, if we begin with the intention of producing several versions of a course, hopefully versions which show increasing effectiveness as information from try-outs is fed into the revision process, we can deliberately design our evaluation procedures to give the appropriate information. Such evaluation is referred to by Scriven as 'formative evaluation', because its purpose is to assist in the development of courses, as contrasted with 'summative evaluation', whose purpose is to evaluate completed courses [12]. In the more normal summative evaluation the emphasis is on reliability and validity, but in formative evaluation the emphasis has to be on obtaining the kind of information which leads to genuine improvements in the revised version of the course. One is more interested in the reason why a student failed to grasp a concept than in precisely how many students failed to grasp the concept.

THE INITIAL BRIEF

This introduction to the process of course development can be summarized by listing the essential components of a brief for a course development team:
1. The logistic input for the course itself and a list of the constraints affecting its allocation (this includes the operational costs allowed for the course, limitations on space, personnel, etc.).
2. An estimate of the student input in terms of numbers, levels of attainment, etc. (this may need to be made more precise in an early stage of the course-development process).
3. Guide-lines on the intended outcomes of the course (these also will need to be refined later).
4. Guide-lines on what is to be optimized; i.e. is the cost to be reduced, is the effectiveness to be improved or are the outcomes to be expanded to include more ambitious objectives?
5. A budget for the course-development process itself, including the costs of the time to be contributed by each member of the course-development team.
6. A commitment to the use of formative evaluation for a least some parts of the course, i.e. to at least one substantial revision of some of them.

The first four components are necessary in order to define the system. The development budget is necessary if the development costs are to be appropriately allocated, if the course development process itself is to be evaluated and if the institution's policy is to be suitably adjusted in the light of the results. The commitment to formative evaluation is necessary if the purpose is course development and not just course design.

AN OVERVIEW OF THE COURSE DEVELOPMENT PROCESS

Figure 3 summarizes the main stages of the course development process. These will be briefly explained in this section and then described in greater detail in the following sections.

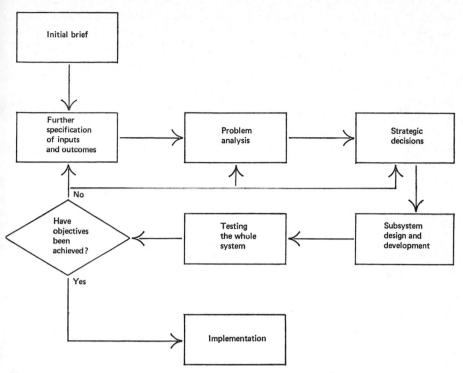

Fig. 3

After the initial brief it is necessary to specify the objectives of the course in greater detail and to develop appropriate methods of assessment. Also important at this stage is a more useful analysis of the student input which may well involve some testing of students to see what knowledge and abilities they bring to the course. Only then is it possible to set out the main teaching problems inherent in a course of this type and to estimate which areas of the course are likely to cause the greatest difficulty. After this preliminary problem analysis the main strategic decisions can be taken. These decisions involve: (a) separating the course into parts or subsystems and defining the intended outcomes of each subsystem; (b) making broad decisions about the kind of teaching to be used in each part of the course; (c) allocating the operational costs of the course after implementation in the light of the above; and (d) deciding how much attention the course development team should give to each subsystem and allocating resources from the development budget accordingly.

Each subsystem can now be designed or developed. Some may go through a number of revisions but others of less priority may just be designed and implemented without further change. Often the development budget will be too small for all the subsystems to undergo the expensive and time consuming process of trial and revision. Finally the whole course is assembled, tried as a whole, and implemented if the try-out is satisfactory. If the try-out is unsatisfactory the process may be repeated (provided that the funding is sufficient!). Clearly the extent to which the development team allocate funds to the further revision of the total course will depend on whether they anticipate the main problems to lie within the various subsystems or in the linking together of the subsystems to form a total course. It should be possible to anticipate this when they make the strategic decisions about allocation of the development funds.

FURTHER SPECIFICATION OF INPUTS AND OUTCOMES

The further specification of outcomes follows the general pattern suggested in Chapter VII for the definition of objectives. This is based on the Scriven model and proceeds from the conceptual level to the manifestational level to the operational level. After the initial formulation of objectives at the conceptual level, each change in level is accompanied by a further selection from the set of possible objectives. An objective at the conceptual level can lead to many different objectives at the manifestational level not all of which will be feasible or even desirable outcomes for the course and an objective at the manifestational level can lead to many objectives at the operational level. At the operational level, objectives are defined in terms of performance measures, conditions of performance and standards of performance. So this third stage in the specification of outcomes gives the criteria by which the course as a whole will be considered to have succeeded or to have failed.

It is also important at each stage to assign priorities within the set of selected objectives. This allows the less-important objectives to be omitted later if pruning should be necessary. And it gives some guidance for the allocation of resources. Priority objectives can then be given more teacher time or more development time when the strategic decisions are made.

In a typical academic situation there is considerable variation in the achievement levels and capabilities of the students entering a course. An accurate assessment of this range of student input is often necessary for the development of a successful course and some special testing may be necessary to secure it. It is particularly important in this context to avoid making the usual assumption that all the students should be required to go through all the course. Fitting a course to the average student can sometimes lead to disaster. The below-average student may be baffled and the above-average student may be bored. It may however be necessary to maintain a minimum entry standard for a course, and this is one possible reason for instituting a pretest. Another reason for having a pretest could well be to allow students with the appropriate knowledge to omit sections of the course or in extreme cases to allow a student who was already proficient to omit the whole course. Obviously these different needs would require different kinds of pretest.

PROBLEM ANALYSIS

The purpose of this stage in course development is to locate objectives or areas of the course which are likely to cause problems for teachers or students. For example, there may be two potentially conflicting frames of reference, a difficult proof, or a topic where there is no suitable text or article to provide additional help. Sources of information on likely problems include the following: research literature on teaching and learning; previous performance on the course or on similar courses (a careful analysis of examination performance may be necessary); interviews with students who have taken the course or similar courses; experience of other institutions.

If the expected problems coincide with priority objectives they may need special attention, but if they are of low priority they may be eventually omitted and time should not be wasted on them during the early stages of development.

STRATEGIC DECISIONS

These decisions are primarily concerned with the selection of teaching methods and the allocation of resources. In the light of the anticipated problems, the objectives of the course, and the resources available for operating the course when implemented, preliminary decisions about teaching methods and the allocation of these operating resources have first to be made. The implications of these preliminary decisions are then carefully examined in order to determine: whether the course as planned is compatible with logistic factors such as the availability of appropriate manpower, learning spaces, special equipment, or support costs; whether the teaching roles assumed require a training course for some of the teachers involved; which parts of the course need extended development by trial and revision; and whether the development budget is sufficient to cover the estimated costs of subsystem development and teacher training.

This further scrutiny may show that certain aspects of the course could not be implemented as planned, and some of the preliminary decisions will need to be modified. The final result of the strategic decision phase of the course development process will be a set of subsystems and a brief for the further design or development of each subsystem. This brief will include: a precise definition of the student input and the expected learning outcomes of each subsystem; a description of the teaching methods to be used and the learning materials to be developed; the operational costs for each part of the course when implemented; and the resources available for the design or development of each subsystem.

SUBSYSTEM DESIGN AND DEVELOPMENT

Resources for subsystem design and development will usually be limited and subsystems which are easy to design or of low priority will probably be designed rather than developed. But those for which sufficient resources are available will proceed through the development cycle outlined in Figure 4. The design process is not a cycle and follows the dotted arrows in the diagram.

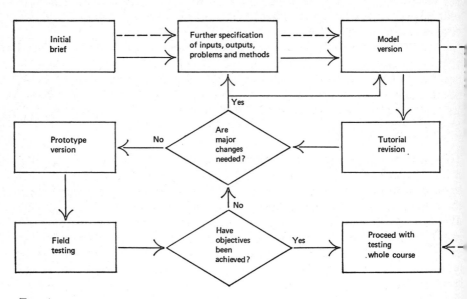

FIG. 4

The further specification of inputs and outputs, problems and methods will probably be only a slightly expanded restatement of the brief, prior to the commencement of work on the preparation of a model version of the subsystem. Once prepared, the model version is ready for trial and revision and the emphasis is on formative evaluation. Since the purpose of this formative evaluation is to obtain information that will be useful in preparing a revised version, it is usually best to submit the model version to tutorial revision rather than field testing in the initial stages [11, 13]. In the tutorial revision situation the model version is tried out on individual students or small groups of students. Whenever difficulties are encountered the tutor probes the sources of the difficulties, collects student comments and tries alternative approaches. When these approaches prove successful they can be incorporated into the revised versions. Though field testing on large groups of students is necessary, it provides much less useful information during the initial stages of development. As mentioned earlier, it is more important initially to find out why a

164

student failed and to remedy it than to know how many students failed. Only when a prototype version is ready which is considered to be a close approximation to the final version is it necessary to change the emphasis to summative evaluation and field test on large groups of students under typical academic conditions.

TESTING AND IMPLEMENTING THE WHOLE COURSE

The last stage in the course development process is the assembling of the subsystems and the testing of the course as a whole. If this gives satisfactory results then the course is ready for implementation. If not some recycling will be necessary (see Figure 3, page 161). The implementation stage may involve further production of duplicate materials and training of some of the teachers involved. It should also include a provision for the regular review of the course and the incorporation of any further changes which might be shown to be both feasible and desirable.

WHEN SHOULD A COURSE BE DEVELOPED?

The simple answer to this question is when a cost-benefit analysis shows it to be profitable. This may mean that the development cost is recovered by a decrease in the operating costs of the course over a number of years while standards are maintained, or it may mean that the development cost is converted into improved standards of performance and the ensuing benefit is considered to be worth the extra expenditure. Less obvious benefits such as the effect on the faculty involved and their colleagues, their attitudes towards teaching and the general climate of the institution should also be taken into account. A less predictable method of recovering the development cost would be through the publication and sale of some of the materials developed. It might also prove possible to share some of the costs through inter-institutional co-operation. Many of these possibilities will be discussed at greater length in the next chapter.

It may often be desirable to carry out a feasibility study before committing resources to course development. Such a study would be concerned with formulating objectives, analysing teaching-learning problems and assessing the probable cost and benefit of applying the full course-development procedure. A series of such feasibility studies would enable resources for course development to be assigned to those areas which promise the maximum pay-off.

MEMBERSHIP OF THE COURSE-DEVELOPMENT TEAM

We are convinced that the bulk of the work involved in course development can only be done by members of faculty who are experts in the subject-matter area concerned. Any attempt to use less-qualified personnel is likely to result in loss of quality. It is also important if the course is to be successfully implemented for these subject-expert members of the team to have the full confidence of their colleagues. When the development of a course is perceived as a departmental or institutional venture rather than a private venture or an administrative plot, the course is more likely to be successfully implemented and to have beneficial side-effects on teaching in general.

Also needed in the team is a course-development consultant with experience in this kind of work. His job is to guide the faculty through the stages of the course-development process, to discern their needs for special consultancy help, and to be responsible for bringing other consultants to the group whenever their advice and expertise seem likely to be advantageous. He avoids bringing in consultants just for the sake of it and makes sure that when they do come they are properly briefed and address themselves to the problems of the course-development team and not their own special interests. Our advocacy of a single course-development consultant is in marked contrast to the multi-consultant nature of most American course-development teams [10]. Our reasons are the following: (a) it keeps the team as a reasonably small working group in which roles can be clearly defined; (b) it keeps the subject-matter experts dominant, and it is they who teach the course; (c) it is highly economical in its use of consultant time; (d) it helps develop a special breed of consultants, whose prior commitment is to the success of the course and not to the advancement of any particular theory and who have to use a language that can be readily understood by teachers; (e) such consultants can be trained by an apprenticeship scheme without necessarily having had formal training in the social sciences; (f) it ought to be possible in the future to use course-development consultants who were originally trained in the discipline of the course being developed.

EFFETCS ON THE ROLES OF TEACHERS, STUDENTS AND ADMINISTRATORS

Our discussion of course development has hitherto ignored the question of its general acceptance as a desirable kind of activity. A fundamental change in attitude will be necessary for most teachers before the concept of course development can become meaningful [10]. They will have to accept criticism of teaching in which they are involved as a possible contribution to our knowledge of teaching and not as a personal attack. There is no teacher who cannot improve his performance, knowledge about teaching is embarrassingly small, and constructive criticism and rigorous evaluation is the only way to improve what we are doing.

The long-term effect of adopting a systematic approach to teaching problems is likely to be a growing professionalization of the teaching role in higher education. By making teaching itself subject to research and development, it is likely to raise its status. Contributions to the improvement of teaching may become readily recognizable and much work in this area could be publishable. The range of skills used in teaching is also likely to increase and there may be some specialization in order to enable teachers to make the kind of contribution for which they are most suited. Teacher training may become normal in higher education but could be quite different from the present patterns. The combination of an apprenticeship with a course-development team and attendance at a micro-teaching workshop to improve performance skills (in discussion groups and tutorials as well as in lectures) could well be a useful possibility.

Many of the changes in teaching and learning methods that we have been discussing in this book would also have far-reaching implications for students in higher education: implications in terms of their attitudes, their role as learners, their relationship to their teachers, and the part they might play in the design, the operation and the evaluation of the courses they take. To put it briefly, if some of the developments we envisage are implemented, students will be expected to be much more active participants in the teaching-learning process than is the case at present when, in many institutions, they are still seen as passive objects of teaching and examination procedures.

It is not possible, however, to trace out these implications in detail at this stage, partly because there are very few institutions of higher education which have yet begun to employ these new procedures and experience of them is still very limited, and partly because possibilities inherent in greater student participation in the academic process are only just beginning to be glimpsed. Even the students themselves have hitherto concentrated their criticisms on the defects of the present conventional system, and have devoted much of their agitation to more political demands, such as participation in the decision-making, administrative and disciplinary processes, or the need to change the content of the curriculum to secure greater 'social relevance'. Yet there can be little doubt that, within the next five years, there will be increasing student pressure for academic participation, and that some of the concepts reviewed in this book may provide opportunities for them to influence decisions about the ways they are taught and the manner in which they learn. This is not a matter of making a *pro forma* concession to student demands: it is rather a question of intelligent anticipation of the direction in which progress could be made and of guiding student concern with the management of their own education into constructive channels. This should be regarded as a positive development for students are the last untapped resource in higher education. They have a distinctive contribution to make, both by bringing their own knowledge and experience into the class-room situation and by providing the kind of feedback which enables faculty to revise the content of courses, the manner in which they are taught, and the means by which they are evaluated [6, 7, 14]. We believe that much can be gained by giving students a more dynamic role to play in any learning system, gains in an academic sense as well as in terms of the efficient use of resources and an improvement of morale.

A number of institutions have begun to take initiatives of this kind. One example is a psychology course at the University of Groningen in Holland, where credit is given to students for their contribution to the design and administration of the course as well as for their academic performance in it. In two or three French institutions of higher education experiments are now being made in co-operative 'workshop' courses, where the students taking part are regarded as part of the available resources for the learning situation rather than as the objects of instruction. Various American colleges are following up earlier experiments at Antioch, Colorado, Michigan and Pennsylvania State and are trying out schemes of 'learner-based' courses which put a strong emphasis on problem-solving by group activity rather than on individual performance. And English universities are making increasing use of project work both on an individual and on a group basis. But these are little more than the first harbingers of a major change of emphasis that is bound to come. The point here is not to predict the precise form in which it will come but to recognize that it is possible and desirable, and that it could well provide a means both of enhancing learning and of securing a change for the better in the social relationships of institutions of higher education.

Much of this, however, will depend on the capacity of administrators to create the framework within which improved teaching is possible [10]. Apart from the obvious need to pay greater attention to teaching skills in recruitment and promotion, there are two major problems: providing the right resources (specialist personnel, learning spaces, materials, equipment, etc.); and allocating special resources to course development. For course development implies a capital investment in teaching resources whose pay-off is either an increased return on recurrent expenditure (i.e. a qualitative improvement) or a saving in recurrent expenditure (i.e. quantitative improvement). These administrative problems form the substance of the last three chapters.

REFERENCES

1. AXELROD, Joseph. *Model building for undergraduate colleges: a theoretical framework for studying and reforming the curricular-instruction subsystem in American colleges.* Washington, D.C., U.S. Dept. of Health, Education and Welfare, 1969.

2. BARSON, John. *A procedural and last analysis study of media in instructional systems development.* Michigan State University, 1965.

3. ———. *Instructional systems development—a demonstration and evaluation project.* Michigan State University, 1967.

4. BEARD, Ruth M. (ed.). *Innovation and experiment in university teaching methods.* London, Society for Research into Higher Education, 1968.

5. ERAUT, Michael R. An instructional systems approach to course development. *AV communication review* (Washington), vol. 15, spring 1967.

6. FALK, B. The use of student evaluation. *The Australian university* (Melbourne), vol. 5, no. 2, 1967.

7.   GAUVAIN, S. The use of student opinion in the quality control of teaching. *British journal of medical education* (London), vol. 2, no. 1, 1968.

8.   GILPIN, J. Design and evaluation of instructional systems. *AV communication review* (Wash.), vol. 10, 1962.

9.   HAMREUS, Dale G. The systems approach to instructional development. In: Jack V. Edling (ed.), *The contribution of behavioral science to instructional technology*. Division of Teaching Research, Oregon State System of Higher Education, 1968.

10.   * HANEY, John B.; LANGE, Phil C.; BARSON, John. The heuristic dimension of instructional development. *AV communication review* (Wash.), vol. 16, no. 4, 1968.

11.   MAGER, R. F. On the sequencing of instructional content. *Psychological reports* (Missoula, Mont.), vol. 9, 1961. Reprinted in: John P. De Cecco (ed.), *Educational technology*. New York, Holt, Rinehart & Winston, 1964.

12.   SCRIVEN, Michael. The methodology of evaluation. In: R. Stake (ed.), *Perspectives of curriculum evaluation*. Chicago, Rand McNally, 1967.

13.   SILBERMAN, Harry; COULSON, John. *Use of exploratory research and individual tutoring techniques for the development of programming methods and theory*. Santa Monica, Calif., Systems Development Corporation, 1964.

14.   SIMPSON, Ray H. The use of self-evaluation procedures by lecturers in educational psychology. *Educational review*, vol. 18, no. 1, 1965.

15.   SMITH, R. G. *The design of instructional systems*. Washington, D.C., Human Resources Research Office, 1966.

16.   STEWART, Donald K. A learning-systems concept as applied to courses in education and training. In: R. V. Wiman and W. C. Meierhenry (eds.), *Educational media: theory into practice*. Columbus, Ohio, Charles Merrill, 1969.

Part four

The management of resources

Authors' note. We are indebted to Mr. G. L. Lockwood, Planning Officer of the University of Sussex, for considerable assistance with the preparation of this section of the book.

XII. Investing in new learning materials

In earlier chapters we discussed the role of media in the teaching and learning process, and considered how new methods might be employed to design, develop and evaluate learning sequences for students. The production and dissemination of appropriate learning materials in higher education, however, remains a serious problem to which far too little attention has hitherto been devoted. Certainly, within a given institution, the establishment of production units, preferably on a multi-media basis and including a printing capacity, can ensure that members of faculty have the necessary technical facilities on call, and the scale on which materials are produced for internal use simply becomes a function of the staff, time, money and physical resources available —and of the faculty's desire to produce new materials for use in their courses. But most of such work is likely to remain at the level of aids to teaching, and to depend upon random and small-scale projects generated by those with enthusiasm or special presentation problems.

Quite different issues are raised when, as a result of systematic development procedures, an effort is made to produce integrated and large-scale learning sequences. The academic, financial and organizational implications of such an effort may be so great that individual institutions are unlikely to be able to mount more than two or three major projects at any one time, and even these may require substantial external funding to meet their original development costs. Even where the effectiveness of such projects has been demonstrated, cost and other factors are unlikely to make them economic unless they can be used for large numbers of students repeated over a period of years, or made available for use in other institutions or for private study. The end product, that is, needs to have either a large market or continuing relevance in a more restricted market.

Both these objectives are difficult to achieve in higher education, where— if teachers are actually available—it is likely to be cheaper in many cases to add more 'live' teaching than to produce relatively more expensive sets of learning materials with a life of about three to four years. Such programmes must be justified either on grounds of greater convenience or more effective learning, so long as they are confined to a single institution or to particular departments within it. It follows that the profitable direction of development seems to lie in increasing the market through inter-institutional arrangements [7, 13]. The arguments for this approach are greatly strengthened by the fact that the skills and physical resources required are at present very scarce, and that much more experience is needed before new learning materials are produced within institutions of higher education or by commercial publishers on a significant scale. The case for inter-institutional co-operation is even greater in countries where teaching and learning resources are still very inadequate.

The educational need for inter-institutional co-operation in this field finds additional support in the search, in all countries, to reduce the *per capita* cost of educating a student. All over the world there is a rapidly growing demand for higher education; it is a demand which must be met. Even the most prosperous nations cannot afford to meet that rapidly increasing demand at the present levels of unit costs, and new means of reducing the unit costs are urgently needed. One possible approach is to produce the basic 'core' of a wide range of courses in all disciplines through the use of television, film, sound recordings, slides and a wide variety of printed materials. If the core were properly designed in modular form, individual institutions and individual faculty would be able to add their own distinctive and locally produced material to it. In any event, nationally or regionally based courses would not amount to a majority of the courses in any degree programme, and there would be no serious danger of reducing the autonomy and academic freedom of individual institutions and their faculty. Yet the savings could be very considerable. Faculty salaries form by far the largest element in the costs of a course, and the provision of common course elements could cut the faculty salary element in costs, provided that the savings were really ploughed back into the system and not used merely to reduce teaching loads.

Any development of this kind is bound, in the initial stages at least, to encounter scepticism and even hostility from some faculty members, objections based on academic grounds as well as habit and a reluctance to accept a new style of work. Yet, there are gains to be made, and some of these gains could be attractive to both faculty and students: the latter could well favour changes which, overall, might allow more members of their generation to benefit from access to higher education. Resistant faculty have also to bear in mind that many of the alternative proposals for cost-reduction, which are under consideration in many countries, are likely to disturb current academic assumptions and arrangements even more dramatically. The position has to be accepted that the *status quo* is not on the list of choices open to us: it is a matter of distinguishing those proposals for cost reduction which have educational merit from those which have not.

We state the potential advantages which lie in the co-operative design, production and use of learning materials in general terms because very little has yet been done to demonstrate their value in practice. The first steps in this direction have usually been *post hoc* attempts to arrange for the exchange of materials between institutions after they have been created in one institution for its own purposes. Examples of this kind are the libraries of television recordings and films which have been established in the United States and some small-scale experiments elsewhere, such as the pilot exchange scheme involving nine universities in the United Kingdom [10]. The drawbacks of this approach are obvious. The initiative usually lies with media centres in the institutions concerned, who are anxious to find other users for their materials and to strengthen their own base by importing television and other materials from outside; they are placed in the position of trying to find academic clients, rather than of seeking material to meet defined academic needs. It is largely a matter of luck whether any of the imported material happens to make a good 'fit' with the needs and standards of the institution which receives it.

The point can be put the other way round. Universities and colleges which produce original materials themselves become subject to many of the same limitations that are imposed on commercial and other producers for a wider market. For the market in higher education is almost invariably confused and fragmented. Even in higher-education systems with a high degree of centralization there is a considerable difference between the courses actually offered in one institution and another, and autonomous systems are even more idiosyncratic. In most systems academic staff seem very reluctant to use materials originating outside their control, and jealous of their right to select what they want to use. They are almost equally unwilling to co-operate with colleagues in other institutions in the definition of common objectives and the production of mutually usable materials. A further constraint is simply inexperience. Until enough good examples of such learning materials are available, either from commercial or national public agencies or individual universities, institutions seem hesitant to commit their own resources of academic manpower, money or physical facilities, to expensive ventures which do not promise fairly quick returns either in lower unit costs, or more effective learning, or both. The result is a vicious circle: even those who have expensive inventories of equipment often find themselves stranded for lack of sufficient materials to fuel the plant they have installed. A more sophisticated approach involves prior consultation and agreement between institutions before courses are designed or learning materials produced. For the reasons given above, this is difficult but not impossible to achieve. It requires a group of similar departments in, say, half a dozen institutions, to identify common elements in their courses, to agree on common objectives and teaching methods, and to arrange for the production of appropriate learning sequences, either by a division of labour between them or by contracting the task to one of them which has suitable professional staff and equipment. Agreement on common objectives and on co-operative evaluation is an essential pre-condition of this process, and where this is achieved there is some guarantee that the materials produced will be used and properly integrated into the academic programme. A case in point is a project for the co-operative production of materials for undergraduate biology teaching which has been launched by a group of five universities in the United Kingdom; all five professors of biology worked together to define the areas of need and to allocate each section of the project to the institution most capable of dealing with it.

As the scale of such work increases, it begins to raise questions about the relationship of universities to the world of publishing [6]. It will be very difficult to overcome long-established divisions between the academic institutions and publishing enterprises and to create a good working partnership between them. Yet this must be done because academic institutions usually lack production know-how and publishers (whose prime aim is the sale of their products) do not possess the skills or opportunities, and in many cases the resources, to design their materials close to academic needs. There are two lines of approach implicit in this concept of partnership. The first, and most familiar, is that publishing and education should engage in joint ventures. The second is that some universities might become mini-publishing houses, possibly on a regional basis, developing new curricular materials in new combinations of media. In the context of the United Kingdom, there are already signs that in time the Open University may emerge as a special publishing base for higher education, linking with the various publishing houses on specific contracts.

There has also been an imbalance between equipment and materials for reasons connected with the structure of the industry: that is, the separation between manufacturers of hardware and producers of software. In the United Kingdom, to take an interesting example, the Ministry of Technology is able to give development grants for new devices, but cannot support the production of materials to go with them, while the Department of Education and Science can use research funds to support the design of new learning materials but cannot underwrite the production of prototypes of educational equipment. The need to overcome this separation has led of late to agreements and even mergers between enterprises operating in these two fields. In the United States, over one hundred such combinations have been made in recent years, some of them involving the largest electronic and publishing corporations.

A third type of approach can be identified. Higher education planning authorities in a number of countries are now beginning to take appropriate action to promote the common use of expensive materials, albeit on a small scale as yet. We have already referred to the libraries for films and video tapes which have been set up in the United States, and a number of regional co-operative schemes are coming into being there [1, 4]. The Swedish university system has set up a special agency (TRU) which is endeavouring to produce centrally film and television materials which can be used in all Swedish universities [2]. A similar project in the Netherlands is based upon a special institute constructed at considerable expense in Utrecht to provide a central production facility for all Netherlands universities [3, 11]. The Open University, which commences operations in the United Kingdom in January 1971, will be producing (in partnership with the BBC) integrated courses of university level for home study, using broadcast television and radio as essential components of its teaching system [9, 12].

This development, like those in Sweden and the Netherlands, has considerable long-term potential. Once a central national agency exists which is regularly producing materials of university standard, and possesses its own academic and professional staff whose primary function is the design and production of such materials, there is the possibility of a breakthrough. It is no longer necessary to find the resources from within one conventional institution, and if the materials are of sufficiently high quality, then it seems probable that some of them at least will find their way into and influence the courses offered by existing universities and colleges. There is also the likelihood that such learning materials could provide a significant source of material for universities in other countries: it is already envisaged that the Open University programmes will be made available—either in broadcast form, or as video tape or other forms of television recordings—to overseas universities wherever English is a possible language of instruction.

Inevitably, this process of development will be slow. Even where the will exists, the design and production of learning sequences takes time, their validation takes longer, and their wide acceptance takes longer still. Most universities and colleges have not yet taken the preliminary steps in this direction. Even those that have presentation capacity, ranging from slide and film projectors, to audio facilities, and to basic television equipment, do virtually nothing systematic to identify external sources of materials relevant to their teaching programme. It is often left to the individual teacher to find and to arrange for rental or purchase of materials he needs, and experience has shown this to be a very haphazard and unsatisfactory process. Despite the difficulties that obstruct effective exchange it has been shown that where a university library, or some special media agency, is charged with this task, a significant increase in the use of 'imported' materials does occur within a fairly short space of time.

At the same time that there is a shortage of suitable materials, there is also an unfortunate waste of them; it is the result of copyright and commercial factors, as well as of poor organization. A broadcasting system, such as the BBC in the United Kingdom, annually produces a large volume of television and sound programmes of potential value to university teaching, such as talks on literature and social problems, drama, science documentaries, political programmes and even direct educational series. Yet these are seldom used in

British universities and colleges, and they are certainly not used systematically. In the first place, information about the content of such programmes (unless they form part of a regular education series) is normally not available much in advance of transmission, and in any case they are usually broadcast outside the normal teaching hours of a university. By the time a university or college teacher has seen or heard a programme and decided it might be relevant to his course, the opportunity to use it has passed. In some countries, such as Britain, copyright constraints—and in most countries lack of suitable recording facilities—prevent such material being recorded or subsequently offered for replay in recorded form. Though there are signs that this situation will change in the next few years, as matters stand very large sums of money and considerable intellectual effort is put into programme materials which disappear once they have been transmitted. At a rough estimate, more materials suitable for university use are produced and lost by the BBC and the ITA companies in a month than have been produced by all British universities and colleges since they became interested in media—and the quality of these professional productions is immensely higher. Similar considerations apply in almost all countries with developed broadcasting systems. Much, therefore, could be done to increase the range and standard of materials at the disposal of educational institutions generally if the relationship between broadcasting agencies and the education system could be clarified, simplified and developed to ensure that the biggest single source of media software is not grossly neglected.

Quite apart from the special problem of broadcast materials, there are other copyright constraints on the more extensive use of media [5, 8]. There are the rights of teachers, and universities and colleges themselves, in materials that they produce. There are also, in free-market economies, the rights of commercial publishers, which have become difficult to protect as the technical capacity to copy print, sound and visual recordings has increased. Producers of language-laboratory programmes, for instance, find it difficult to prevent unauthorized copying of their tapes, and the reproduction of books and other printed materials is now so easy that publishers feel their market is thereby threatened. As a matter of practice, it might be true that the obstacles to the use of new media for teaching and learning can be arranged in a hierarchy of difficulty, in which pedagogic and technical considerations rank lowest, followed in ascending order by the costs and effort of producing suitable materials and capped by organizational and copyright constraints. For the moment, however, copyright problems of this kind do not appear to be seriously hindering the progress of curriculum development within institutions of higher education, largely because the scale of production of new kinds of material is still at a relatively low level in most countries.

There are three fairly distinct situations with respect to academic contributors which can be identified:

1. The situations where materials are prepared by an academic (in return for

payment) on behalf of a publisher or other agency external to the university or college. In this case the copyright clearly belongs to the academic concerned, and he should (though frequently he does not) negotiate for the use of any facilities he requires from his own institution by offering either direct payment or a share in any royalties.

2. The situation where materials are prepared by an academic as a normal part of his teaching responsibilities and without involving him in work above and beyond his normal teaching load. In this case the copyright should presumably belong to the institution, which may or may not choose *ex gratia* to offer a share in the royalties to the academic concerned.

3. The situation where an academic develops materials by extra work above and beyond his normal teaching load. The materials may be developed either partly or totally in this extra time. In this case the copyright should be vested jointly in the institution and in the academic concerned (a 50-50 share in the royalty would seem appropriate). This is the policy in a number of American universities.

In so far as the teaching of students is a primary function of any institution to which all faculty and other persons employed are committed, either directly or indirectly, there can be no question of payment twice for contributing to this function. Consequently, where media producers, course designers and teachers co-operate in the preparation of teaching and learning materials for use within the institution it could be argued that they are merely showing a proper professional concern for a major activity which they undertook upon accepting an appointment. It may be necessary in the next few years to revise conditions of service to take account of this situation.

Were materials are produced in the first instance for the institution (as a part of normal duties) then there is no reason why the institution concerned should not make what use it wishes of them, including exchange, or sale of copies without repayment to anyone. It is the institution which bears the burden of expense for salaries, equipment and materials. It is the institution which underwrites the inevitable production facilities. It is the institution which carries the cost of installation and maintenance of production, plant and support staff. It is the institution therefore which, in theory at least, should have first claim on copyright. However, one must at this point consider a wider aspect of the problem. The main aim of the institution in its effort to provide facilities for the production of teaching and learning materials is to improve teaching-learning activities. An over-zealous defence of its claims to copyright might well arrest the very process it hopes to promote. If the promise of royalties or some alternative incentive would encourage faculty to attempt the production of their own teaching-learning materials on a scale previously unfamiliar, then it has to be considered as part of a strategy of innovation, or little progress may be possible.

The use of faculty time, or rather of university or college time, and facilities for official as opposed to personal purposes, is an extremely complex and as yet unresolved issue in many institutions all over the world. The complexity is increased since more and more team-work is involved in many of these projects. In most countries the individual faculty member has hitherto had the expectation that he is entitled to supplement his earnings by any combination of these activities, usually with the sole vague proviso that they do not interfere with his 'academic obligations'. However, unless and until there is a more precise definition of hours of work and academic duties, it will be impossible, even if it were desirable, for university or college authorities to impose any viable or comprehensive control system to ensure appropriate financial or product return for the investments made in faculty, support staff and facilities.

There is a further problem that we note at this point. That is, the right of the 'author' to impose restrictions upon further use of materials he has produced, especially since they may date. For instance, one could envisage a three-year limitation upon repeated use, without revision, of any recorded teaching materials, or a restriction of use to within the institution, express permission being required for any proposed exchange. This problem, however, can only be resolved if the essential copyright issues raised earlier have been tackled first.

This raises fundamental questions about the operating philosophy of the individual institution. One familiar concept is that the university or college is the title of a loose umbrella organization within which departments and individuals can operate with relative independence. Provided they contribute the basic minimum teaching requirements made of them, many members of faculty use the resources of the department or of the institution to conduct whatever research or projects they wish, using the name of the university or of the college to add status to their work. This concept is frequently justified by the argument that anything the individual does accrues automatically to the credit of the institution, as well as enhancing the reputation of the individual concerned. The alternative concept is that the university or college is a corporate unit, consisting of interdependent parts with interlocking activities, staffed by employees of the institution. Here the activities of a department or an individual must be integrated within an agreed programme of work and shown to benefit the institution in some explicit way or other, as well as achieve the objectives of the department or institution. In other words, either the time and effort of the individual faculty member is at the disposal of the institution or he is a quasi-private entrepreneur who has merely contracted to provide a specified number of teaching hours for thirty weeks a year. If this dilemma remains unresolved, course development on the scale described in Chapter XI will be difficult to achieve, not least because release time for faculty to spend on the design, production and evaluation stages has to be paid for, and may well represent a contribution of time and effort over and above the standard teaching load. The time allocation to course development has to be bought and negotiated officially, whilst activities other than those relating to teaching can often be accepted by the individual faculty member without consultation.

REFERENCES

1. BROWN, James W.; NORBERG, Kenneth O. *Administering educational media.* New York, McGraw-Hill, 1965.
2. COMMITTEE FOR TELEVISION AND RADIO IN EDUCATION, (TRU). *Television and radio in Swedish education.* Stockholm, 1969.
3. DE VOGEL, W. *Thinking about university video centres in the Netherlands.* Utrecht, Scientific Film Institute, 1969.
4. HODGE, Carle. Educom. *Audiovisual instruction* (Wash.), vol. 12, no. 4, April 1967.
5. MCINTYRE, Charles J. *Responsibilities, rights and incentives for faculty with respect to televised instruction.* Urbana, Ill., University of Illinois.
6. MACKENZIE, N. Education and the new technology. *Technical education and industrial training* (London), vol. 8, no. 12, December 1966.
7. ——. The challenge of new teaching techniques. *New statesman*, 7 November 1969.
8. NATIONAL COUNCIL FOR EDUCATIONAL TECHNOLOGY. *NCET and the rights of producers and authors in new media: rights in recorded material.* London, National Council for Educational Technology, 1969.
9. OPEN UNIVERSITY. *First prospectus.* Milton Keynes (England), 1969.
10. PERRATON, H. D.; WADE, D. A. L.; FOX, J. W. R. *Linking universities by technology.* Cambridge, National Extension College, 1969.
11. VAROSSIEAU, Jan W. The use of closed-circuit television and scientific films for university teaching in the Netherlands. *Impact of science on society* (Paris), vol. 18, no. 1, 1968.
12. VENABLES, Sir Peter (chairman). *The Open University. Report of the Planning Committee.* London, HMSO, 1969.
13. *Abstracts of instructional developments.* Ann Arbor, Mich., Committee on Institutional Cooperation, Center for Research on Learning and Teaching, 1969. (Report No. 5.)

XIII. Organizing support services

So far as higher education is concerned, the introduction of new methods of teaching and learning has hitherto been randomized, haphazard and on a relatively small scale; it has been left largely to individuals, small groups of faculty or specialized centres, and there are comparatively few cases where innovations have been the result of strong and coherent policy on the part of the institution. One reason for this is that new techniques tend first to appear at the margin of the conventional teaching pattern; a process of creeping change whose origin may well be accidentally determined by the presence in a university or college of individuals who happen to be interested in a specific innovation. Another reason stems from the fact that there is a great deal of confusion between innovatory support services, such as television and multi-media centres, and actual innovations in teaching, learning or methods of organization and decision-taking. It is true that support services are often the most obvious focus of innovatory activity, and their staffs tend to appear among the most active innovators; yet there is an ever-present risk that innovations in teaching and learning may too easily be exclusively identified with them. When this happens, it may well increase the resistance of many academics to innovations, which they associate with mechanical and electronic devices, and isolate (rather than integrate) valuable support services from the teaching system as a whole.

We stress this point because there are important theoretical as well as practical matters at issue here, although they have seldom been discussed in the literature. On the one hand, when a multi-media services unit is regarded as the main innovatory centre within an institution, it inevitably grows in a lopsided fashion, and its staff will be perpetually forced to seek means of influencing their academic colleagues towards innovation, if only to make sufficient work for themselves. On the other hand, it must be recognized that in a significant number of United States institutions the creation of such centres represented the first point of entry both for new ideas and for new techniques, and this precedent may well be followed elsewhere. At a later stage, other innovatory strategies may prove possible, and the innovatory initiative may then shift away from its original location within a media-based unit. All the same, the role of media and materials as carriers of innovatory activity should not be minimized. The real need is to avoid too strong an early commitment, both of attitude and resources, to this particular and unavoidably costly strategy, and to retain in the constitution and relationship of any media unit, sufficient flexibility to permit a change of role once other groups in the institution begin to involve themselves in any systematic process of innovation. More case studies of service and support units, and of the part they have played in stimulating (and biasing) innovation within their institution are urgently required to provide guide-lines for other universities and colleges.

Once the institution as a whole begins to be concerned with innovation, however, support services are able to operate in a new and more dynamic context. It is no more a question of trying, from a media base, to persuade individuals or departments to try out new methods of presentation: a media unit no longer needs to play the role of change agent for the institution in default of anyone else, and it can adopt the more comfortable posture of a partner in the change process rather than forcing itself into the stance of a promoter. At the same time, a whole range of other support services besides those concerned directly with teaching have to be reviewed. It becomes necessary to reconsider the design and use of buildings, the character of library (and computer) facilities, and, not least, the part that psychologists, educationists and other specialists can play as consultants to the emerging needs of faculty groups that are gradually becoming committed to innovation in teaching and learning.

THE DESIGN OF TEACHING AND LEARNING SPACES

We can see some of these implications if we consider how the development of new resources for learning affects the physical design and use of university and college buildings. There is a direct relationship between the architecture of universities and their academic pattern; where they are in balance, academic work can run smoothly, but where they are in conflict all kinds of difficulties and inconveniences arise. In a period of rapid change, such a balance is particularly difficult to secure or to maintain, because the academic pattern (and indeed the general demands made upon university accomodation) alter more rapidly than the physical environment. For academic buildings are usually built to endure, and large sums of money are invested in them, though the design that is frozen into them at the moment of construction may only reflect a transient conventional wisdom (or even a passing fashion) about what is the most suitable accomodation for teaching and learning.

183

The facts of high initial cost and of relative permanence may not have mattered too greatly in the past, when neither the essential characteristics of teaching nor of university architecture changed greatly over the years: there are many universities in Europe which are still using buildings erected a century or more ago. Where the provision of space for teaching is largely a matter of offices for faculty, class-rooms, lecture theatres, laboratories and libraries, there is little reason to make basic changes in what may be called the educational content of the architecture. Thus a good number of colleges and universities have been built, even in the last decade, which are little more than architectural variations on old themes; the differences between them have often been more a matter of appearance than function.

There are now clear signs that this is no longer likely to be the case. The experience of new universities in several countries shows that even within a few years they have had to make (often at some cost) significant alterations in their original designs, simply because they have found that the developing patterns of use conflict with the solid limitations of the buildings which they have erected. At the same time, older universities have had to modify and rebuild their premises to meet fresh demands, not merely to house and service more students but also to accommodate new types of scientific equipment, computers, library facilities and, not least, new resources for teaching and learning based upon educational media [8, 11].

Some of the alterations that are required by new media are, of course, marginal. They are simply a matter of ensuring that new tools can be used in the class-room and lecture theatre and of providing such elementary amenities as adequate electric power, black-out for projection, reasonable acoustics and storage space for equipment. Some are more substantial: the installation of ducts and wiring facilities for television and sound distribution systems clearly involves greater expense and effort. Also, as one moves up the scale, changes may be required in the shape and disposition of teaching rooms, in the space allocated by libraries for independent study [3] (especially those forms of it which use multi-media presentation), and in the accommodation which is required for the systematic production and dissemination of teaching and learning materials.

It is possible to make some of the necessary modifications to existing buildings as new needs develop. When, however, designs are being drafted for completely new buildings, it is much more difficult to decide what to do, because it is difficult to guess, let alone predict with any accuracy, how far and how fast the introduction of new methods will proceed even in the coming decade. Many new university buildings reflect an attempt mainly to rectify weaknesses that use has demonstrated in old ones, others are valiant but sometimes mistaken efforts to anticipate what is likely to be needed in the future. The lack of adequate knowledge about impending developments means that educational planners who must write the briefs are understandably unsure what they should say to the architects. How far should they commit themselves to providing for new teaching methods or creating new kinds of learning environments that are as yet untried or at least sufficiently unproven, with all the risks of making extensive and possibly irretrievable mistakes if their forecasts prove to be wrong? Conversely, even where architects are aware that new types of building may be needed, they may be equally unsure how far they should encourage their educational clients to experiment with novel (and possibly costly) conceptions. It is clearly safer for both parties to try and hedge their bets, and to strike some kind of compromise between conventional and innovatory designs.

Whatever decision is taken, on our present level of knowledge, it will be a matter of luck whether the brief, or the execution of it, will be successful, or have the intended results. For experience shows that architectural and technical decisions about academic accommodation may affect the educational pattern and also social behaviour within it in unforeseen ways, just as changes in curriculum and teaching concepts may make buildings obsolete. There is no doubt that some of the more novel teaching spaces that have been put up in recent years rest on a somewhat shaky educational foundation. This is to be expected in a transitional period in which the principles of systems design, which integrates educational, architectural and technical forecasts into a coherent unit, is still a novelty; until more experience has been gained in this respect, it is inevitable that some operationally imposing projects will turn out to be misconceived or actually undesirable. It should not automatically be assumed that some of the new structures which have been erected during the last decade in the United States have already proved themselves and that they are therefore desirable models. It is as difficult to secure reliable information about the utility of some of these buildings as it is easy to secure imposing plans and photographs of them.

This caveat must be borne in mind in examining the plans of new campuses, such as those of Florida Atlantic University at Boca Raton, Simon Fraser University in British Columbia, the University of California campus at Irvine, or that of Oral Roberts University in Oklahoma; or new conceptions of individual lecture theatres such as the early experimental Forum building at Penn State University or the design studies undertaken at Rensselaer Polytechnic Institute in New York. While many of these examples can stimulate thought and open new perspectives, they are not yet definitive solutions to the emerging problem of how to adapt university accommodation to all the possibilities that are opened up by new methods. What one can say is that they begin to reflect certain types of need:

1. To provide suitably equipped learning spaces in which both conventional and new methods can be used effectively and economically.
2. To profit from the ability of new media to transmit educational communications over distance and to repeat them at will as teachers and students require them.
3. To provide greater flexibility in the use of spaces, to permit alterations in

the size of teaching or learning groups as the academic pattern itself becomes more flexible.

4. To offer a greater number and variety of 'learning situations', to provide space for study carrels equipped with multi-media resources (which permit the students to study independently) and also to set aside suitable spaces for team or project work rather than straightforward presentations by the teacher.

5. To provide student access to a much wider range of learning resources than the library, class-room or laboratory.

6. To build adequate central service facilities such as computer data processing and audio-visual resource centres, television studios and recording banks for dial-access systems.

7. To design new types of library facilities, which include means of access to automated and electronic information retrieval devices.

In any discussion of the types of accomodation that may be required in the future, it is essential that attention be given to three objectives. The first is to retain the maximum flexibility of use that is possible, even though this is technically, operationally, financially and psychologically difficult. The second is to identify those elements in a structure which may be taken as relatively fixed and those where both physical growth and changes in method may demand modification within relatively short time spans. Very few universities have found it possible (not least because of the manner in which funds for buildings are made available) to designate 'free' areas within which flexible partitioning [10] and other devices may be used to change the configuration as required. (One of the handicaps in this respect has been the lack of suitable light and acoustically satisfactory partitioning, though this problem is now being tackled.)

The third objective is perhaps the most important. That is to devise procedures which can link forward curriculum and logistic planning to the construction programme [6, 9]. This involves sophisticated analysis of the range and character of room sizes that are required on different assumptions about the subject-teaching method-student numbers 'mix' in order to ensure maximum effective use of available space, and to enable an institution to get all the elements in phase. Where, as in the British system, the budget for recurrent (or teaching) costs is settled on a five-year basis, the capital budget (from the same source) is fixed on a different cycle, and a university enjoys considerable autonomy in the way it decides to teach or in deciding what buildings to erect, it is very difficult to get such planning. Comparable difficulties exist in other systems (Sweden, for instance, has recently been facing a similar problem). Important though it may be to plan buildings for the new media and methods, it is even more urgent, in terms of economy and effectiveness, to establish the right planning context in which these and all other problems relating to the provision of expensive accommodation can be tackled systematically rather than piecemeal.

THE ROLE OF THE LIBRARY

At this point it is necessary to remind ourselves that the largest, the most traditional and the most accepted organizational form of support service is frequently forgotten in discussions about innovations in teaching and learning. This is the library.

In recent years libraries have begun to consider the use of learning materials which are not in the form of books but take a variety of different forms— films, audio tapes, video tapes and tape-slide combinations—'non-book materials' as they are somewhat derogatorily called. They bear little resemblance to the book; often the information they contain cannot be retrieved or displayed without the aid of specialized and complicated equipment. A tape recording, for example, gives no visible indication of the nature of its contents or whether it contains a message at all. Even a film, the individual frames of which can be seen, does not begin to communicate effectively until it is projected.

This development implicitly raises a major policy issue which most institutions have not yet really faced. What should be the role of the library in the organization of teaching and learning, and what should the relationship be between libraries and new media centres? It is not merely that the book has been the major influence on library organization and policy, but that libraries have frequently interpreted their roles within educational institutions in a rather passive sense, waiting for requests to emerge once curricular plans have been determined. It seems fair to say that the majority of libraries in universities play very little active part in the design and renewal of curricula, conceiving their role to be that of an agency established to order, catalogue and supply books after the academic decisions have all been taken by others.

The Parry Report on university libraries in the United Kingdom is a significant example of traditionalism, and the assumptions on which it rests are undoubtedly shared by many librarians in higher education. Though it is of recent date (1967) [14] it does not recognize the creative role that a university library can play as an active participant in the design and administration of learning materials, and it does not perceive how an institution's library policy can be related to its over-all policy of resource allocation. It is still, apparently, a novel idea to suggest that library provision should be closely linked to student numbers and teaching methods; far too often, moreover, highly qualified librarians spend much of their time on purely custodial and clerical functions. It would be too radical a departure from our brief to discuss the important conceptual and technical changes that are taking place in information science, or the new thinking that is beginning to influence the training of information scientists [12], but we do need to note that they conflict very sharply with the traditionalist attitudes which continue to dominate many libraries and librarians.

Confronted by these various changes, a university librarian today is understandably uncertain about his relationship to new methods and materials, not least because the field as a whole seems to be in a state of flux, and he usually has more than enough to do to cope with the flow of new books which are flooding his space and eroding his budget. He may well sympathize with academic colleagues who believe (especially in a period of rapid expansion) that there is no case for adding new 'non-book' burdens to the library when it cannot manage to fulfil its classical role adequately. That point of view is taken by many librarians who refuse to spend any part of their budget on film, audio or even graphic materials on the grounds that these lie outside their area of responsibility and that, anyway, the demand for books is so great it must always be given priority. Such an attitude erects the double barrier of theory and finance to block attempts to widen the role of the library as a basic support service.

This 'segregation by form' approach by librarians is becoming less and less easy to justify. For many years some 'non-book' materials—illustrations, slides, gramophone records—have been admitted to library shelves. The 'new materials' (despite their name) cannot be treated as if they are in some way of lower status than books. True, they are different, but in certain respects they may actually be superior to the printed word. For example, a film or television recording of a surgical operation can constitute a primary source of information. Such materials, moreover, are increasingly being produced in conjunction with printed matter which the conventional library cannot ignore. Excellent examples of such packages are already provided for schools in the United Kingdom by the BBC, and in the United States by educational publishers, and the British Open University project is preparing a large range of multi-media packages for its students. It is impossible for libraries to accept and store only the print component, and reject the remainder of the package.

The emergence of multi-media learning materials poses a problem for any library, and one which will increase in scale over the next few years. In terms of organization, it seems logical and desirable that the conception of a library's role should reflect this change, and that it should assume a very wide range of responsibility for the production, storage and use of learning materials in institutions of higher education. The alternative, which United States experience indicates may be unsatisfactory over a period of time, is to set up media materials centres quite separately from the library. When this is done, the two activities tend to develop in isolation, and even in competition with each other, forging different but overlapping links with staff and students and becoming rivals for funds [16]. The media centre is driven increasingly towards an emphasis on hardware, as its distinctive feature, and in the library there is a defensive retreat to classical bibliographic tasks. All the evidence available to us suggests that the user's interest will best be served by an integrated approach to the whole range of educational media, including print. This view is reinforced by the fact that the professional training and experience of the librarian, which includes the administrative skill needed to

188

run a daily service in close touch with faculty and students, should make for the efficient handling of learning materials of all kinds. There are, after all, many novel problems of classification and access involved [7], and the librarian is at least trained to tackle these.

We are thus clearly led to the conclusion that universities and colleges would do well to consider the case for an integrated organization of learning resources, and to estimate the disadvantages of allowing new media centres and libraries to operate independently of each other. For there are strong grounds for such an integration:

1. It overcomes immediately the print-media dichotomy.
2. It simplifies the access routes to teaching and learning resources for teachers and students, and facilitates the improved organization of the flow of information to faculty and students.
3. It provides the framework within which television (which almost invariably tends to run off operationally and cost-wise on its own) can be brought into a more balanced relationship with other media.
4. It provides an integrated production base for internal publications, teaching and learning materials, irrespective of the combinations of media required.
5. It helps turn the library into a much more dynamic agency, more integrally involved in institutional resource planning, and with the total process of teaching and learning.
6. It thus creates a university-wide integrated resource system capable of combining flexible growth and administrative efficiency, also making possible economies of scale by centralization of appropriate manpower and technological plant.

We have been looking some way ahead in this brief summary, for few libraries in higher education are as yet disposed to assume this kind of role; even when the disposition exists, the lack of funds and of suitably trained staff impose serious constraints upon the conversion of the traditional library into the core of an integrated resource centre. Yet such a development seems to us a legitimate and desirable goal, and it would be regrettable if progress towards it were to be obstructed either by conservatism on the part of librarians or isolationism on the part of media specialists.

MEDIA SUPPORT SERVICES

An isolationist attitude on the part of media specialists may be part of the price that must be paid initially when a separate centre to control media support services is established. While media specialists, from photographers to graphic, audio, film and television professional staff, are attached to a single department (such as a medical school) they are clearly in a dependent and subordinate position, providing the services desired by their academic employers. Once they achieve the status of a separate organization, with its own director, budget, staff and operating objectives, their relationship with their academic colleagues changes. They now have a wider responsibility for the provision of media support services to the institution as a whole.

This evolution occurred first in a number of United States institutions, which have experimented with different forms of media centre during the last decade [4]. But it is now being widely copied in United Kingdom, European and Commonwealth universities; whatever the merits of such a model, there is no doubt that it is currently a fashionable one. Some explanation for this may be found in the impetus given to it by the Brynmor Jones report [5], in which an official British inquiry into the use of audio-visual aids in higher scientific education specifically concluded that 'central service units' were the best means of promoting and controlling the use of media in institutions of higher education. After the publication of the report in 1965, a number of universities in the United Kingdom were given special financial grants for this purpose during the period 1967-72 (nine out of forty-two were designated as 'high-activity' centres, and others received smaller allowances). At the same time, a broadly similar policy was adopted in respect of colleges of education, with a special emphasis on television units which were primarily intended to facilitate class-room observation by teachers in training [11].

Thus the general principle of central units was officially endorsed in the United Kingdom and it appears to have been taken up in Europe and Africa, where the line taken in the Brynmor Jones report reinforced the impression created by much of the United States literature on the organization of support services. It is interesting to note, in view of the time-lag that seems to exist in this field between North America and Europe, that the tide of opinion seems to be moving against such segregated centres in several United States institutions at the moment when it is clearly still moving in favour of them elsewhere. It may be wise perhaps, to regard the central unit as essentially a transitional form, necessary to protect and nurture the media interest in its early days, but possibly unsuitable when an institution develops a more widely based interest in new methods of teaching and learning.

There are, of course, a bewildering variety of models for such media centres [13], varying from one institution to another and even, over quite short periods of time, within one institution. For our present purposes we broadly define a central unit as one whose jurisdiction covers the whole institution (on the model of a university library) or at least a significant part of it; which provides or supervises all or a group of such services as projection, sound recording, graphic and photographic, television and programmed learning; which has its own academic, professional and technical staffs, and the necessary equipment and accommodation for them; which has its own place in the administrative structure and its own budget; which is specifically charged with planning work in this field for the institution as a whole, and co-operates with the faculty in improving the development and use of teaching and learning resources.

Institutions of higher education, however, differ in size, design, age, academic objectives, structure and attitude, needs and resources. Older institutions with strong departmental traditions may find an innovation of this kind more difficult to achieve than newer institutions which can, to some extent at least, make advance provision for it. Some will necessarily give more emphasis than others to a television system as the core of their central provision; some will be more concerned with developing audio-visual techniques in selected fields, such as language teaching; some will devote themselves to programmed learning, or graphic services (medical and scientific illustration, for instance) or become involved in course development and resource planning; some will be able to offer training facilities; some will develop particular lines of research; and some will be more heavily involved than others in co-operative ventures with other branches of education. This diversity is necessary and desirable, not least because at this stage there is a need for as broad a range of experience as possible, though it must be said that the efforts by many of the existing central units derive less from an institutionally agreed brief concerning curricular and teaching problems than from vague experiments with media 'to see what happens'. The process often has much in common with the traditional means of founding a new academic unit, that is, appoint one or two senior scholars and let them develop the unit more or less according to their personal professional interests.

Such a process is certainly not systematic: anything can happen. One important reason for this is the fact that little or nothing has been done rigorously to evaluate the accumulated experience of central service units, and it is therefore difficult to provide reliable guide-lines for any institution which is thinking of establishing one. In particular, no one has yet derived from the general experience a set of analytical questions which any institution can use to determine whether it really needs a central media unit, whether it can afford it, what form it should take, what its relationship should be to other units, and what it is expected to do. In the absence of such an analysis it is not surprising that quite large sums of money have been spent on staff and equipment which, on later consideration, might well have been spent differently or not at all.

We suggest that much more documentation of experience is needed on this matter, as a matter of urgency. In the interim we set out a series of questions to illustrate the kind of issues we feel that any policy committee should attempt to answer before committing itself or its institution to establishing a central media support service. This list is not exhaustive: some of the questions, moreover, need to be formulated differently and in a different order of priority, according to the situation within a given institution:

What are the resources currently devoted to work of this kind, i.e. staff, space, equipment, materials, annual expenditure?

Who disposes of these resources? Departments? Special centres and research units? The university or college as a whole?

Who controls decisions about the use of these resources, authorizes equipment purchases and employs staff?

Is it possible to deploy these resources between departments or are they exclusively used by one department? How is this arranged and financed, and what is its extent?

How effectively are these resources used? Are equipment and staff underused? Is there unnecessary duplication of equipment or staff in different parts of the university? Do faculty make the best use of the resources available?

Are the resources disposed to support established patterns of teaching? Or are they being deployed to solve the problems of teaching courses with large numbers of students, courses with special content problems, courses where their use could secure national improvements in teaching and learning, and areas of the university where economies might be secured?

Why create a new central unit? What is the educational rationale?

What jurisdiction should the central unit be given? That is, how widely should its activities range within the broad field of educational technology?

How far should it be regarded as a service unit, responding to calls made on it, and how far should it be encouraged to play an independent creative and planning role within the university?

On what scale can such a unit operate within the university? What can be done at once, what can be done in the short run, and what is the objective for the longer term?

What criteria should be used in assessing the work of such a unit? How are cost and effectiveness to be measured, and how far should account be taken of more nebulous 'academic' considerations, such as 'improved' teaching or learning? How can the claims of such a unit be usefully compared to those of other divisions of the university which are seeking more funds, more staff, more equipment, more space, etc.?

There is a purpose behind these questions. Any group of policy-makers which considers them seriously will rapidly discover that they are unanswerable solely in terms of a support service unit, and that such a unit could not itself begin to answer them without involving many other sections of the university or college. They demonstrate, in fact, that a service support unit which is isolated from the academic structure and the system of institutional management is unlikely to be effective and may not even be viable. It certainly cannot indefinitely sustain the onerous role of innovator-at-large; we are far from sure whether, if alternative strategies are available, it is wise for it to attempt that role at all.

CONSULTANCY SUPPORT

The publicity given to media-based innovations in recent years, moreover, has tended to distort their relative importance as sources of educational change, and to distract attention from alternative strategies. There are, within most institutions of higher education, human resources which are usually inadequately used: teachers with special skills or researchers with special knowledge who could deploy these in support of their colleagues [1]. Sometimes it is difficult to identify such people; sometimes they are reluctant to take on more work; sometimes neither they nor their institution know how to bring their talents into effective use. Potentially, at least, such people have a role to play as consultants to their colleagues, listening, guiding, suggesting and sometimes demonstrating: they may well prove to be among the most important sources of innovation in teaching and learning if they are properly used.

We have already referred to this point when we were discussing the means of systematic course development, and we return to it again here because we feel that many of the changes we have been considering in this book vitally depend upon the creation within each institution of a small cadre of consultants who have some time set aside to support the innovatory endeavours of their academic colleagues. The form, size and composition of such a group will clearly vary from one institution to another, as will its location in the administrative structure. Yet, in the long run, the presence of such a group, and its location close to the centre of the decision-taking machinery, could prove to be as important as the presence of any professional media specialist [15].

In this chapter we have briefly considered four types of support service which can be used to assist innovations in teaching and learning. We regard this as no more than a preliminary review of a sadly neglected field of study. But even on limited experience it seems clear that, to be really effective, all four types of service need to be co-ordinated within an over-all strategy, and such a strategy can only be developed when the institution as a whole is governed by a system of management that promotes and guides change into constructive channels. In the next chapter, therefore, we turn to consider some of the management requirements for effective innovation in teaching and learning.

REFERENCES

1. ABERCROMBIE, M. L. J. The work of a university education research unit. *Universities quarterly* (London), vol. 22, 1968.
2. BALANOFF, Neil. New dimensions in instructional media. In: P. H. Rossi and B. J. Biddle (eds.), *The new media and education: their impact on society*. Chicago, Aldine, 1966.
3. BENYON, John. *Study carrels: design for independent study space*. New York, Educational Facilities Laboratories, 1964.
4. BROWN, James W.; NORBERG, Kenneth O. *Administering educational media*. New York, McGraw-Hill, 1965.

5. JONES, Sir Brynmor (chairman). *Audio-visual aids in higher scientific education.* London, HMSO, 1965. (Committee Report.)

6. BULLOCK, Nicholas; DICKENS, Peter; STEADMAN, Philip. *A theoretical basis for university planning*, Cambridge, University School of Architecture, 1968.

7. CHIBNALL, Bernard; CROGHAN, Antony. *A feasibility study of a multimedia catalogue.* University of Sussex, 1969.

8. DUNCAN, C. J. (ed.). *Modern lecture theatres.* Newcastle upon Tyne, Oriel Press, 1966.

9. EDUCATIONAL FACILITIES LABORATORIES. *To build or not to build: the utilisation and planning of instructional facilities in small colleges.* New York, 1962.

10. ——. *Divisible auditoriums.* New York, 1966.

11. HAUF, Harold D. *et al. New spaces for learning: designing college facilities to utilise instructional aids and media.* Troy, New York, Rensselaer Polytechnic Institute, 1961.

12. HEILPRIN, L. B.; MARKUSON, B. E.; GOODMAN, F. L. (ed.). *Education for information science.* London, Macmillan, 1965.

13. MCINTYRE, Charles J.; HANEY, John B. *Planning for instructional resources at a rapidly growing urban university*, Urbana, Ill., University of Illinois, 1967.

14. PARRY, Thomas (chairman). *Report of the Committee on Libraries.* London, HMSO, 1967.

15. * ROURKE, Francis E.; BROOKS, Glenn E. *The managerial revolution in higher education.* Baltimore, Md., Johns Hopkins Press, 1966.

16. SLEEMAN, Phillip J.; GOFF, Robert. The instructional materials center: dialogue or discord? *AV communication review* (Wash.), vol. 15, no. 2, summer 1967.

XIV. The management of innovation

The fundamental task of management, whether one considers a city, a business or a university, is to deal rationally with continuous change. Its purpose is to minimize the disrupting effect of unforeseen developments and to maximize the opportunities for interaction between members of the enterprise to achieve its shifting objectives and programmes as effectively as possible. No institution can remain both static and relevant indefinitely. Institutional managers must be able to adjust the balance between the forces of change and resistance continuously, to select and evaluate the specific options for change, and to determine the rate and speed at which change occurs [4]. The role of management is to achieve these ends, through the collective exercise of reason and foresight, without creating or increasing stress within the institution to an intolerable level. Management must therefore be concerned with the institution as an entity and must consider the totality of its enterprise and activity.

It is fair to say that this concept of management is unfamiliar to the majority of educational institutions. For historical reasons, especially the dominant role of the academic faculty, the style of management of institutions of higher education has largely been a static one. In this style, the institution has a role and objectives which appear to be unchanging; the structure of government and management is normally deemed to be sufficiently stable to be enshrined in detailed legalistic constitutions which are difficult to amend. The main emphasis in the institution's structures and processes tends to be on the protection of the rights of component units and individual members of the institution, both to regulate internal relationships and to protect the institution as far as possible from the vagaries of external pressures. For this reason, therefore, the role of management is often seen as a minimal one of conducting day-to-day administrative duties to maintain the fabric of an institution within which the component parts can act almost independently.

The whole system is significantly analogous to the nineteenth-century liberal concept of the role of the State which prevailed at the time when the basic pattern of European universities was being established.

Thus, in our view, the current management styles of educational institutions usually fail to reflect the fundamental task of management, which is highly relevant to the processes of innovation, whether the innovation concerns teaching, learning, research or community service [1]. We believe, for instance, that the agencies or individuals concerned with the introduction of educational technology and other innovations in teaching and learning must therefore attempt to understand the relevance of institutional management and should then seek to make management itself more conducive to change. As long as attention is concentrated primarily upon physical facilities, such as new devices, and on the organization and methods most closely associated with them, fairly simple analytical techniques for studying innovation can serve a limited purpose. When, however, development becomes more sophisticated and affects the institution as a whole, much more complex questions arise. Isolated innovations can certainly occur within a static style of management, but the planned consideration and integration of innovation in teaching and learning on an institution-wide basis requires a different approach. Those who are interested in specific innovations in limited areas may well find that a strategy of infiltration provides the quickest and most successful approach; a department often uses its traditional autonomy to launch and protect an innovation that is not supported elsewhere in the university. For those interested in more comprehensive innovation, however, there is no escaping the primary task of gearing the management system to the concept of change and its implications [6].

The strategies for innovation we discuss below are concerned with such institution-wide innovation. We have already noted that it is both possible and desirable to develop strategies of innovation at the inter-institutional level; we do not again refer to such developments partly for lack of space and partly because we assume that they will be greatly facilitated once individual institutions have developed their internal strategies. Equally, it is possible for particular faculties, schools, departments, centres and institutes to innovate in the absence of a supporting framework provided by the institution to which they belong; we feel that such sub-institutional strategies represent a necessary fall-back situation if a corporate strategy cannot be formulated.

How, then, can one approach the problem of the institution's management and its role in promoting planned innovation? Three factors need to be taken in account. One is the need to treat interrelated problems as a whole. The next is the need for participative government. The third is the need for devolution of responsibility.

If the organizational structures and processes of an institution are the critical element which determine whether, and how far, it can react positively to changing circumstances, they should be integrated into a single and coherent management system. That should be a truism, but unfortunately it is seldom the case. In most universities there is no certain relationship between the structure of academic sub-units and the structure of the fiscal planning process, or between the admissions control process and the process which allocates resources for teaching [7]. For example, a decision to change the curriculum for a particular course may reside within the authority of a faculty board although the normal resources required for teaching (faculty manpower, materials, costs, etc.) may well be allocated by the senate direct to the departmental level, and the media required for the course may well be the responsibility of a committee controlling a central audio-visual services unit. In this example, the authority for academic decisions and the authority for decisions about the usage and mix of resources lie in different places. Thus, although it may appear to be common sense that a faculty board cannot alter the curriculum without having some effect on the resource patterns of the departments and the central services unit, the organizational structure of the institution does not recognize that interdependence. The traditional constitutional division of financial and academic authority between a board of governors and a senate is the split which has prevented common-sense integration of the total management systems of universities. As it runs down through the system as a deep fissure, it has led to inefficient divisions between finance committees and academic planning committees, between the professional managers responsible for finance and business and the academic administrators responsible for admission and teaching. The key to the creation of an integrated unitary system lies in a recognition that the president or vice-chancellor is, *de facto*, managing director of the institution, fully responsible for all of its activities.

The second question, that of involving faculty more effectively in the planning and development processes, is more complex. The best plans are unworkable unless members of the institution are concerned with their formulation as well as their implementation; and this means that the planning machinery must; provide ways of ensuring this and of creating a climate in which the relevant procedures are politically acceptable to faculty. This is partly a matter of agreeing upon institutional objectives. Unless these exist and exist openly, then confusion, waste, frustration and inefficiency are bound to occur. An educational institution must contain groups and individuals who hold different views on the purposes of the institution. However, those differing views need to be kept in balance for operational purposes whilst remaining in conflict as to the future; the outcome of that conflict can then alter the future balance which will in turn lead to changes in the consensus view of institutional role. Thus the objectives themselves have to be subject to change; this is another reason in favour of continuous planning which results in fixed agreements for only the shortest period essential for operational stability and efficiency.

Educational institutions, we must recognize, are not rational communities

197

of idealistic scholars; they are complex socio-political institutions, and those who promote innovations need to understand the nature of the internal inter-actions and stresses if they are to control the forces that they generate. If this first step is carried out successfully it should result in a shift in the collective attitude of the leadership towards the management of the institution. Five aspects of that attitude can be noted. Firstly, there must be a deep commit-ment to innovation, springing from a recognition that since the institution exists in a dynamic environment it has to adapt the means whereby it fulfils its less-changing purposes to changing circumstances. The social, economic, political, scientific and technological requirements and processes which affect contemporary institutions are changing at an increasingly rapid rate, and these make internal planning much more complex. Secondly, it must be recognized that innovation in management is a prerequisite to other forms of innovation within the institution, for it is a system which consists of interdependent parts in which change to one process or part may have ripple effects throughout the whole system. For this reason, change has to be planned and managed with great understanding and care by those who are in a position to see the entire interlocking structure of relationships within the system. Thirdly, lasting and successful change cannot be forced upon the institution. Without careful pre-paration, in which those who form opinion and take decisions are gradually drawn into the innovatory process, change will be frustrated. Premature changes, or false starts, may actually intensify the resistances within the institution. Fourthly, it must be assumed that the present level of stress, problems and opportunities is unlikely to be reduced in the future: in such circumstances, more may be gained by stressing the opportunities created by change than by dwelling obsessively upon the problems that it brings. Finally, most institutions possess reasonable resources of intelligent and expert man-power which, effectively deployed, can be used to tackle many of their problems and to accept most of the challenges facing them. The crucial condition is that these resources should be mobilized to achieve institutional goals.

The third question is that of devising a suitable system for devolving responsibility. It is necessary to stress that, in our view, effective integration does not necessarily lead to bureaucratic centralization. On the contrary, the good management of a large educational institution not only involves institutional integration but it also provides for internal diversification and devolution to meet the varying conditions in which sub-units have to operate and to promote the different objectives they pursue. If the right balance is struck, by creating a framework within which the sub-units can operate successfully while conforming to the over-all strategy of the institu-tion, then the system as a whole can become dynamically responsive to change.

It now becomes clear why such practices as Management by Objectives and Management by Exception are both relevant; the framework should set clear objectives to the units but the units can exercise initiative to achieve those objectives, seeking approval only for action which deviates from the approved pattern.

The budgetary process can be used to illustrate this point about devolution within a structured system. In a given university, the process could allocate $1 million to the Faculty of Physical Sciences to teach 500 students in a particular year. The faculty could be told that the $1 million is made up: of $500,000 for faculty salaries (arrived at by using a ratio of 1 faculty member to 10 students and by assuming an average faculty salary of $10,000); of $45,000 for secretarial and clerical staff (arrived at by using a ratio of 1 secretary to 5 members of faculty and an average cost per secretary of $4,500); of $300,000 for technical support staff (arrived at by using a ratio of 1.2 technicians to 1 faculty with an average salary of $5,000); and of $155,000 for materials and other costs (arrived at by allocating $310 per student for that purpose). The Faculty of Physical Sciences would thus be informed by the budgetary process of the moneys it would receive for teaching purposes, how these moneys were composed by the university, and what the basis is for the calculation of each element of the moneys. The university would have communicated its views on how these should be spent by the way in which it has constructed the budget. Devolution and localized initiatives can then be built into the process by giving the faculty virtual freedom to spend the moneys in the ways it feels will best achieve the objective of teaching the 500 students in that year. The faculty could, for example, decide to appoint only 9 faculty members and to use the $10,000 saving on faculty salaries to increase the learning resources available to the students. One basic limit would have to be imposed upon the faculty. It should not be able to alter the mix of its spending in such a way that the faculty will necessarily have to be given an increase in its budget in the following year (e.g. by appointing additional permanent staff on funds saved on materials). We hope that the foregoing over-simplified example of a budgetary process provides one illustration of the manner in which a unified organizational system can enable a meaningful devolution of initiative to take place.

It is, however, futile to discuss such procedures if the process whereby the objectives are decided is itself unsatisfactory. Thus the design of the decision-making process is critical. Long decision chains, overlapping or imprecise responsibilities and the division of decisions into their specialist parts all tend to slow down and discourage change [5]. Unfortunately these factors are usually present in abundance in the decision-taking processes of educational institutions; committees exist in large numbers (and sizes) and they are formed into multi-tier structures; decision-making responsibilities are rarely clearly defined; the financial and the academic aspects of a particular decision are often considered separately by different committees or offices. Many devices can be used to make the decision-taking process more flexible without reducing the quality of the decisions that are taken, and without removing policy decisions from the hands of those most directly concerned with their results. It is possible to reduce the numbers of tiers in the committee structure, to devolve clear responsibilities to sectors of the institution, to assign assessment work to individuals or small informal groups and leave only decisions on policy and key issues to the large formal committees, or to use project teams which are responsible for all facets of decision-making on a particular topic. A decision, for example, to replace small-group (two to five students) teaching of traditional economics by a larger group (ten to fifteen students) teaching of econometrics has implications for those members and officers concerned with student assessment, faculty teaching loads and the distribution of faculty resources, curricula, space design and allocation, the time-tabling of teaching and the teaching of allied subjects.

The decision-taking processes of most educational institutions normally allow for two approaches to such a decision. It can be taken by those members directly concerned with the teaching, leaving the others for whom it has implications to 'pick up the pieces'. In the long run, the friction and frustration caused by this approach would probably lead to strong pressures against innovation. Alternatively, in most institutions, those concerned directly with the teaching, say, of economics can recommend the change on academic grounds to a social-studies faculty board; this in turn has to recommend it to the academic board or the senate of the university after referring the recommendation to the other groups concerned for comment (the statistics department, the finance or planning committee, the space-administration office, the dean of students, etc.). The time taken by that approach, and the risks involved in asking a wide range of groups to comment on the proposal in isolation, would probably combine to form an effective barrier to innovation. There is yet another way of dealing with the matter, but it requires a carefully structured institution-wide forward planning process (a macro-process within the institution) and a project process for particular decisions (a micro-process).

An educational institution should formalize planning as a continuous process involving the collective exercise of foresight; it should give each unit or group the opportunity to put forward plans and ideas for change which can then be considered in a structured sequence by all concerned and which results in an agreed institutional plan. Such an annual process underlines the need and fact of change; it should stress the participation of all members (faculty, students, administrators), and it should examine realistically the implications of all proposals for change. The concept of a planning process is firmly established in the world of government and business. The planning process of the University of Sussex in the United Kingdom is similar to many corporate planning strategies developed by industrial companies. The planning system of the University of California makes use of the Planning Programming and Budgetary System (PPBS) [2] developed by the United States

Department of Defense. Within such a planning process the example used above of a change in the teaching of economics would require the officer responsible for economics to consult with the individual officers for whom the decision had implications. A systematic assessment of the effects and costs of the decision could then be fed into the process at the same time as the request for the change.

The micro-process concerning projects has a similar function to the planning process at the level of individual items of development. If we continue to take the proposed change in the teaching of economics as our example, the normal position at present, once a decision in principle had been taken by the institution, would be for the economics faculty group to design a new curriculum; that group would then take their finished product to related groups (e.g. the statistics group), to the educational technologists, to the librarian, to the admissions officer, etc., for them to make marginal specialist comments prior to implementation. It is highly unlikely that systematic evaluation of the results of the change would be part of the process. The idea of the project process is to obtain genuine interdisciplinary and inter-specialist co-operation at the design, implementation and evaluation stages of such a development. In essence, if through the planning process the institution accepted the need for the change, it would then establish a project team under a project leader; the team would comprise members of all of the groups affected by the change; the leader would be given a time-table and a budget for the work of the team; and the team would be jointly responsible for the design, implementation and evaluation of the change.

In briefly outlining the concepts of planning and project processes as one way of improving an institution's ability to plan and implement change effectively and efficiently, we have moved across the boundary we drew earlier between the decision-taking and the implementation structures. The latter are very important. Decisions become effective only when they are acted upon. The degree of flexibility in the structures and processes concerned with decision implementation is a major factor in the institution's ability to change and to change in time. The nature and the structural relationship of academic units can either inhibit or encourage change. A structure which is highly specialized along disciplinary lines with a large number of separate small departments tends to be less adaptive than a structure which is less divisive, which contains units which straddle the boundaries of disciplines, and which contains larger units. For example, relatively small departments of physics, chemistry and mathematics would find it more difficult to develop genuine interdisciplinary curricula, would be more under influence of the national professional bodies and groups concerned with these disciplines, would be less likely to come to agreements about relative priorities for development in the three subjects, and be less economics in the provision of common services than would a school of physical sciences which included these three disciplines. Equally, as we have outlined earlier, the separation of the

201

library, the computing centre and the media or educational technology centre into separate units is a less efficient and less adaptive mechanism than the placing of these functions within one management unit.

It is also necessary for the responsibility for implementation and for evaluating the effects of the implementation to be clearly assigned. In regard to curriculum renewal, for example, an educational development office with a very small permanent staff of specialists in curriculum development, innovation theory, media-resource utilization, etc., but with a larger budget, can use some of its funds to buy time from the faculty groups. The individuals thus released can then systematically implement decisions in curriculum change and can keep those changes under review [3]. If necessary, the financing of such an educational development programme could be obtained by slightly reducing the teaching resources allocated to faculties, schools and departments. Curriculum renewal and evaluation is one of the functions for which teaching resources are at present given to departments; the above proposal simply suggests that the resources allocated for those functions should be given to the educational development office (rather than direct to the departments) in order that the office can use it to ensure that specified members of each subject group do obtain time to carry out those functions, and carry them out in co-operation with a specialist and interdisciplinary team.

How does a management structure of the kind we have briefly summarized bear upon the problems of teaching and learning? The critical factors are: (a) having sufficient information; (b) providing regular review of the problems and (c) being able to make planned changes as appropriate.

We feel that perhaps the most helpful approach to the information problem is to set out a framework of considerations and questions which should be answered by any institution that wishes to commit itself to a regular programme of review and development of teaching and learning. The approach adopted offers no more than a basic framework; the order and priority will be best determined by local circumstances, since the politics of the phasing, timing and form of any such institutional analysis is of paramount importance.

The first stage would have two component aspects, namely the collection and co-ordination of quantitative data on current teaching practices, and a statement or restatement of internal procedures relating to teaching. The task of assembling all this data is frequently undertaken in United States universities by offices of institutional research attached to the central administration [4]. If it is assumed that material of this kind should be prepared each year, it raises important questions concerning the training, briefing and work-loads of existing educational administrators, who may well have to assume responsibility for this exercise. Too often, administrative effort is almost exclusively geared to the day-to-day servicing of committees or dealing with problems as they arise rather than to the institution's programme of teaching, research or community service.

DATA COLLECTION

Teaching

Use of faculty time

Teaching loads of each member of faculty in contact hours over a typical year; the size and frequency of the groups taught; the spread of the load over the academic year; the titles of the courses taught; an assessment of the amount of preparation required to teach each course and of the time taken to comment on the written or project work produced by students on the course.

Similar information for non full-time faculty who contribute to teaching (fellows, visiting tutors, graduate students, etc.).

Quantitative assessment of the amount of written or project work, related reading and its frequency, required from students for each course and option.

The teaching methods used for each course and option, the frequency of teaching sessions and the distribution of faculty inputs within each course.

Quantitative information on the other activities of full-time faculty, i.e. research, student admissions, personal tutorship, administrative and committee work, examinations, public and community service.

Courses

Course schedules. The objectives for each course, the contact hours for students, their sequence and form.

Course list. An analysis of all courses and options on offer, the percentage of teaching input into each course by subject group of faculty; a weighting for the course in terms of its role in the final assessment of a student; and a classification of the teaching methods used for each course.

Course material. The supporting material prepared for each course, with indications of total costs involved.

Student load

The contact hours in the teaching situation received by the average student in each major each term in each year of his course; the size of group in which he would be involved in each of these contact hours; the spread of hours over the term; the amount and spread of written or project work in each term.

The utilization of learning facilities by the students in the various groups, e.g. the average number of items borrowed from the library by a history student, or the number of hours of laboratory work required per year by each chemistry student.

Characteristics of students and faculty

Students
Breakdown of intake by faculty, departmental or subject categories, for year of study.
General data on socio-educational characteristics of students.
Wastage rates.
Examination results, by grade and school or subject.
Placements.

Faculty
Breakdown by subject group.
Experience of any in-service teacher-training programmes for faculty.

Supporting units

Library. Number of qualified librarians; roles and relationships with academic units; information flow to faculty and students.

Production facilities. Availability and disposition of various media facilities; staffing; training; patterns of use; information flow to faculty and students.

Counselling services. Range of services for admissions, health, educational, careers advice, etc.; relationship of services to each other and flow of information about them to faculty and students.

Curriculum commitments. Availability of curriculum developers, or educational technologists or learning psychologists; extent of involvement to date.

Administrative. Disposition of support for time-tabling of teaching; statistical support, etc.

Technical. Laboratory support services; disposition.

Secretarial services. Access for teaching services, such as typing and distribution of essays, notes, etc.

Other resources

Teaching spaces. Number, location, distribution, size of spaces; pattern of utilization.

Library provision. Reading spaces, provision of duplicate copies, access to non-print material; utilization of library facilities; and bottle-necks.

Computer. Use of computers for teaching or learning.

Teaching laboratories. Distribution and number of laboratories; patterns of utilization; and bottle-necks.

Study spaces. Number, size and distribution of supplementary study facilities.

Audio-visual resources. Disposition of central and local facilities, patterns of use.

Financial allocation. Recurrent expenditure by subject group on supporting materials, expressed as proportion of departmental expenditure; library budget; special fund for teaching and learning projects.

Plans for expansion

A summary of plans for expansion of student numbers should be prepared, giving anticipated breakdown of additional students by subjects and faculties, with an indication of level of expected unit costs by subject and faculty.

STATEMENT OF PROCEDURES

Students

Form of guidance on selection of faculty or subject.
Means of transferring from faculty or subject.
Advice on 'study' problems.
Records of student progress, and on wastage.
Assessment and examinations.

Faculty

Selection criteria in terms of teaching experience and interest.
Weighting in promotion criteria of teaching contribution and performance.
Internal training or workshop programmes for faculty.
Variety of functions and responsibilities to be performed by faculty, e.g. administration, teaching, research, student counselling, examinations, etc. Who or which bodies or individuals assess each category of students? At what intervals? Is there a range of assessment techniques used?

Curriculum review

Is there a systematic structure of decision-making regarding the introduction of new curricula in terms of its various implications on space, equipment, materials, manpower, spread of courses, examination procedures, etc?

Is there a regular review of courses undertaken by subject groups? What form does this take?

What happens if a course option has not been taken for, say, three years?

The study of the data and restatement of existing procedures should familiarize senior members of the institution with the scale and diversity of teaching practices and indicate some of the pressure points in the total system. This is essentially the quantitative and descriptive phase of the operation. It needs to be built into the second phase, which is the systematic review involving all faculty groups and academic units in the institution. It is envisaged that these participative discussions would be based firmly on an understanding of the quantitative material and this would relate to the methods of creating a climate for innovation described in the previous chapter.

Each faculty group or unit should be asked to comment on the data and on the guide-lines prepared by the senior academic and administrative officers, and then prepare a statement on the following points:

1. The rationale for its present pattern of teaching, with an indication of what changes in method have occurred in the last few years.
2. The view of the group as to whether, at its present level of faculty and student numbers, the present sequence and pattern of teaching is regarded as the most effective and appropriate from an academic and educational standpoint.
3. The changes considered necessary, if any, and special problems which are causing concern to faculty and/or students.
4. The most critical teaching-curricular problems facing the group, and possible approaches to them.

Certainly in the first year of any such institutional review, this stage of participation by groups of faculty is of course much more complex than might appear on the surface, not least since they will be expected to cover the major, optional, elective and service courses in which they are involved. It is also open-ended: recommendations concerning faculty recruitment, unit costs and course organization could well emerge from it. Nevertheless, it is the kind of exercise which occurs all too rarely in institutions of higher education, and should provide the base from which the systematic organization of innovations in teaching can be developed.

The third and vital phase now becomes self-evident. This is the planning and implementation of specific innovations designed to achieve the goals or solve the problems identified in the two earlier phases. These innovations may be at the level of the department, the institution or even a group of institutions. Where changes in resource allocation are needed these may be achieved either through the main planning process or an educational development programme.

We have not described in detail the application of such a process to any of these three levels, though we touched on some of its essential principles at various points in this book and specifically in Chapter XI where we discussed course development. What we have sought to do is to indicate its general features in order to place the problems of teaching and learning in the wider context of the institutional system as a whole, and the problems of the institution in the still wider context of a society's pattern of higher education. More specific case studies are now required to fill out the details of this framework. We have, however, thus completed the logical sequence we set out in Chapter I, where we indicated that it was essential to move from an immediate concern with the problems of teaching, through the repertoire of resources and procedures which are relevant to them, to the innovations in management which are required to apply those resources effectively. In the next decade, all institutions of higher education will need to move through this sequence in some form or other. On the degree to which they do so intelligently and creatively will depend the effectiveness of their teaching, their organizational stability and their ability to adapt to the demands which society and their students will make upon them in the next age of expansion.

REFERENCES

1. BARON, George; TAYLOR, William (ed.). *Educational administration and the social sciences.* University of London, 1969.
2. FIELDEN, John. *Analytical planning and improved resource allocation in British universities: a critical evaluation of American PPBS and its potential in Great Britain.* University of London, November 1969.
3. JOHNSON, F. Craig. *An evaluation of educational development programs in higher education.* Michigan State University, 1968.
4. ROURKE, Francis E.; BROOKS, Glenn E. *The managerial revolution in higher education.* Baltimore, Md., Johns Hopkins Press, 1966.
5. STEWART, Rosemary. *The reality of management.* London, Pan Books, 1967.
6. UNESCO/INTERNATIONAL INSTITUTE FOR EDUCATIONAL PLANNING. *Planning the development of universities.* Paris. (In press.)
7. WILLIAMS, Harry. *Planning for effective resource allocation in universities.* Washington, D.C., American Council on Education, 1966.

Publishers of journals cited in references

Acta psychologica. European Journal of Psychology, North Holland Publishing Co., Box 3489, Amsterdam (Netherlands).

American educational research journal. American Educational Research Association, 1126 16th Street N.W., Washington, D.C. 20036 (United States).

American sociological review. American Sociological Association, 1001 Connecticut Ave., N.W., Washington, D.C. 20036 (United States).

Audio-visual instruction. National Education Association, Department of Audio-visual Instruction, 1201 16th St., N.W., Washington, D.C. 20036 (United States).

Australian university. Melbourne University Press, Carlton N.3, Victoria Australia).

AV communication review. National Education Association, Department of Audio-visual Instruction, 1201 16th St., N.W., Washington, D.C. 20036 (United States).

Bookseller. J. Whitaker & Sons Ltd., 13 Bedford Square, London, W.C.1 (United Kingdom).

British journal of educational psychology. Methuen & Co., 11 New Fetter Lane, London, E.C.4 (United Kingdom).

British journal of medical education. Association for the Study of Medical Education, BMA House, Tavistock Square, London, W.C.1 (United Kingdom).

British journal of psychology. British Psychological Society, 200 Euston Road, London, N.W.1 (United Kingdom).

Economist. Economist Newspaper Ltd., 25 St. James's Street, London, S.W.1 (United Kingdom).

Educational record. American Council on Education, 1785 Massachusetts Ave., N.W., Washington, D.C. 20036 (United States).

Educational research. National Foundation for Educational Research, England and Wales, Tower House, Southampton Street, Strand, London, W.C.2 (United Kingdom).

Educational review. Institute of Education, University of Birmingham, 50 Wellington Road, Edgbaston, Birmingham 15 (United Kingdom).

Harvard educational review. Harvard University, Graduate School of Education, Longfellow Hall, 13 Appian Way, Cambridge, Mass. 02138 (United States).

Impact of science on society. Unesco, Place de Fontenoy, 75 Paris-7ᵉ (France).

Industrial training international. Pergamon Press, Headington Hill Hall, Oxford (United Kingdom).

Journal of educational psychology. American Psychological Association Inc., 1200 17 th St., N.W. Washington, D.C. 20036 (United States).

Journal of educational research. Dembar Educational Research Services, 2018 N. Sherman Ave., Box 1605, Madison, Wis. 53701 (United States).

Journal of educatioal technology. Councils & Education Press Ltd., 10 Queen Anne Street, London, W.1 (United Kingdom).

Journal of experimental education. Dembar Educational Research Services Inc., Box 1605, Madison, Wis. 53701 (United States).

Journal of general education. Pennsylvania State University Press, Old Main, University Park, Pa. (United States).

Journal of programmed instruction. c/o Mr. Lincoln E. Hanson, 453 Strawtown Road, West Nyack, N.Y. 10994 (United States).

Journal of psychology. Journal Press, 2 Commercial Street, Princetown, Mass. 02657 (United States).

New scientist. Cromwell House, Fulwood Place, London, W.C.1 (United Kingdom).

New statesman. Statesman & Nation Publishing Co., 10 Great Turnstile, London, W.C.1 (United Kingdom).

NSPI journal. National Society for Programmed Instruction, Trinity University, 715 Stadium Drive, San Antonio, Tex. 78212 (United States).

Psychological reports. Box 1441, Missoula, Mont. 59801 (United States).

Review of educational research. American Educational Research Association, 1126 16th St., N.W., Washington, D.C. 20036 (United States).

Science. American Association for the Advancement of Science, 1515 Massachusetts Ave., N.W., Washington, D.C. 20005 (United States).

Science education. John Wiley & Sons Inc., 605 Third Avenue, New York, N.Y. 10016 (United States).

Scientific American. Scientific American Inc., 415 Madison Avenue, New York, N.Y. 10017 (United States).

Technical education (formerly Technical education and industrial training). Evans Brothers, Montague House, Russell Square, London, W.C.1 (United Kingdom).

The Times educational supplement. The Times Publishing Co. Ltd., Printing House Square, London, E.C.4 (United Kingdom).

Universities quarterly. Turnstiles Press Ltd., 10 Great Turnstile, London, W.C.1 (United Kingdom).